S. Grant

MW01057978

The Domain Game

The Domain Game

How People Get Rich From Internet Domain Names

David Kesmodel

Copyright © 2008 by David Kesmodel.

ISBN: Hardcover   978-1-4363-3228-6
                Softcover   978-1-4363-3227-9

All rights reserved. No part of this book may be reproduced or transmitted in any form
or by any means, electronic or mechanical, including photocopying, recording, or by
any information storage and retrieval system, without permission in writing from the
copyright owner.

This book was printed in the United States of America.

To order additional copies of this book, contact:
Xlibris Corporation
1-888-795-4274
www.Xlibris.com
Orders@Xlibris.com
47650

Contents

Introduction..9

Chapter One: Speculators 15

Chapter Two: From Dirt Bikes to Domains 34

Chapter Three: Name Dropping 55

Chapter Four: Click, Click, Click........................68

Chapter Five: Better Late Than Never 94

Chapter Six: Big Money....................................110

Chapter Seven: The Domain Craze........................130

Chapter Eight: Shenanigans in Cyberspace...........163

Chapter Nine: The Future 177

Appendix I: Big Deals: The Twenty-Five Largest Domain Sales.........193

Appendix II: Resources for Investors 195

Acknowledgments 199

A Note on Sources..201

Endnotes..203

This book is dedicated to my parents, who taught me to do what I love.

Introduction

In the fall of 2002, a thirty-three-year-old man living in the Cayman Islands made a rather unorthodox financial decision. He took all of his family's savings, which totaled about $200,000, and invested it in thousands of Internet domain names.

The move terrified his wife, who phoned her in-laws to warn them that something might be wrong with him. But the man, normally conservative with money, kept remarkably calm throughout his domain-buying binge. He'd done lots of research and was convinced he was doing the right thing. "Don't worry, honey," he said repeatedly.

At the time of Frank Schilling's big bet on Web addresses, the Internet economy was in the doldrums. Silicon Valley and Wall Street were reeling from the dot-com bust of the previous two years. Billions of dollars had been lost on ill-formed business ideas. Thousands of jobs had evaporated. Wall Street analysts and the media were crucified—and justly so—for hyping shoddy companies.

A little-noticed by-product of the dot-com implosion was that many owners of domain names, the real estate of the New Economy, let their names expire. They figured, why continue paying annual renewal fees of as much as $35 for something that seemed worthless? So, just like Internet stocks, online real estate was left for dead.

For Schilling, a college dropout from Canada who'd dabbled in several careers, the timing couldn't have been better. He believed that generic, easy-to-remember domain names would be in demand when the Web economy rebounded. He was also among a small group of people who recognized that, even amid the dot-com crash, a new Internet business model was starting to catch fire. It was called pay-per-click advertising. Under that model, a marketer only paid for an Internet ad when a user clicked on it and landed on the marketer's site. It was an incredibly compelling proposition for advertisers. Within a few years, a company called Google would leverage the appeal of pay-per-click advertising to become one of the world's most successful companies. Schilling signed up with ad networks run by Google, Yahoo, and others that let domain owners display small text ads on their sites and receive a share of the revenue. The ads were relevant to the domain name; for instance, spavacations.com would feature ads for spa resorts. Everything was automated, so Schilling needed no sales force and had few expenses.

Schilling's high-stakes gamble was a classic case of buying at a market's nadir, just before a boom phase. Between 2002 and 2004, he watched with delight as individuals and companies let domains expire by the hundreds of thousands—some intentionally, some by accident. Schilling and other shrewd speculators battled to grab the names in what they viewed as a rare window of opportunity in the Internet's history. Domains "fell like pennies from heaven," Schilling told me.

Working twenty hours a day in a dimly lit wing of his two-story house on Grand Cayman Island, Schilling scooped up more than 250,000 names in about two years. His hair grew to his shoulders, and he became rail thin consuming little but shots of double espresso. He ventured outside into the blazing Caribbean sunshine so rarely, he said, that he "was the whitest man on Grand Cayman." Most of his domains were simple, generic terms, such as chapter11.com, apartmentlisting.com, antarctica.com, and eatingdisorders. com. Schilling placed little content on his sites except pay-per-click ads. People landed on his sites by typing the domains directly into their Web browsers, bypassing search engines in their quest for information. In 2004, only two years after Schilling began focusing on domain investing, his revenue—all from people clicking on his ads—topped $10 million, and 90 percent of it was profit. By 2006, his revenue and profit more than doubled. Several companies offered to buy his domain portfolio for more than $100 million. He started driving a Mercedes-Benz and bought a stake in a Gulfstream IV jet.

Schilling, one of the world's most successful domain investors, was obsessed with Web addresses. He likened his affection for his names to his love of his two children. But he was hardly alone. His passion was matched by thousands of other people who jumped into the domain game in the 2000s. "I can't look at a sign, I can't watch a TV show, I can't do anything in life without thinking of it from the perspective of a domain name," says Adam Dicker, another college dropout who became a millionaire in the domain market.

The name trade had made headlines amid the Internet mania of the 1990s, when wallstreet.com fetched $1 million, wine.com $3 million, and business. com a staggering $7.5 million. But the market of the 2000s was different. Investors began stockpiling names by the tens of thousands and primarily filled them with ads, no longer needing to sell their names to make money with them. Critics complained that the sites were transforming the Internet into the virtual equivalent of a gaudy, billboard-laden commercial strip. But investors insisted they were helping Web users find relevant information. It was a modern land rush, and speculators were sticking billboards onto their new properties as quickly as they could acquire the lots. By 2007, ad revenue in the domain market reached about $1 billion.

The new scramble for Web addresses began quietly, with a few people like Schilling and Dicker placing big bets on names. Then, as word spread online that domains could be turned into virtual money-printing machines, more and more people entered the fray. By 2007, at least ten thousand people worldwide actively invested in domains, and at least five hundred did it full-time, estimated DNJournal.com, the industry's main trade publication. A new profession was born. A new word was even created to describe its people: "domainers."

Many domain investors worked from their homes in a pair of shorts or a bathrobe, not unlike the day traders of the stock-market boom of the 1990s. Dozens became millionaires. And it didn't take long for their success to capture the attention of major players in America's financial markets. In the mid-2000s, the U.S. economy flourished, and a lot of private-equity dollars sloshed around, awaiting the next big idea. The Internet again became a hotbed of investment, and domains were part of the frenzy. Investment firms backed by the likes of former presidential candidate Ross Perot and Starbucks Chairman Howard Schultz invested in new media companies that amassed giant portfolios of domains by sweeping up the holdings of smaller investors. A Seattle-based public company, Marchex, helped ignite the land rush when it paid $164 million to acquire 100,000 names from a reclusive Chinese-born speculator. Marchex and other large domain owners began adding editorial content and other features to their sites to make them more appealing. In the wake of the Marchex deal, several individual domains garnered hefty prices, including vodka.com ($3 million) and diamond.com ($7.5 million).

As professional investors entered the market, they accorded legitimacy on an industry that had long suffered a negative reputation because of the activities of its worst participants: cybersquatters. Cybersquatters bought addresses associated with the trademarks of famous brands and tried to profit from them, which gave rise to thousands of legal fights.

But the professional investors struggled to burnish the industry's image. Cybersquatters continued to acquire domains in massive quantities and exploited the pay-per-click advertising boom themselves. Some major

trademark holders were furious, and filed lawsuits. The industry's effort at
an image makeover wasn't helped, either, when some large, reputable domain
holders were found to be engaging in cybersquatting.

Like early participants in other financial markets, successful domain
investors benefited from being first to identify a moneymaking opportunity.
They also benefited from loose regulation of the Internet. And they worked
hard, toiling for days at their computers to determine which names were
valuable, how to get them, and what to do with them. Many worked in
extreme secrecy to preserve a competitive advantage, refusing to share their
techniques with other investors.

They were a motley crew, these domain junkies. Mostly men, they came
from a wide range of backgrounds. Some had dropped out of high school
or college; others had graduate degrees in fields such as computer science
and engineering. They tended to have several traits: they liked working for
themselves, were skeptical of large corporations, and were fiercely competitive.
Many also had the self-awareness to realize they might never be this good at
anything else. "One of the reasons I love this crowd so much is these are all
the wrong kind of people," John Berryhill, a lawyer for domain investors,
told me one day at an industry trade show. "These are not the people who
went to the right schools, who had the right social connections."

I stumbled onto the domain game while working as a technology
reporter for The Wall Street Journal's online edition. I became obsessed with
understanding how the market worked. I wanted to know how people like
Frank Schilling had become multimillionaires in a few short years by splurging
on Web addresses.

I quickly learned that many of the people who invested in domains had
no interest in sharing their stories. They didn't like to tell each other much,
let alone a writer. This only strengthened my conviction that the story of the
domain game needed to be told. This book is that effort. It seeks to shed
light on a little-understood market, and one that is important to the future
of one of the world's greatest inventions, the Internet. Domain names are an
essential part of the Web. As the Web evolves in many ways in the coming
years, its real-estate barons will have a big influence on what happens.

Besides tackling the inner workings of a mysterious universe, this book will
arm readers with information they can use to invest in domains themselves.
The market isn't for everyone. It's generally riskier than other financial markets,
such as stocks. However, Web addresses are still in their infancy, and they're
likely to appreciate in value over time as more people use the Web and do
business on it. That's particularly true of short, generic terms that describe an

industry or product. Domains are now woven into the fabric of our society and culture, appearing everywhere from T-shirts to the sides of buses. They're here to stay. There's also a relatively low barrier to entering the market. New domains can be obtained for less than $10, and the median sales price for an old name is roughly $1,000. The secondary market, where previously registered domains are bought and sold, is growing rapidly, reaching $700 million in sales in 2006, according to Sedo, a name broker. The combination of revenue from ads and sales in the secondary market means the domain market generates annual revenue of about $2 billion. "There's still a ton of money to be made for persistent people," says Garry Chernoff, who ditched a career as an electrician on his way to making millions from domains.

Chapter One

Speculators

All Scott Day ever wanted to do was run his family's watermelon farm.

As a boy, Scott tagged along as his father, Frank Day, ran Red River Farms in Terral, Oklahoma, a sleepy town of four hundred people about a mile from the Texas border. Red River Farms was one of the largest producers of watermelons in Oklahoma. Frank had taken the reins of the two-thousand-acre operation in the early 1980s from his father-in-law, Olen Weatherly, who, after turning sixty, asked Frank for help. Red River Farms took its name from the mud-colored waterway that divided Oklahoma and Texas. The farm shared the same road as Terral's tiny town center, which featured the minute headquarters of the phone company, an elementary school, and a white, one-story building housing both city hall and the fire department.

When he wasn't in school, Scott walked the watermelon fields with his father, who was his hero almost from birth, as he studied the soil to make sure it was properly fertilized to grow the sweet, succulent fruit. During the harvest each summer, he watched his father shout instructions to seasonal workers loading the melons onto trucks that hauled them to produce markets in New York and Chicago, and to grocery stores throughout the country. And Scott sat quietly in the farm's one-room office—also known as "the shed"—while his father took calls and wrote down orders for melons on large sheets of yellow paper.

When Scott began high school and was big and strong enough, he joined the other workers in the field. For six weeks from late June until early August, they picked, carried, and boxed watermelons from sunrise until midnight. The watermelons were some of the tastiest produced in the United States. According to Frank, mild weather conditions and the sandy and fertile soil of the Red River Valley yielded superior sugar content in the melons, making them sweeter than those from rival states.

On some days, Scott and the other workers filled twenty eighteen-wheelers with watermelons. Scott worked as hard, if not harder, than the other workers. He showed that even though he was the owner's son, he received no special favors and did not take the tasks lightly. After a full day of work on the farm, sleep came easily, but was always too brief. Frank tried to give everyone as many Sundays off as he could so they could attend church, get much-needed rest, and wash their clothes. Still, on many Sundays, everyone worked.

As a rural Oklahoma farm boy, Scott became heavily involved in Future Farmers of America (FFA), a national organization that promoted agricultural science education. Here he developed a flair for public speaking about agriculture, delivering speeches to as many as ten thousand farmers. Poised and straightforward, he won many speech contests, including state and national awards from FFA and other groups. Scott was also active in his Baptist church, earned A's and B's in school, and was gifted in sports. He attended Waurika High School, twenty miles upriver from Terral, earning all-state honors in football and basketball. (He was the football team's main running back and the basketball team's point guard.)

Frank Day, a man with broad shoulders, a broad smile, and a few strong convictions, expected a couple of things from Scott and his older brother, Steve. Frank expected the boys to earn college degrees, and to leave the comforts of home for a little while. For Scott, that meant heading off to Oklahoma State University in Stillwater, about a three-hour drive from Terral. His high school sweetheart, Stacy Wallace, joined him at OSU. Scott earned a degree in agricultural education in the spring of 1994, and married Stacy two weeks later. The couple moved to Arnett, a town of five hundred in northwestern Oklahoma, where Scott took a job at the high school, teaching agricultural education. He taught there for two years. Around that time, Olen Weatherly, Scott's grandfather, died, leaving only Frank to run Red River Farms. Scott had been itching to move back to Terral to join his dad in the business, and, when Olen died, it was time.

Scott's goal was to find ways to expand the business. Red River Farms was selling plenty of watermelons. Frank and Scott not only sold their own melons, but also acted as brokers helping a few other farmers sell their harvests in south Texas and in Oklahoma. Meanwhile, the Days supplemented their income by growing wheat and raising cattle. But Scott had a few ideas for bringing more revenue into the farm's coffers.

The first idea didn't go very far. Scott wanted to raise ostriches. He'd called around to a few farmers in the region who appeared to be making pretty good money selling ostrich eggs and meat; ostrich meat was lower in fat and cholesterol than other red meat, which appealed to some consumers. Scott was convinced it was a good idea and broached it with his father. Frank wasn't so sure, but he figured they ought to explore it. The other ostrich farmers seemed to be doing so well, Frank recalled, that they were "all going to be rich and never be broke again." Ostriches went for about $25,000 to $50,000 a pair. So Frank paid a visit to his banker and asked for a loan. "I said, 'Joe, how about loaning me $25,000 to buy me some ostriches?'" Frank said. The banker balked. According to Frank, he replied, "Ain't gonna do that, but if you got some cattle you want to put up [for collateral] for the $25,000, I'll be happy to loan you $25,000 against the cattle. But not against the ostriches." That was enough to make Frank cool to the idea, and he called it off. And that was a good thing, Scott said. Within a few years, the ostriches in the Red River basin largely had become money losers, and some were let free to roam the countryside. "Heck," Frank said, "there've been ostriches running out here for years."

Scott's next idea proved much more fruitful.

In May 1996, Scott and Frank drove south on Texas Highway 281 to Falfurrias, a little town in south Texas, for their annual ritual of brokering sales of watermelons harvested by farmers in the Lone Star State. They worked out of a room in the three-story Antlers Inn motel, right off the state highway. During a stop on their journey, they visited an electronics store. An employee showed them a computer connected to the World Wide Web. Neither father nor son was familiar with the nascent Web, though both were comfortable with computers. Scott's only memory of being online was in high school, when Frank let him use a CompuServe account to access a virtual library to help him write a paper. The experience was memorable in part because the phone bill for the access cost Frank more than $200. In college at OSU, Scott used his own Macintosh, a hand-me-down from his dad. Frank favored Macs, and kept one in the office. But the Days were amazed when they saw the Web for the first time. When they returned to Oklahoma later that spring, they signed up for dial-up Internet in the office so they could surf for business and pleasure, though there was little time for the latter. "It was extremely fascinating to us that we could sit here in Terral, Oklahoma, and see what was going on through the whole world," Scott remembered.

After the Days finished the watermelon harvest that August, Scott spent a few weeks in Weatherford, Oklahoma, about a three-hour drive from Terral, earning money helping another farmer sell his harvest. During his time off, Scott spent hours trolling the Web at the local public library. When he returned to Terral, he broached a new idea. Why not get the Web addresses watermelon.com and watermelons.com, and use them to sell melons all over the world? In addition, they could offer space on the sites to other watermelon farmers. Scott would design Web pages for the farmers for a fee.

Frank thought it was a fine idea. So then Scott had to figure out how to register domain names. Little did he know then, but his days in the watermelon patch were numbered.

What's a Domain Name, Anyway?

Domain names date to the early 1980s, when the Internet was the province of a small number of academics, scientists, and government officials. Computer scientists at the University of Southern California's Information Sciences Institute invented the domain-name system, or DNS, to serve as the Internet equivalent of a postal system, ensuring that information reached its intended destination.[1] Every computer connected to the Internet is assigned a unique series of numbers known as an Internet protocol, or IP, address. But words are much easier for humans to remember than numbers, so the computer scientists created a hierarchical naming structure in which words served as aliases for IP addresses. Today, when an Internet user types a domain name into a Web browser, computers running in the background translate it into the IP address associated with the name, and the user is able to access the Web site.

The pioneers of the Internet, which began in 1969 as a communications project of the U.S. Department of Defense, didn't regard domain names as investments. No one called them "virtual real estate." Domains principally served a technical purpose. Also, commercial use of the Internet was prohibited until Congress amended a decades-old federal law known as the National Science Foundation Act in 1992.[2]

Not surprisingly, large computer companies were among the first businesses to register domains. They'd been active participants in the nascent Internet, and were encouraged to adopt domains when the domain-name system was implemented. IBM.com, Intel.com, and HP.com (for Hewlett-Packard) were all registered in 1986. Apple.com followed suit a year later. The first name registered in the .com extension, or top-level domain, was Symbolics.com, adopted by Boston-area computer manufacturer Symbolics in 1985. (The .com suffix was designed for commercial entities, while federal government agencies were assigned to the top-level domain .gov, and educational institutions to .edu.) Defense contractors were also early domain owners. Northrop.com was registered in 1985, followed by Boeing.com in 1986 and Lockheed.com in 1987.

The swift and dramatic transformation of domains into prized economic assets coincided with the explosion of the World Wide Web in the 1990s. The Web—a user-friendly platform for distributing information over the Internet—was invented in 1989 by Englishman Tim Berners-Lee, a software engineer at the CERN physics research laboratory in Switzerland. The Web represented Berners-Lee's vision for a democratic system that would allow any computer user to connect to the Internet and send and receive information. The Web went online in 1991, but it didn't explode in popularity until the mid-1990s, after a Silicon Valley start-up company, Netscape Communications, began offering a graphical Web browser that enabled users to easily navigate Web pages by pointing and clicking.

At the beginning of 1993, only 21,000 domains had been registered worldwide.[3] In the next two years, the number more than tripled to 71,000, as Internet start-up companies and speculators clamored for parcels of virtual land.[4] By the time Scott Day obtained watermelons.com in early 1997, the number had surged to nearly one million.[5] Some equated the frenzy to the nineteenth-century gold rushes in California, Canada, and Australia. Others compared it to the Land Run of 1889 in Day's home state, when tens of thousands of white settlers lined up to claim former Indian territory.

The company responsible for assigning domains ending in .com, .org, and .net was Network Solutions, then a small firm in Herndon, Virginia. Network Solutions won a five-year contract to manage registrations in 1993 from the National Science Foundation, a U.S. government agency that oversaw the nonmilitary use of the Internet. Neither organization was prepared for the sharp and sudden rise in demand for Web addresses, which came soon after the agreement was signed.[6]

At first it cost nothing to register a domain with the InterNIC, the registration system managed by Network Solutions. Names were doled out on a first-come, first-served basis. Initially Network Solutions told registrants that only one domain could be registered per person or company. To sidestep this policy, some early investors created multiple fake companies. One such investor was CES Marketing Group, a three-person team in Vancouver, British Columbia. The company successfully registered scores of domains in 1995 using an assortment of aliases, according to cofounder Christopher Wall. Another early speculator, Chad Folkening of Indianapolis, said he got around the rule in part by using many different Hotmail e-mail accounts for his contact information.

Eventually Network Solutions' tiny staff—it had less than a handful of people devoted to registration—became so overwhelmed by the flood of e-mailed applications that it was unable to carefully screen each request. Applications surged from about 3,600 a month in December 1994 to 14,000 a month in October 1995.[7] Network Solutions gave up trying to prevent multiple registrations by the same person or company. It also dropped efforts to allocate domains to specific types of registrants (i.e., .com for commercial, for-profit organizations; .org for nonprofit organizations; and .net for businesses and groups involved in Internet infrastructure).[8] It was basically a free-for-all. Any name could be grabbed by anyone, regardless of trademark considerations or other factors.[9]

Ultimately the National Science Foundation decided that Network Solutions should charge a fee for each domain registered. The foundation had been subsidizing the cost of administering domains and could no longer afford it. In September 1995, Network Solutions began charging $100 to register a new domain for two years and $50 thereafter to renew it. But the company didn't require immediate payment upon registration.

Trademark-Lawyer.com

Besides an avalanche of applications, Network Solutions faced a mounting crisis over how to deal with legal disputes. Hundreds of early speculators registered domains associated with trademarks—names or symbols used to identify a company's goods and to distinguish them from those sold by others. The classic tactic was to register a domain, do nothing with it (create no Web site), wait to hear from the trademark holder, and then offer to sell it for a high price. The practice came to be known as cybersquatting. Some trademark holders agreed to pay the name owner. Others, angry at being held for ransom, threatened or filed lawsuits. The disputes arose in part because many large corporations were slow to recognize the significance of the Internet medium and failed to register sites matching their trademarks.

In the fall of 1994, writer Joshua Quittner brought the issue to light in an article in Wired magazine.[10] Quittner pointed out that the hamburger chain McDonald's had failed to register mcdonalds.com, and that anyone could grab it. He also discovered that only one-third of Fortune 500 companies had registered the addresses matching their names. Quittner called a McDonald's spokesperson to find out why there were no Golden Arches on the information superhighway. The spokesperson didn't know and told him she'd check with company officials and get back to him. (During the call, she asked, "Are you finding that the Internet is a big thing?") Quittner never received a response from McDonald's. So, with the backing of Wired officials, he registered mcdonalds.com and began receiving e-mail at ronald@mcdonalds.com, where he invited readers to send him tips about what to do with the site. About half said he should extort as much money as possible from McDonald's, while the other half said he should use the address to promote vegetarianism.[11] Quittner wasn't interested in being paid for the name; he merely wanted to illustrate by example how corporations were overlooking the Web. McDonald's wasn't amused. It asked Network Solutions to yank Quittner's registration of the address. Quittner objected on the advice of Wired lawyers. Eventually, the parties reached a settlement: Quittner forked over the domain, and, in exchange, McDonald's donated $3,500 to an inner-city New York school for underprivileged children so the students could have faster Internet access.

Dozens of other big companies, from MTV to Taco Bell, became embroiled in domain disputes in the mid-1990s. In some clashes, the trademark holder's adversary was a rival corporation, rather than a speculator. In 1994, Princeton Review and Stanley H. Kaplan Educational Centers, competitors in preparing students for standardized tests, butted heads. Princeton Review had registered kaplan.com and created a Web site listing differences between the companies. Later, Princeton Review's management said its principal motive was to annoy its nemesis. It certainly worked. Kaplan sued Princeton Review in a New York federal court. The sides agreed to arbitration, and in October 1994 an arbitration panel ruled that Princeton Review had to surrender the address. Princeton Review's president, John Katzman, said the company offered to give up the name for a case of beer, but Kaplan demurred. "Clearly, the folks at Kaplan have no imagination, no sense of humor, and no beer," Katzman said.[12]

Initially Network Solutions took a primarily hands-off approach to intellectual-property considerations, leaving antagonists to settle their issues in or out of court. The company's beleaguered staff didn't have time to scrutinize each application, nor did it think it should make such judgment calls. However, Scott Williamson, a supervisor at Network Solutions, told Quittner it did try to block "obvious" cases of a company registering another's trademark. Sometimes it erred in that analysis, however, Williamson said. For example, at one point, three requests for mci.com came in almost simultaneously—one from phone giant MCI, another from rival Sprint Communications, and a third from another company with the initials MCI. A Network Solutions employee gave it to Sprint. "It was a fluke," Williamson told Quittner. Within a few weeks, the name was reassigned to MCI.[13]

Network Solutions changed its approach in the summer of 1995. The company, having itself been named a codefendant in a lawsuit over a domain, decided to adopt a formal domain dispute policy, aimed in part at insulating the company from future suits. The policy required applicants to certify that the names they intended to register did not interfere with trademarks or other intellectual-property rights. If a trademark holder contested a registration, Network Solutions asked the domain owner to present evidence that it had trademarked the name. If no proof was provided, the name was placed on hold, which meant it couldn't be used by either side until the dispute was resolved. If proof was provided, the name's owner could continue using it—but only if the owner agreed to indemnify Network Solutions in any lawsuit.

The policy drew a flurry of criticism from domain owners and legal experts. One objection was that Network Solutions only recognized U.S. federal or foreign trademark registrations, ignoring state trademarks and rights a Web-site owner might have gained over time under common-law use of the name. Critics also said the policy was biased in favor of challengers because they could get a name placed on hold—which, in some cases, shut down an entire business—without any ruling by a judge on the merits of their case.

Hundreds of disputes were initiated under the policy. Some trademark holders got away with suspending legitimate registrations of domains, including generic words like "prince" and "roadrunner," which gave rise to the term "reverse domain name hijacking."[14] Some domain holders fought back, filing suit against their foe, Network Solutions, or both. Network Solutions tweaked the policy several times, but it remained highly controversial.

The bullying tactics brought negative press to some trademark holders. In one well-publicized incident, Prema Toy, which held trademarks for the Gumby and Pokey bendable toys, tried to use Network Solutions' policy to wrest pokey.org from a twelve-year-old Pennsylvania boy, Chris "Pokey" Van Allen. His father had registered the name for him as a birthday present, and he used it for his personal Web site. It contained no content related to the Pokey toys, but rather pictures of his puppy and photographs of the planet Mars. After the media covered the story, Van Allen was showered with support from thousands of people around the world. Following some legal wrangling, seventy-eight-year-old Art Clokey, the creator of Gumby, intervened. He declared that Van Allen could use the address "in the spirit of Gumby."[15]

Domain names raised a host of new and perplexing questions in the field of intellectual-property law, especially when it came to trademarks. One problem was that only one company could register a domain, whereas under trademark law, multiple companies were entitled to use the same name, as long as they operated in different industries. That's why United Airlines, United Van Lines, and other companies using "United" could peacefully coexist.[16] But only one entity could register united.com. Trademark law also allowed for companies in different regions to share a name, but that was not practical on the borderless Internet.

It was by no means clear in the early days of the Web whether it was illegal to register trademark-associated domains in an effort to profit. But the question became less cloudy after companies sued Dennis Toeppen, a speculator from Champaign, Illinois. Toeppen was one of the first notorious cybersquatters. Over the years, scores of others would mimic him, while adding their own wrinkles. In doing so, they tested the skills—and patience—of lawyers representing famous brands.

Toeppen, who ran a small Internet service provider, registered about 240 domains. A few, including hydrogen.com, were generic English words, but many represented the trademarks of famous brands. The list included intermatic.com, panavision.com, deltaairlines.com, britishairways.com, and eddiebauer.com. Toeppen sought to profit by reselling the names to trademark holders or others, or by licensing them. "Many even-tempered folks purchased domain names and went on their way," Toeppen wrote later on his Web site, toeppen.com. "Others sued me."

Intermatic Inc. sued him in a Chicago federal court and won. In the 1996 ruling, the court found that Toeppen had diluted Intermatic's trademark for electrical and electronic products. Toeppen had displayed only a map of Champaign-Urbana on intermatic.com. However, he'd admitted to registering the name in hopes of selling it to Intermatic. That was crucial to Intermatic's winning the case, because under federal trademark law, a plaintiff must show commercial use of its marks. The court ruled that Toeppen's desire to resell the name was sufficient to meet that test.

On Oct. 3, 1996, in the case of *Intermatic Inc. v. Toeppen*, the court itself established a written description for the term *cybersquatters*. It called them individuals who "attempt to profit from the Internet by reserving and later reselling or licensing domain names back to the companies that spent millions of dollars developing the goodwill of the trademark."[17]

Panavision also sued and defeated Toeppen. He'd only displayed an aerial view of Pana, Illinois, on the site. But, according to a ruling by a California federal court, he'd offered to sell the domain to Panavision for $13,000. The court ruled, just as the Illinois court had, that the action constituted commercial use and that Toeppen had diluted Panavision's trademarks.

Soon after the defeats, Toeppen disposed of all domains associated with trademarks, according to a statement on his Web site. Fittingly, given his role in early domain-dispute law, one of Toeppen's addresses was trademark-lawyer. com.

"I Just Think They're Neat."

Contrary to popular belief, not all early domain speculators were cybersquatters. A number of them focused on scooping up generic addresses. One was CES Marketing Group, the Canadian firm. The company went after popular English words. In all, it registered about a thousand at no cost in 1995, including chocolates.com, suits.com, desks.com, and earrings.com. Neither CES nor other early investors could say with certainty that their names would be worth something one day, but at an acquisition cost of zero, they had little to lose.

And not everyone who registered multiple domains in the Web's infancy did it in a calculating way. Some collected a few on a whim, thinking they'd be fun to have even if they didn't end up being worth a dime. Mike O'Connor, who co-owned gofast.net, an Internet service provider in St. Paul, Minnesota, registered eleven names in 1993 and 1994, thinking they might be good for creating online discussion groups or easy-to-remember e-mail addresses. His names included television.com, bar.com, company. com, and ing.com. Five years later, he sold both company.com and ing. com for six-figure sums. When O'Connor registered his eleven domains, his friends thought he was "completely crazy" to get that many, even though he ran with "a pretty geeky crowd," he said. Meanwhile, the operator of a large Internet service provider in the Twin Cities expressed shock when O'Connor registered more than one name. "He was going, 'Well, that's not the way the Internet was designed. It wasn't designed to have any single entity having more than one name. What are you thinking of?' And I was going, 'I don't know, I just think they're neat.'"

Speculators weren't alone in acquiring large numbers of domains, nor were they the only ones to come under criticism for it. Procter & Gamble, the multinational consumer-products giant, registered hundreds. It grabbed names associated with its brands, but also collected many generic words, such as cough.com, underarms.com, pimples.com, and badbreath.com. For this activity, sibling authors Ellen and Peter Rony gave Procter & Gamble the dubious award of "Cyberserk Corporation" in their 1998 book, *The Domain Name Handbook*. "In our opinion, a corporation has a right to protect its registered trademarks, and this is one way of doing so, at minimal annual cost," they wrote. "On the other hand, if this becomes standard practice, all the meaningful words in the English language will be gobbled up, leaving latecomers to make do with odd names and abstruse fabrications . . . we have a clear case of corporate excess." For its part, Procter and Gamble said, "We are providing ourselves with more than one avenue to reach consumers with helpful information. We make 'Sure,' 'Secret,' and 'Old Spice.' Underarms are important to us."[18]

It took little time for the .com extension to become the most popular in the world. As big companies chose .com—after all, they were commercial entities—and advertised their sites on television, in print media, and on billboards, small businesses and individuals followed suit, believing .com was the Park Avenue or Rodeo Drive of domain suffixes. The makers of some Internet browsers helped fuel demand for .com by making it the default extension whenever a user typed a name into the address field of his browser and failed to list an extension. (For example, typing "games" would default to games.com, rather than games.net or games.org.) In addition, the administrators of domain extensions representing other countries, such as .jp for Japan and .fr for France, imposed tougher restrictions on who could get a domain—and how many—than Network Solutions did, heightening interest in .com abroad, too.[19]

But it took several years before prized .com domains—generally defined at the time as short, easy-to-spell, everyday words—began commanding hefty prices in the resale, or secondary, market. In 1996, CNET, an Internet media company, paid a total of $30,000 to acquire tv.com and radio.com, in one of the first reported sales of domains.[20] It was considered a huge amount of money. But CNET had been willing to spend even more than that for O'Connor's television.com alone. In the spring of 1996, it offered him $50,000 for it. He was about to sign the deal when a friend suggested that he might be shortchanging himself. Perhaps, the friend told him, there were other potential buyers. O'Connor panicked, called off the deal, and decided to hold an auction for two weeks. He contacted all the major TV networks, inviting them to bid. They didn't bite; their reactions ranged from "Huh?" to "We'll get back to you."[21] Nobody submitted a higher bid than CNET's, so O'Connor decided to hang on to the name. "I basically threw a party to which nobody came," he recounted.

Fertile Land

To learn who owns a domain, Web users search sites that publish the "Whois," a directory of Web addresses. In the mid-1990s, the InterNIC site run by Network Solutions let users search the database by typing in a domain, a domain owner's name, or an e-mail address, among other options.

When watermelon farmer Scott Day ran searches on watermelon.com and watermelons.com in late 1996, he found out they'd already been registered to CES Marketing. So he placed a phone call to the Canadian company. He explained that he raised watermelons, which made him ideally suited to own the domains, and asked how much it would cost to buy them. He was taken aback when CES Marketing suggested a figure of about $3,500 for both. The price seemed unreasonably high. After all, Scott knew it cost $100 to register a new name for two years. He talked it over with his father. "We were kind of blown away at first," Frank recalled. "We thought, *Good grief, is this going to cost this much?* And then we backed off for a bit and thought about it, and then we decided, well, maybe this would be a good thing to start and try."

The parties agreed to an unusual transaction. Red River Farms would pay CES Marketing $3,000, and send it a crate of watermelons. The Days sent the check, but CES Marketing was still waiting for the melons in 2007, a decade later. "Every day I expect this huge pallet of watermelons to arrive on my front yard," CES Marketing's Christopher Wall said with a chuckle.

The transaction sparked a long friendship between Scott Day and CES Marketing, which also made $5,000 in the mid-1990s selling icecream.com to ice-cream giant Dreyer's. The men in Vancouver—CES was an acronym for the owners' first names: Christopher, Eric (Woodward), and Scott (Musgrove)—always enjoyed talking to Scott and hearing about life on the farm. "We found him to be quite fun and cordial," said Wall. "He loved to chat." Wall and his city-dwelling colleagues were amused when they'd call for Scott and someone would have to locate him in the field on his tractor.

After securing watermelon.com and watermelons.com, Scott's next order of business was to start building Web pages. He studied HTML, or hypertext markup language, the computer language used to create Web pages, and designed watermelons.com as a portal for watermelon farmers. (Watermelon. com displayed the same content.)

On March 3, 1997, The Packer, a trade journal for the produce industry, published an article about Red River Farms' online venture. Watermelon. com "includes information about growers and shippers, packaging, seeds, transplants, industry associations, transportation, and supplies," it wrote. "[Frank] Day said he does not expect his company to 'make millions' off the site, but he does hope the site will boost the overall profitability of the industry."[22]

But selling other watermelon farmers on the importance of having a presence on the information superhighway wasn't easy. In early 1997, Scott set up booths at two conventions of watermelon farmers: the Oklahoma-Texas trade show in McAllen, Texas, and a national convention in Lake Tahoe, California. He signed up only a handful of customers. The farmers paid $250 for one year for Red River Farms to design a Web page for them. Scott went back to Terral and built their sites. But it took him hours. "I was spending way too much time developing a Web site for little to no money," he said. "HTML took me too long to learn." He realized that the Web-development business "would never really blossom into what I wanted it to be."

He also experimented with the idea of building an online agricultural directory, listing farms throughout the country. But that, too, was going to be extremely time-consuming, and Scott scrapped the concept before it got off the ground.

The one idea that Scott thought might have some promise was to invest in domains themselves. If a farmer was willing to spend $3,000 for watermelon.com and watermelons.com, "what would a business pay for a really good domain name?" he wondered. "That is kind of when a light bulb went off."

Although Day was a few years behind other speculators, his timing was fortuitous. In 1997, Network Solutions canceled thousands of domain registrations for nonpayment, making the addresses available for anyone to seize on a first-come, first-served basis. Many popular English words suddenly were up for grabs.

Why had so many people failed to pay for their names? For one, it wasn't clear they were worth much, if anything, so some owners didn't want to cough up $50 per year to keep them. (It cost $100 to register a new domain for two years, and $50 to renew an old one for one year.) Others didn't think it was fair that Network Solutions had begun charging for names. But in many cases, owners either didn't receive their bills or didn't take seriously Network Solutions' threat to cancel their registrations. Part of the problem, according to several early investors, was that there was confusion over Network Solutions' billing practices. The company began charging for domains as of September 14, 1995, but it took months for it to send out bills, typically by mail. And many invoices came back "return to sender," because the domain holder's address had changed since the original registration. There'd been little reason for owners to update their mailing addresses prior to the move to charge for domains. Also, some owners didn't keep good records of all their domain registrations and didn't alert Network Solutions to address changes after the company began charging fees. "There was just mass confusion," recalled CES's Christopher Wall, whose company lost some names by not closely monitoring all of its roughly one thousand registrations.

Adding to the disorder, when customers did mail their payments to Network Solutions, it took the company months to process them. The delays made some investors question how serious Network Solutions was about bill collection. Some investors registered scores of names they knew they couldn't afford, thinking they could wait and see if someone came along and offered to buy them before Network Solutions got around to demanding payment. Network Solutions didn't require payment immediately upon registration; instead, according to its rules, under "normal conditions" it sent out an invoice by postal and electronic mail within seven days of activating a domain, and payment was then due within thirty days. As of June 1996, the owners of about 25,000, or 10 percent, of the 250,000 domains registered since Network Solutions began charging fees had yet to pay for them.[23] The company began cutting off names for nonpayment, and made a few mistakes along the way. In one high-profile case, it briefly disconnected MSNBC.com, the online news site run by Microsoft and NBC, even though MSNBC had sent in its payment.[24]

Things were so chaotic at Network Solutions that huge stacks of mail piled up in its offices, unopened for weeks or months. The company had to hire several dozen temporary workers so it could start culling through mail, processing checks, and completing other routine administrative tasks. "We had some huge challenges," said a former Network Solutions employee. "We had boxes of returned mail . . . It was just a horrendous situation to catch up with."

When Network Solutions got around to deleting thousands of names for nonpayment, it played right into Scott Day's hands. But it wasn't easy to figure out how to identify and acquire newly deleted domains. Scott scoured the Web for information. He also made a few phone calls to other speculators. Soon he began to piece together a rough timeline of how Network Solutions went about releasing expired names. In the Whois record, Network Solutions published a domain's "status." If it was listed as "on hold," that generally meant the previous owner had not paid to renew it, and soon it would be released so that anyone could register it. Network Solutions' rules said a domain owner generally had sixty days after his name was deactivated to pay his bill and reactivate. If the time expired, the name would be released. A few companies compiled voluminous lists of on-hold domains and allowed users to access them. Few people knew about such lists, and even if they had, it's unlikely they would have cared. It was mostly a small group of domain speculators who religiously monitored such lists.

Scott was one of them. He began printing out "on-hold lists" each day and marking the names that appealed to him. Then he went about trying to register them as soon as they were released. That proved to be arduous. First, it was hard to anticipate when Network Solutions would release a name from on-hold status. A speculator had to constantly enter queries on the InterNIC Web site to see whether a name was available. As soon as a desired name was released, the speculator needed to move quickly to register it in case others were vying for it. And registration wasn't a simple, one-step process. Users had to fill out a template on the InterNIC site, listing the name they wanted, as well as their contact information. After completing the template, they waited for an e-mail from the InterNIC, with a copy of the information. They then had to verify that the information was correct by sending it back to the InterNIC by email. Domain applicants also could use a text version of the template and e-mail it directly to the InterNIC. But in either case, e-mail, rather than a direct request on the InterNIC's Web site, was the form by which names were registered. Confirmation of a successful application came by e-mail—typically within twenty-four hours.

Catchy generic names could attract competition from a half-dozen or more speculators. The winner had to be lightning-quick at zapping e-mails to Network Solutions. To improve their odds, some speculators wrote computer programs that automatically sent e-mails on their behalf.

The release of the expired names became known as the "drop." When a name was released, it "dropped" into the pool of available names. Investors who competed for such names became known as "drop catchers."

Scott was among the first drop catchers, and he was exceptionally good at it. He didn't work alone, however. While contacting other speculators for help, he formed a friendship with a Florida man who became his business partner in catching names. The partner was more skilled than Scott at the technical functions of the Internet, and together they made a formidable team.

At the farm each day, Frank Day gave Scott latitude to scout for domains whenever he could find time between other chores. He worked on an old Macintosh computer in the farm's wood-paneled office, which contained several dusty brown desks, a fan, some power tools, and watermelon-print curtains, sewn by Scott's mother, Jeannie. At home each night, Scott spent a few hours after dinner with his wife and daughter. Then he went to work on his computer, and often stayed up all night. On several occasions, Stacy Day said, Scott pretended to be asleep while lying next to her, only to rise once she'd fallen asleep, to boot up his computer.

Scott believed he had at most a two-year window of opportunity to register quality names. He related domains to farmland: "You have got to have quality land to build or grow a crop, and there's only so much good, fertile land," he said. And "there were only so many good dot-com domain names available."

Scott brainstormed about which words would be valuable one day, and enlisted Stacy's help. He sometimes handed her a notebook and said, "Here, write down anything you can think of. Anything. Just write down words." Stacy was baffled by the entire endeavor. She also got frustrated at times, because she didn't get to see much of her husband. "What are you doing?" she asked him on more than one occasion. "You're wasting time."

Scott focused on simple, straightforward names. He considered himself "a simple guy," and this trait paid off. In a short but frenetic period of his life, he grabbed hundreds of popular generic words that became available in the drop. The names included:

Scott Day-owned Domains

dress.com

tile.com

trips.com

prescription.com

moviereviews.com

webdesign.com

bathingsuits.com

chairs.com

cook.com

decorations.com

bed.com

computergames.com

penpal.com

desserts.com

Scott liked the names because most described a product or business. He thought he might be able to sell them one day to businesses for a handsome profit. He liked common English words because they could appeal to lots of potential buyers. In contrast, some early investors collected names that were too cute or complicated, such as WErSTOCKSANDBONDS.com and WErCLASSACTIONATTORNEYS.com (actual domains people registered and tried to sell).

But when Scott snagged his names, it wasn't clear he'd be able to make any money from them. Web addresses were highly speculative investments. The value of a domain was some unknown dollar figure that a buyer *might* pay for the name at some undetermined point in the future. It was akin to buying land in a remote area, hoping that one day a developer would offer money for it to build housing. Scott, of course, was confident that somebody would want to pay for one of his domains to build a business on it. After all, he'd paid $3,000 for watermelon.com and watermelons.com. Surely there'd be an increasing number of buyers like him as the Web expanded. But the secondary market for domain sales barely existed when he began investing. Few significant sales had become public knowledge by early 1997. That made it difficult to estimate the value of a domain. Three deals that had been reported were tv.com and radio.com (for $30,000 combined), grocery.com ($9,000), and search.com ($7,000).

But the prospects of riches resulted in fevered competition among at least a dozen ardent drop catchers in 1997. Day felt he needed to be near his computer almost every waking hour to seize names before his foes did. He became obsessed with winning. Few drop catchers were able to match his success. And they were puzzled by how Day pulled it off. Speculators commiserated by saying, "You've gotta get up pretty early to beat the watermelon farmer from Oklahoma."

"Scott Day, more than any other person or player, was able to register any domain that came on hold and dropped," Wall said. "We were all running [computer programs] to submit registrations in the middle of the night. [But] Scott registered a lot of domains that a lot of other people were trying to register at the same time. It was frustrating, because we could see these great domains sitting there on hold and not be able to find out how to scoop them."

When asked how he garnered so many coveted names, Scott said he "worked hard." He declined to discuss the details. "There were a lot of sleepless nights," he said. "When they would drop a batch of domain names, I stayed by my computer a lot."

There was little rhyme or reason to the process by which Network Solutions released names, but Day identified some patterns that helped him know when to be at his computer. One Halloween night, he was all set to go trick-or-treating with his wife and daughter when he realized that Network Solutions was releasing a group of names. His wife and daughter went without him.

Paying for the names was another matter. Scott and his father didn't have a lot of money to devote to domains, and at $100 each for two years, the costs mounted quickly. But because payment wasn't required immediately in those days, Scott registered dozens of names without sending in any money. However, one day in August 1997, a Network Solutions employee called him and said the company would delete his addresses if he didn't pay for them. The bill added up to more than $5,000. "For a small watermelon farmer, it was a lot of money," Scott said. And "we were new in the business and weren't real sure if this was going to be a great business to be in." But he resolved the problem by selling a name for $5,000. He paid for the balance of the bill with credit cards.

Scott continued to work for his dad as he compiled more Web addresses, but he spent less and less time on the farm. By 1999, he'd collected about 1,700 domains and formed a company called DigiMedia.com. To earn revenue, Scott redirected visitors to most of his sites to digimedia.com, and signed up for affiliate marketing programs. In affiliate marketing, Web sites display links—often in the form of banner advertisements or smaller ads known as buttons—to other sites that pay a commission for leads. In 1999, sites paid Scott's company under a variety of commission models. Some paid a flat fee for each user who clicked a button on his site and landed on theirs. Others paid only when the user became a paying customer or member of their site. Typically, each referral paid no more than a dollar. Scott signed up for a number of affiliate programs, including several from Microsoft's MSN online service and NextCard, an online credit-card issuer. Affiliate marketing was one of the few ways other than selling domains that a speculator could make some money in the Web's early days. Scott wasn't getting rich from his addresses by any stretch of the imagination, but he was starting to see some encouraging signs.

In the spring of 1999, Scott received an unusual phone call at the watermelon shed. The friendly caller said he represented the George W. Bush presidential campaign and wanted to know if Scott was the owner of georgebush.com. Scott said he was. Scott was a fan of Bush, then the governor of Texas, and had registered the address a few years earlier. The caller said he might be interested in buying the name. Scott, who wasn't doing anything with it (which greatly limited any legal risk he might have), said he'd be happy to give it to the campaign for free. A few days later, he received a follow-up call from the Bush campaign, which said it would gladly accept the domain, and invited him and his wife to attend a small gathering with Bush at the governor's mansion in Austin. Scott and Stacy joined about fifteen other guests at the event, including several dignitaries. The Days were invited to pose for a photograph with Bush. Scott and Stacy framed it when they got home. In remarks in front of the group about his goals for his presidential campaign, Bush mentioned that he was happy to have in the room a watermelon farmer from neighboring Oklahoma.

Who was responsible for acquiring georgebush.com? An Austin-based political consultant named Karl Rove. In the late 1990s, Rove read about domain speculators and decided to grab any names he could think of related to Bush before others could get to them. Rove helped the Bush campaign snag about two hundred, including dubya.net, bushsucks.com, and bushblows. com.[25] Like many early domain investors, the man later called "Bush's Brain" showed a flair for anticipating his competition.

Scott Day's brush with American royalty was quite a thrill. But there was plenty of excitement yet to come for Day and other early domain speculators.

Chapter Two

From Dirt Bikes to Domains

Garry Chernoff was a dreamer. He was one of those people who read the classified listings in the backs of magazines. The ads were filled with possibilities: work from home, get rich quick, own the house of your dreams.

Chernoff was their ideal target. He'd been raised in a middle-class, blue-collar family in rural British Columbia, but he had a feeling—a very real, persistent feeling—that he would be wealthy someday. He just knew it.

As a kid in the 1970s, Chernoff tried all kinds of activities. He played baseball, soccer, and hockey, and he dabbled in collecting stamps, playing guitar, and drawing cartoons. He even formed a slingshot club with his best friend. He also loved riding dirt bikes in the hills surrounding his hometown of Penticton, a charming hamlet bordered by two pristine lakes. Penticton means "a place to live forever" in the language of local Salish Native Americans.

In high school, Chernoff began fancying cars. To afford one, he began working as a restaurant cook on evenings and weekends. His second car was particularly sweet: a candy-apple red 1967 Ford Mustang. Chernoff was a very good student early in high school, but as he shifted his attention to jobs and cars, he began to spend less time on schoolwork. And when his parents split up in grade twelve, school became even less of a priority. Going to college hadn't really occurred to him, anyway. Neither of his parents had finished high school. His father was a plumber and pipefitter, and his mother a homemaker.

After graduating from high school in 1981, Chernoff set out to be a tradesman, like his father. He took a six-month preapprentice course to be an electrician, but when he finished, the economy in western Canada was sputtering, and he couldn't find a job. He languished for a year on unemployment, unable to figure out what to do with his life. Finally, his brother, one of three older siblings, told him he needed to do something and suggested he get a degree in electronics. So Chernoff entered Selkirk College in Castlegar, British Columbia. He earned a two-year electronics degree and followed that up with a four-year electrical apprenticeship. Thus began his career as an electrician.

In 1995, Chernoff was working at Penticton Regional Hospital and living in a small townhouse with his four-year-old son, Jon. He was thirty-two years old, about $50,000 in debt (including his mortgage), and living paycheck to paycheck. He routinely reached the spending limit on his credit card, and often dipped into his overdraft protection to avoid bouncing checks. But he was inspired to earn some extra income when he read a manual called *How to Start and Operate a Profitable Homemade Booklet Business*, by Don Massey. The manual was among a phalanx of books that Chernoff collected over the years dealing with making money from home or getting rich quick. "I always thought booklets would be the easiest way to make money from your home to start, because it doesn't cost anything to write what you know about," Chernoff said. "Everyone knows something other people would like to know."

Chernoff read about the World Wide Web in magazines and had a hunch it was going to be huge. Why not write a booklet about how to make money on the Internet? he thought. He decided to give it a whirl. Chernoff called his booklet *50 Idiot-Proof Ways to Make Money on the Net*.

The Web was so new to just about everyone that Chernoff, who'd used computers primarily to play videogames, didn't fret that he lacked authority to write such a guide. He simply made up the fifty ways off the top of his head. They included creating an online auction service (later a proven winner for a company called eBay); an online trivia game; an astrology charting service; and becoming an online aircraft broker. The booklet required much more work than Chernoff anticipated. It took him nearly six months to finish it, and he had to burn many of his vacation days.

In the introduction to his book, Chernoff wrote a few sentences that sounded very much like a sales pitch. Later, they would come to describe Chernoff's own life.

> You can indeed make money with the Internet, lots of it, and it isn't hard. You will get excited thinking about the potentially unlimited Net income you will earn by being your own boss, answering to only yourself, and getting rewarded proportionally to your own efforts. [1]

To promote his booklet online, Chernoff registered his first domain name. He wanted the name to have something to do with making money, so he loaded a thesaurus program onto his computer and typed in the word "profit." The synonym that caught his eye was "net income." It was brilliant, Chernoff thought. The term referred not only to making money but also to the Net, short for Internet.

"I thought, *My God, how perfect is that?* It was a ray of light from the heaven above," Chernoff recalled. With the help of the man who ran the local Internet service provider, Chernoff registered netincome.com. He called his company Netincome Ventures.

Chernoff earned only about $10,000 selling roughly five thousand copies of his booklet through various distribution channels. But he got some publicity for it, including a guest appearance on a Canadian radio talk show and a blurb in Maxim magazine's U.K. edition.

Although the booklet generated little money for all the work it required, Chernoff continued to hunt for other booklet ideas. Many people complimented him on his domain. Also, he'd read news reports about several speculators who'd sold names for thousands of dollars. He decided to pursue a booklet about how to make money selling Web addresses. But once he began his research, he changed his mind. He realized he could probably make a lot more money investing in names than writing about them.

In 1997, Chernoff began checking on whether certain popular English words had been registered, such as cars.com and computer.com. He kept finding that they were. One day, he checked the Whois database for retired. com. The report told him the domain was "on hold." He had no idea what that meant. He sent an e-mail to Edwin Hayward, an Englishman who ran a domain news site, igoldrush.com, out of his home in Tokyo. Hayward told Chernoff that the owner of the address likely had failed to renew the name, and that it probably would soon be available for anyone to register. Every other day for a few weeks, Chernoff checked the InterNIC site to see if he could get it. One Saturday in June 1997, he e-mailed an application for the domain and got it. He was thrilled.

At that point, Chernoff concluded that identifying common English words that were in on-hold status could be a route to success. But he didn't know where he could find a regularly updated list of on-hold names. Hayward told him he didn't know where such a list could be obtained—that it was the holy grail of domain research. "I thought that was the key," Chernoff said, because so many good domains already were taken. "I asked around, and people told me it didn't exist, that they were looking for that, too. I posted a message on one of the Usenet newsgroups, and one person said where to find it. I couldn't believe it."

The site was SAEGIS.com. SAEGIS was a service used by intellectual-property lawyers to find uses of trademarks online. The site allowed users to search all Web addresses currently in on-hold status. If the user clicked on a name to view its Whois record, SAEGIS charged 25 cents. But Chernoff didn't need that information. He just wanted to know what names were about to expire, so he could go to Network Solutions and try to grab them as soon as they became available.

Like Scott Day, Christopher Wall, and others, Chernoff spent hours poring over on-hold lists. When names became available, he e-mailed Network Solutions as fast as he could. And he was able to grab a number of potentially valuable domains, including cabinets.com, refinance.com, babyfoods.com, and gourmetfood.com. But he needed a way to make some money off the names to cover his costs. One day, he noticed autoglass.com was about to drop. "Nobody sells auto glass online; that's no good," he recalled thinking at the time. "I couldn't understand what they'd use it for. But I thought, it is the name of an industry, so it must be worth something." He registered the name and contacted several large auto-glass manufacturers to see if any would buy it. A big Canadian company asked him to name a price. Figuring he had nothing to lose by throwing out a big number, he asked for $5,000. "They said, 'We'll take it. How do we send you the money?'" Chernoff said. "So they sent me a check for $5,000 U.S., and at that time it was like winning the lottery. I was living on overdraft, I had credit cards racked up, and here's $5,000 for just a few days' work."

The transaction convinced him that being a speculator would pay off. *If someone is going to pay me $5,000 today, what are they going to pay for these things ten years from now?* he recalled thinking. He flipped other names and used the profits to register more names. For example, he paid $100 to register taxshelter.com for two years, and then flipped it for $600. Aside from netincome.com, where he listed domains for sale and links to information on the Web, Chernoff didn't build Web sites on his addresses.

Chernoff stole as many hours as he could at his computer before and after work. The purring sound of his dial-up modem became his son, Jon's, lullaby. Jon knew that his dad was close by and all was well when he heard the modem churning. If Chernoff was doing something else and wasn't at his machine, Jon grew worried. "Dad, why aren't you up here in your office?" he'd ask.

There weren't many people spending hours snapping up newly expired Web addresses. So when Chernoff checked Whois records to see who'd grabbed a domain he'd been chasing, he kept seeing the same people's names. And the one that seemed to come up most often was that of a watermelon farmer in Oklahoma. "That darn Scott Day guy! His name came up way too many times," Chernoff said.

Even as Chernoff acquired and sold names, he worried about the long-term prospects of being a speculator, especially as competition for names increased. By 1998, he owned about a hundred addresses. At $100 apiece for two years, registering many domains cost a lot of money for a person of modest means. Things got a little better in April 1998, when Network Solutions lowered the registration price to $70 for two years and $35 per year after that. But speculators had to be patient to see a return on their investment, and it wasn't certain that the Internet would be a commercial hit. Domains "were very expensive," Chernoff said. "And there was no way to make money on the traffic. I was just hoping to sell them."

Chernoff brainstormed ways to generate cash. One idea was to lease names to businesses. He figured that if he could collect a steady stream of rental income, he might be able to quit his day job, where he earned about $40,000 Canadian per year (about $29,000 U.S. at the time). He desperately wanted to stay home so little Jon wouldn't have to go to day care. Chernoff asked a lawyer to draw up a standard lease agreement for domains. For the lawyer, it was a first, but he did it.

The move proved wise. With persistence, Chernoff was able to lease about forty names, including retired.com, barstools.com, refinance.com, and bowlingballs.com. He started out charging $50 a month, but steadily raised the price to $100 or $200. He typically gave the tenant an option to buy the name at a fixed price. Chernoff began earning enough money from leasing to strongly consider quitting the hospital.

The Domain King

While most early domain investors, like Garry Chernoff, chugged along, gradually building their portfolios and hoping for a big killing one day, a loquacious former furniture salesman, Rick Schwartz, raked in huge profits. How did he do it? In a word: porn.

Most industries on the Web struggled in the mid-1990s. Even the celebrated dot-coms that went public mostly bled red ink. Pornography sites were an exception, and they were willing to part with lots of cash to advertise their wares on other Web sites. That's where Richard H. "Rick" Schwartz came in. He hawked advertising space on his slate of adult-oriented domains, including porno.com, ass.com, dirtysites.com, and voyeur.com. Schwartz didn't produce pornography himself; he funneled Web users to porn sites. He drew so much traffic that he didn't need to sell his domains to make money from them.

Schwartz, who lived in south Florida, said he recognized the potential to profit from domains because he'd invested in a similar industry in the early 1990s: the 1-800 business. Schwartz owned several hundred toll-free vanity numbers, such as 1-800-MAKEOUT and 1-800-SIR-LOVE. He arranged for calls to be forwarded to phone-sex services, and received a cut of the sales. The calls went to "live party lines" that were "not hardcore adult in nature," he said.

Schwartz was among a number of entrepreneurs who saw parallels between vanity phone numbers and Web addresses. "While I was late to enter the 800 game," Schwartz said, "I was right on time for domain names."

Schwartz attributed his success partly to his years of education in a wide range of industries, from fast food to liquor to manufacturing. Schwartz was born in New Jersey in 1953. He grew up in a hardworking, middle-class family. At an early age, he was driven to succeed financially. His father, Hyman Schwartz, had jobs in the federal government and the private sector that required the family to move often—Schwartz refused to say what his father did. Growing up, Schwartz lived in a half-dozen states, including Maryland, Massachusetts, and California. He attended three different schools his last three semesters of high school. Having to change schools frequently and make new friends caused Schwartz to yearn to leave school and enter the job market. He attended a community college in California for about eighteen months before dropping out. He entered the furniture business, first in retail, then in wholesale. His experience in furniture sales helped him see the value of simple, straightforward domains—the kind people would type into their Web browsers to search for relevant information, he said. "I've been in enough businesses in my life to know how hard it is to get people in your front door," Schwartz said. "Even on a busy day in the furniture business, you may only get fifteen to twenty customers coming into your door. So that would basically be my threshold [for deciding whether to buy a domain]. How could I have that guarantee of traffic even before I unlock the door?" In the domain market, the traffic became known as type-in traffic.

Schwartz was a consummate salesman. For about a decade, he traveled the U.S. selling furniture for a wholesaler. In his thirties, he struck out on his own in various business lines. But he foundered while running a company selling novelty advertising items, including hot-air balloons and blimps. In 1989, Schwartz filed for Chapter 7 bankruptcy. He was thirty-six, single, and living in Truro, Massachusetts, near the tip of Cape Cod. In his bankruptcy filing, he listed $123,000 in liabilities, including more than $100,000 in credit-card debt spread over about twenty-five cards. He had $17,000 in assets, including his year-old Mercury Cougar and $7,350 in business inventory. Schwartz received a gift from a family member to pay his attorney. Under the bankruptcy laws, he was able to discharge all of his credit-card debt. However, one credit-card issuer, Chevy Chase Federal Savings Bank, sued him, claiming he'd grossly misrepresented his income on an application. Schwartz had listed annual income of $96,000 plus a bonus. But in his bankruptcy filing, he said his income for the same period in which he applied for the card was $14,250. Schwartz denied falsifying the application, explaining that he'd included the income and assets of his business. But a federal judge ruled against him, saying his explanation wasn't credible because his business reported only $996 in net income in 1986 and a $236 loss in 1987. Schwartz was required to repay the $9,400 he owed the bank.

Several factors led to the bankruptcy, Schwartz recalled. He was new to running a business and "had a lot to learn." He also ruptured a disc in his back and couldn't attend some of the trade shows where he struck deals. In addition, the U.S. economy was stumbling. "I would go to the shows, and the attendance was way off, and sales would not even cover my hotel and travel expenses," he said. "I just got to the point where I was in over my head."

Schwartz soon rebounded from his financial woes.

He registered his first domain, lipservice.com, on Dec. 27, 1995, paying only the $100 registration fee. It wasn't poised to be a big moneymaker, but Schwartz liked it because he believed word-of-mouth advertising was the best kind, and he believed the Web was the "ultimate word-of-mouth machine," he said. The choice—at least the "lip" part—was apt. The word had to do with talking, and Schwartz liked to talk. In fact, he talked so much about his passion for domains that over time he became a leading ambassador for domains and the people who invested in them—a group that, thanks to cybersquatters, had a major image problem.

Schwartz plowed some of the profits he made from porn ads into buying more domains. When critics told him he was wasting money, his retort was that he was capitalizing on a once-in-a-lifetime opportunity. He told them, "Your father didn't have this opportunity and his grandfather didn't have this opportunity." [2]

Schwartz used the Whois database to look up and contact the owners of names he wanted to buy. He grabbed ass.com from a man in Germany for $12,500. He paid a mere $15,000 for men.com in 1997; he later sold it for $1.3 million. "Can't get much better than men.com. It's half the population of the planet," he quipped in 1999.[3] He was a buy-and-hold investor, but sold a few names. In the late 1990s, he sold escore.com to Stanley H. Kaplan Educational Centers for $100,000, and used the proceeds to buy his mother an oceanfront condominium in Fort Lauderdale, Florida.

In the middle and late 1990s, Schwartz bought about two thousand adult-oriented names. Many were vulgar, like slut.com and whore.com. Some were the type that might only be printed in X-rated publications. Schwartz also bought about one thousand mainstream names, such as wholesalejewelry. com, tradeshows.com, and discountreservations.com. But his revenue was largely in the adult names.

The layout of porno.com in late 1998 was typical of his adult sites. The top of the page said "Porno.com Presents" in bold turquoise letters against a black background. Below it, the phrase "The Very Best Adult Sites" blinked in bold green letters. The site instructed viewers in all caps that it was for "adults only." And it featured large, flashing links to a handful of porn sites. Each time a customer clicked on a link and ended up on one of the sites, Schwartz received a commission. He worked on a flat rate that was paid in advance, he said. It was a variation of online affiliate marketing, which was pioneered by adult companies. Porno.com warned visitors that "minors and easily offended people MUST exit"; if users clicked on the exit link, they were directed to Schwartz's tradeshows.com, of all sites.

Schwartz bought porno.com—his most lucrative name—for $42,000 in 1997, from a man who'd bought it only a week earlier for $5,000. People familiar with the transaction "wanted to take me to the insane asylum," Schwartz recalled. However, thanks to affiliate advertising revenue, he recouped the cost of the name in only two months. In 1997, Schwartz's second full year as a speculator, he earned more than $1 million in revenue. He'd hit the jackpot, especially considering he'd set aside just $1,800 to invest in domains when he started.

"In those days it was impossible to monetize mainstream traffic, so basically I had no choice but to focus on adult," Schwartz said. "They were paying for the traffic; they understood the nature of the traffic. To this day I don't know if mainstream has quite caught up to where adult was in 1997." Today, porno. com alone earns more than $1 million a year from ads, Schwartz said. Dick. com, which Schwartz bought for $100, makes $100 to $200 a day.

After building a successful portfolio, Schwartz posted long-winded commentaries about his feats on erealestate.com, a portal he designed to showcase his business. He touted his smart purchases and chastised large companies for failing to recognize and appreciate the power of domains. He later created a private online forum for investors. Schwartz was an industry leader, and that made some domain investors nervous. Some didn't like the fact that he made most of his money from ads for adult content, and others didn't like his ego. On the other hand, Schwartz was friendly and outgoing, and spent hours sharing advice with newcomers to the trade.

Schwartz, who wore a goatee, glasses, multicolored shirts, and flashy jewelry (including a diamond-studded Rolex), called himself the "Domain King." The beginning of his e-mail address was "mr800king." Schwartz said someone else gave him the Domain King moniker, but he did little to quell its use. He labeled erealestate.com "the worldwide virtual home of the domain king!" The site, mostly developed in the late 1990s, included tips and resources for investors. It was filled with lots of puffed-up prose, such as this paragraph:

> While others lose millions, we make millions and prepare to make billions! That is the strength of a plan that is well thought out and easily and quickly adaptable to changing times and conditions. While I sit back and watch this chaos, I am able to spot great opportunities and capitalize on them within minutes. Patience really is key.

But the site also featured insightful observations—information that earned Schwartz the respect of many investors. He was ahead of the curve, for instance, in his recognition of the value of type-in traffic.

> While others depend on search engines for traffic or paying for traffic from third parties, we are self-sufficient. We get our hits from direct "type-ins" on the browser bar. This is because many folks will first attempt to bypass the search engines and they input our URLs directly into the address line on the browser they use. The result is the most potent and targeted traffic anyone on the Internet can pull. Our sites are destinations.

Schwartz "has an ego as big as a house," said Richard Meyer, an investor in Ellicott City, Maryland, but "you and I in our lifetime would like to be as successful as Rick Schwartz."

Schwartz relished preaching his views to neophytes. He helped many become successful. One was Roy Messer of Tallahassee, Florida. Messer had owned his own retail flooring business for more than twenty years, and it had been, in his own words, a "roller coaster ride." In some years, he earned six figures for himself, and others much less. Like Schwartz, he'd filed for bankruptcy. Messer began investing in domains in 1998 after reading an article in USA Today about the market. "The idea seemed simple enough to try," he said. "It turned out not to be so simple—lots of long-hour days searching and mining for domains." One day, Messer called Schwartz, told him he was in south Florida, and asked if he could pay a visit. Schwartz happily gave him his view of the universe. It paid off for Messer, who became a big player in the market with names such as vodka.com, razors.com, and furniturestore.com.

Leap of Faith

If Rick Schwartz had an equal when it came to salesmanship and marketing savvy in the domain business (and at times, bluster), it was Marc Ostrofsky.

Like Schwartz, Ostrofsky began selling things at a young age, and never let up. While a marketing major at the University of Texas at Austin in the early 1980s, Ostrofsky sold real estate on weekends, often to parents of students. He also bought jewelry from a wholesaler and peddled it to sororities, sometimes pocketing $1,500 for a few days work. The son of a business professor at the University of Houston, he loved figuring out ways to earn a buck. "I made a lot of money while my friends were out having parties on the weekends," he said. "I loved it."

Shortly after college, Ostrofsky and his then-wife, Sara, started a trade magazine about the pay-telephone business out of their one-bedroom Houston apartment with $5,000. Within a few years, they turned the publication, Pay Phone Magazine, into a multimillion-dollar business. Journalists covering telecommunications regularly called Ostrofsky for quotes because he was one of the nation's foremost experts on the pay phone market. Ostrofsky said he sold the company for $7.5 million in the early 1990s. Then he built another successful publisher of telecommunications magazines called MultiMedia Publishing, which he sold for $35 million in 1999 to New York publishing giant Primedia.

In 1995, Ostrofsky's sister, Keri Pearlson, a professor at the University of Texas, invited him to speak to her class. At one point during the visit, she showed him how she was researching the Internet. Ostrofsky, always curious about possible new lines of business, asked how one went about acquiring "one of those names" she kept typing into her browser. They went to the InterNIC site and looked up a few addresses. Ostrofsky had just rented a car, so they looked up whether Avis.com and Hertz.com had been taken.

Avis.com was gone, but Hertz.com was available. Ostrofsky wondered if he ought to explore registering some domains. However, he thought, if they were valuable, why hadn't they all been snatched up by big companies? He returned to Houston and continued to chew on the idea. Finally, one night in May 1996, the thirty-four-year-old registered about one hundred names on the InterNIC site. It took him all night because he was using dial-up Internet access, and it was tedious filling out each application. The names included ebusiness.com, eflowers.com, eradio.com, and etickets.com. The registration fees totaled about $10,000. "It was a leap of faith, but I believed that one day those names might be worth a lot," he said.[4]

Ostrofsky didn't know what to do with the names, so he hung on to them and waited. In the meantime, he recognized an opportunity to help large corporations, many of which didn't understand Web addresses, register all their corporate names and brands in the many different domain extensions. At the time, a few hundred countries had their own suffix, known in industry parlance as a country-code top-level domain. Ostrofsky started a company to register names on behalf of big businesses, teaming up with a fraternity brother from the University of Texas, Pinkard Alan "Pinky" Brand. They'd gotten reacquainted in the early 1990s through the Young Entrepreneurs Organization in Houston. Ostrofsky struck Brand as the rare businessman who wasn't afraid to fail, said Brand. "We all talk about things, but very few of us go out and act on our dreams," he said.

They formed idNames.com in June 1996, while Ostrofsky continued to run his media company. They landed McDonald's, America Online, and other large companies as clients. Brand found Ostrofsky brilliant, but said he could be tough to work with. They sometimes got into screaming matches, but Brand said he always walked away knowing it was merely business, and they remained good partners. "Marc can be abrasive," Brand said. "He's mellowed out a lot over the years. He's just a hypercompetitive guy."

In 1997, Ostrofsky came up with the idea of starting a business-oriented portal called business.com. When he checked the Whois database, he found it was owned by a British computer company, Business Systems International, or BSI, which had registered it for free several years earlier. Ostrofsky decided to place a big bet on the name. In April 1997, he paid BSI a whopping $150,000. It was believed at the time to be the most money ever spent for a domain. Later that spring, a media company, Mecklermedia Corp., paid more than $100,000 for internet.com, but neither it nor the seller disclosed the exact price.[5]

Ostrofsky saw the purchase of business.com as an opportunity to promote idNames.com, so he and Brand issued a press release in June 1997 saying "Texas firm pays world-record price for domain name."[6] They said idNames.com had "handled" the transaction (i.e., brokered it), but they did not mention anywhere in the release that Ostrofsky was the buyer. And when contacted by reporters, Brand refused to reveal the purchaser.

The press release even quoted Ostrofsky referring to the mysterious buyer. "Our client was pleased to have the opportunity to purchase one of the few 'instant brand names' available for sale," Ostrofsky was quoted as saying. The release said Ostrofsky was the person who'd handled the transaction.

Brand said it was a publicity stunt of sorts. "Marc has always been good about getting press," he said. "This was something that Marc wanted to do because he knew that domain names would be popular, and he knew that this would get us press that we couldn't possibly buy by going out and buying ads for idNames."

Ostrofsky said a key reason he didn't want to be named was that he was concerned he'd look like "a fool." The perception at the time, he recounted, was that only an idiot would pay $150,000 for a Web address. "We were pleased that we didn't disclose it," he said. "And it was a brilliant PR move."

In the spring of 1998, Ostrofsky sold idNames to Network Solutions for an undisclosed price, and Brand moved to Virginia to run Network Solutions' idNames division. Network Solutions had been spun off into a public company by its former parent, Science Applications International, in September 1997.

Ostrofsky's purchase of business.com was important to the domain market. It led more people to invest in names, believing they might be able to sell them at similar prices. And it helped trigger a string of six- and seven-figure sales over the next several years. The deals also reflected the enthusiasm for all things Internet in the go-go late 1990s. Some deals were prudent and yielded long-term benefits to the buyer; others didn't work out particularly well.

Fledgling domain brokers, such as GreatDomains.com, Afternic.com, and HitDomains.com (later known as Moniker.com), also helped fuel the dealmaking. The brokers solicited private bids or held auctions, sometimes advertising lists of names in major financial publications like The Wall Street Journal or Financial Times. They listed domains on their sites by price or topic, and parties typically negotiated by e-mail. Some brokers offered escrow services, and some sold appraisals to help customers try to assign values to their names. The appraisers took into account such factors as the length of the name (the shorter the better), whether it ended in .com (the preferred extension), and whether it drew significant type-in traffic. Auction giant eBay also became a popular place to peddle names. Hundreds of thousands of domains were listed for sale on brokerage and auction sites at the peak of Internet euphoria. But the buying and selling on eBay and some other sites came with risks. There was no regulation of domain transactions, and buyers and sellers sometimes duped each other. Some sellers took their cash without transferring the name to the buyer, and some buyers managed to acquire names without paying. Some bidders never materialized. This was highlighted when the apparent $10 million winning bid for Year2000.com on eBay at the turn of the millennium turned out to be a hoax. The more reputable brokerage sites like GreatDomains.com, founded by a California real-estate broker, used contract and escrow procedures similar to those used in real-estate transactions.

Roughly a dozen sales of at least $1 million were reported in the dot-com boom. There were certainly others, but most transactions are kept confidential by the parties for reasons of business competition or privacy.

One of the first million-dollar domain sales involved a twenty-four-year-old. While in college in Arizona, Matthew Grossman had registered about one hundred domains, many of which corresponded to corporate trademarks. He routinely handed over names to trademark holders in exchange for gifts. He got a vacuum cleaner for dirtdevil.com, a case of Seven-Up and a T-shirt for 7up.com, and a case of ice cream for breyers.com.[7] In April 1999, he hit the jackpot.

Grossman co-owned wallstreet.com with Eric Wade, a former Albuquerque stockbroker, and Ehud Gavron, Wade's friend, who'd registered the name in 1994. The three partners decided to hire New Commerce Communications, a merger and acquisition service, to auction off wallstreet.com online. It was an ideal name for many different businesses, from an investment bank to a financial news outlet. And it drew a lot of type-in traffic. "Between 4,000 and 17,000 people a day would just type 'Wall Street' into their browser," Wade said. "We called it background noise. People were just typing it in to see what would happen."[8] Wade's wife, Ana Montoya-Wade, likened the domain to the "most prime beachfront property on the Internet."[9]

The sellers set a minimum bid of $300,000. Suitors included adult-entertainment companies, gambling companies, individual investors, and investment firms, said Monte Cahn, who ran the domain brokerage HitDomains.com in Pompano Beach, Florida, and helped New Commerce Communications arrange the auction. "Interest in the name was quite phenomenal," he said. It was a live, six-round auction. An Internet marketing company in Saint Kitts, an island in the Caribbean, won the address with a bid of $1.03 million. The company said it planned to set up a gambling game based on stock performance. When the name sold for more than $1 million, "people just couldn't believe it," Cahn said. Wade and his friends were inundated with phone calls from the media. (It wasn't the first reported domain sale in the millions of dollars. In 1998, a strange set of circumstances led altavista.com to be sold for $3.35 million.)

Another major transaction in 1999—the sale of drugs.com—underscored the differences of opinion that existed between speculators and much of corporate America about the value of generic domains. "Drugs" is a common English word, and it's a mere five letters. The name also represents a multibillion-dollar industry, pharmaceuticals. And if viewed in the context of the world's drug problem, it's easy to see why it might appeal to an organization focused on combating that crisis.

But when Bonnie Neubeck of Minneapolis tried to sell drugs.com to pharmaceutical companies in early 1999, the fifty-one-year-old was rebuffed. "I was sure drug companies would jump at this domain name right away," said Neubeck, who registered it in 1994. "But amazingly they didn't realize what a great investment it would be."[10]

So Neubeck, working with a twenty-one-year-old partner, Eric MacIver, who'd purchased an option to buy the name from her, decided to put the name up for sale that summer through an online auction conducted by GreatDomains.com. The auction was held over several weeks. At first, it drew mild interest and a number of pranksters. A bogus "Bill Gates" submitted six offers.[11] Some analysts speculated that the name wouldn't appeal to major drug companies because they historically focused on building brand names. "I wonder if the name is so general as to not communicate any brand names, so I'm not sure how valuable it is," said Lauren Levitan, an investment analyst.[12]

"Whatever drugs.com sells for will be a bargain," Rick Schwartz, the Florida investor told Wired News. "The mainstream hasn't figured out the power of the domain yet."[13]

The auction picked up steam on the final day. In the last thirty minutes, bidding rose from about $300,000 to the winning bid of $823,456. The victor was Venture Frogs, a new San Francisco technology investment company run by two entrepreneurs in their twenties, Tony Hsieh and Alfred Lin, and named after their friend's pet, Frisky the Frog. The men, who'd sold a company to Microsoft a year earlier for a reported $250 million, planned to develop drugs.com into a pharmaceutical shopping portal. At a news conference in San Francisco, the chief executive of GreatDomains.com, Jeffrey Tinsley, called the sale "history in the making" and bragged about the nationwide media coverage it attracted.[14]

The auction, however, was tinged with controversy. Schwartz and a group of about twenty-five other adult Web-site owners were prepared to bid more than $1 million on the last day. Schwartz submitted a bid of $850,000, but GreatDomains.com said it arrived a few minutes too late. Schwartz claimed his coterie was shut out because of their involvement in the adult-entertainment industry. "We could have turned that million into a profit in twelve months," he said.[15]

Wine.com fetched about $3 million in September 1999, but two months later Marc Ostrofsky, the Houston entrepreneur, shattered all previous records for domain sales by unloading business.com in a cash-and-stock deal valued at $7.5 million. The price was emblematic of the Internet bubble. Ostrofsky sold the domain to Santa Monica, California-based eCompanies, an incubator of Internet businesses founded by Jake Winebaum, who previously ran Walt Disney Co.'s Web operations, and Sky Dayton, founder of Internet service provider Earthlink. eCompanies aimed to use the name for a directory of online services for businesses. In the domain market, the deal was the shot heard 'round the world. No other publicly reported sale had even reached $4 million. But around the same time, Ostrofsky said, he also sold ebusiness.com to another Internet incubator, Idealab. The price topped the sale of business.com, he said, but couldn't be disclosed because the parties signed a non-disclosure agreement. Ostrofsky declined to reveal the price, saying only that it was "many millions." An Idealab spokeswoman declined to comment for this book, citing the confidentiality agreement.

The sale of business.com received worldwide media coverage, and cemented Ostrofsky's place in Internet lore.

When the sale was announced, some branding consultants were highly skeptical of eCompanies' decision. "It's a huge amount of money for something that might be a commodity in six months," said Allen Adamson, managing director of branding consultancy Landor Associates. "Owning generic domain names will not be a long-term play in branding and marketing."[16] That was a common refrain for branding experts during the dot-com era. Years later, they'd have ample reason to reconsider their theories. Case in point: in 2007, phone-directory company R.H. Donnelly Corp. paid an eye-popping $345 million for business.com and the marketing company Winebaum and Dayton had built on it.

The 1999 business.com sale was followed by several other multimillion-dollar transactions. CarsDirect.com paid $2.2 million to buy autos.com from an Atlanta businessman in late 1999, and Bank of America, one of the few large U.S. companies that showed a keen interest in owning a generic name, acquired loans.com for $3 million from a California businessman who'd registered it for free in 1994.

New Regulation

As speculators and entrepreneurs rushed to secure domains, Network Solutions' lucrative monopoly on assigning Web addresses met with growing criticism. Users complained its customer service was poor and the price of registering an address too high. Many, too, were dissatisfied with its dispute-resolution policy. The Clinton administration also faced growing pressure from abroad to give other countries a greater role in Internet governance. So in response to these concerns, the administration sought to open the registration business to competition, and to transfer oversight of the Internet from federal research agencies to a private, not-for-profit international corporation. In June 1998, the Commerce Department released a "white paper" asking the private sector to come up with proposals to oversee the Internet. After soliciting and reviewing public comments on several proposals, the government in November 1998 entered into a memorandum of understanding with the Internet Corporation for Assigned Names and Numbers, or Icann, a newly created organization that had been spearheaded by the late Internet pioneer Jon Postel, one of the inventors of the domain-name system.

The Commerce Department retained oversight of Icann, with the ability to veto decisions. From its birth, Icann, based in Marina del Rey, California, was mired in controversy. Its board quickly developed a reputation for secrecy by making big decisions behind closed doors. The organization sought to build consensus policy from the bottom up, which was one of its mandates, but it was widely accused of being overly bureaucratic and inefficient. Few could understand Icann's Byzantine rule-making procedures. Over the years, it amassed an ever-growing list of critics in the public and private sectors, leading to calls in some corners for a new system of managing the Internet.

Competition came to the registration business in 1999. Network Solutions, which had been reluctant to recognize Icann, agreed to a compromise with the group and with the Commerce Department. Under the pact, Network Solutions won the right to keep managing the coveted directory of .com, .net, and .org addresses, known as the "registry." Icann accredited other companies, known as "registrars," to sell domains to consumers. These retailers paid Network Solutions a wholesale price of $6 per year (it was $9 until Jan. 15,

2000) each time they registered a name for a customer, then marked up the price. Network Solutions was also allowed to operate a registrar business, but was supposed to sell its controlling stake in either that entity or the registry within eighteen months. The company's victory in getting to maintain the registry was significant; even though the price per domain fell to $6 from $35, it was a steady, lucrative business. Some in the Internet community were concerned that the registry remained in the hands of a for-profit business. One influential group involved in the creation of Icann argued the public trust would be better served if all domain registries were nonprofits owned by competing registrars.[17]

When the registration market opened to competition, most registrars charged an amount close to Network Solutions' price of $35 a year. But eventually, prices fell. Go Daddy, launched in late 2000, offered the most aggressive pricing, charging only $9 a year, and grew to become the world's largest registrar in terms of domains under management.

Icann's first substantive policy—and, according to some, its biggest accomplishment—was to create a relatively quick and inexpensive way to settle cases of alleged cybersquatting. The group introduced the Uniform Domain-Name Dispute Resolution Policy, or UDRP, in late 1999. The system allowed any person or company in the world to challenge a domain registration by launching an arbitration proceeding. Cases could be filed with one of several dispute-resolution service providers, including the World Intellectual Property Organization, a branch of the United Nations. It cost roughly $750 to $3,000 to bring a case. The cases were adjudicated by e-mail; there were no in-person hearings. In order to win, the "complainant" had to prove three things:

1. The domain is identical or "confusingly similar" to the complainant's trademark.
2. The domain holder has no rights or legitimate interest in the name.
3. The domain was registered and is being used in bad faith.

When consumers registered a name, they were bound under their service agreements with registrars to submit to arbitration under the policy. Complainants won about 80 percent of the three thousand cases filed in the first year and a half of the policy.[18]

Many domain speculators, and some legal scholars, said the deck was stacked in favor of trademark holders. For instance, WIPO, one of the dispute-resolution providers, is a group whose mandate is to promote the protection of intellectual property throughout the world. WIPO also played a major role in creating the dispute policy. Also, the UDRP allows the challenger to choose the dispute-resolution service; that encouraged forum shopping for favorable arbitrators—akin to how ailing U.S. corporations shop for favorable bankruptcy courts. Critics also complained that decisions by the arbitration panels were inconsistent. There were several puzzling rulings. In one case, in April 2000, clothier J. Crew wrested crew.com, a generic term, from an entity called Telepathy. The ruling largely was based on the fact that Telepathy had speculated in about fifty names that included trademarks or common words that might appeal to businesses.[19] One of the three arbitrators dissented. He said his colleagues failed to follow the narrow test Icann had created to prevent abuse by large trademark holders. "The majority seems to assume that a trademark owner has some sort of God-given right to use the trademark to the exclusion of others," wrote G. Gervaise Davis III. J. Crew "does not own all rights to the generic word 'crew' by virtue of its trademark registration."[20]

In two other questionable verdicts, Tata Sons, an Indian industrial company, garnered bodacious-tatas.com, and a German chemical-products company that made a bleached-clay product called Tonsil snared tonsil.com.[21]

In many other cases, individuals hoarded domains that clearly matched or resembled corporate trademarks, and sought to profit from them, resulting in straightforward victories for plaintiffs. For instance, Californian Saeid Yomtobian lost numerous cases in arbitration under the Icann policy. He registered names associated with a wide range of large corporations, including Bank of America and Playboy. Some of the domains he registered were misspellings, including playbooy.com and playbochannel.com—a practice known as typosquatting.

Meanwhile, in 1999, Congress approved the Anticybersquatting Consumer Protection Act, or ACPA, which bolstered efforts by trademark holders to fight cybersquatting by giving more teeth to federal trademark law. The law imposed penalties of as much as $100,000 per domain if a domain holder demonstrated "a bad faith intent to profit" from a name identical or confusingly similar to another's trademark, or that diluted the mark. Winning an arbitration case under the Icann policy yielded no such financial awards.

A Mixed Market

The big domain sales of 1999 and 2000 gave some people the impression that everyone who owned a short, intuitive generic name was getting rich, when in fact six- and seven-figure deals were rare. Most holders of such names had to sit patiently and wait for the prospect of a big payday, or take what they could get at the time. On GreatDomains.com, the average listing price for a Web address in 1999 was $32,000, but the average sale price was $14,500.

One event in December 1999—the same month Ostrofsky's landmark sale of business.com was announced—illustrated the difficulty of reaping big sales. Eric "Wall Street" Wade, one of the sellers of wallstreet.com, organized a twenty-four-hour global auction of hundreds of names.[22] The much-hyped event, which received extensive media coverage, showcased names like jeans.com, airline.com, woman.com, and publicrelations.com.[23] Beforehand, Wade said he expected many names to sell for seven figures and that the auction might reap $10 million in total sales.[24] But the event failed to produce a single sale. Even after the flop, Wade claimed it was a success because it brought publicity to the market.[25]

The press coverage of the auctions and big sales like Ostrofsky's—along with the lofty prices of Internet stocks—did drive interest in domains of all stripes. Registrations surged. More than ten million domains were registered worldwide by early 2000, up from about 2.3 million in early 1998.[26] Icann, the Internet regulatory body, made room for a wider variety of addresses in 1999 when it began allowing up to sixty-three characters in a name (excluding the suffix), compared with twenty-two previously. The characters allowed consisted of the twenty-six letters of the alphabet, the hyphen and the numbers zero to nine.

The English language has about 500,000 words, so one-word domains went fast. In the spring of 1999, Wired News reported that "start-ups, squatters, and speculators" have "bought up all the Internet's prime real estate." It analyzed 25,500 common words in the dictionary and found that only 1,760 were still available to register in the .com extension. "And those were hardly winners," it said. "Who really wants to pay good money for maggoty.com or gluttonous.com?"[27]

Many domain speculators were overly confident about their prospects during the Internet boom. Some hawked subpar domains at astronomical prices, thinking they could match the success of Ostrofsky and other big sellers. There was something of a bubble for domains, just as there was for dot-com stocks. In 1999, someone advertised JewelersMallofAmerica.com on eBay for $2 million.[28] Among other names offered for sale online in the late 1990s and early 2000s were these beauties: 4u2findcomedy.com, sporadicallyyours.com, millenniuMAGIC.com, A1bonfirenight.co.uk, WErWIRELESSDATA.com, and postelectionstressdisorder.org.

One of the biggest risks speculators took was to register scores of names that all began with the same series of letters, such as the "A1" example above. And perhaps nobody else took quite such a risk as did Lieven Van Neste, a Belgian physician. He registered about 200,000 domains, many containing a variation of the phrase "24 hour" or the word "express." The purchases cost Van Neste and his fellow investors several million dollars. Van Neste acquired 24houracupuncture.com, 24houreverything.com, 24hrexpertise.com, and 24hourbanking.com, among others. "For a number of days I had tried to think of a good prefix, and this one just popped into my head," he recalled. "I traveled frequently to the States, and you found that everywhere. You found 24-hour banking, 24-hour service. It made sense (to register the domains) because it really gave a characteristic about the Internet, which ran 24 hours." When he did his research and found that many of the names hadn't been registered, he said, "I couldn't believe my eyes." He did find a few that were taken, such as 24hournews.com and 24hourleasing.com. Those discoveries were helpful, he said, because they assured him that he wasn't the only person on earth who thought such names might be valuable. "I really felt that I had stumbled onto something."

Van Neste's domain-buying spree ran from 1999 through 2001. He formed an investment company called 24hournames.com. He hired a small staff and brought in another investor as a senior executive. They listed their names for sale on their site and on auction services like Afternic.com. They became one of the five largest domain holders in the world. They registered so many names that Belgian postal workers regularly hauled enormous bags stuffed with hundreds of invoices from Network Solutions into Van Neste's office. His goal was to make about $10 million to $20 million to build a global healthcare center focused on natural healing and fitness treatments. But the business was a big flop, and a personal catastrophe for Van Neste. He ended up losing his investment and leaving the company. But he insisted the failure was largely the result of a dispute with his main partner, which turned into a legal battle, and less about the company's often poor choices of domains. Ultimately a Belgian court appointed a government official to oversee the company. It became "a painful and expensive lesson," Van Neste said. Before things went awry, "we were increasingly becoming efficient in reselling individual names . . . Now I'd be lying if I said that 100 percent of our names were all top names."

Another company that placed a big bet on a numerical prefixes—and foundered—was 4Anything.com. The Philadelphia-area Web company, founded by Vincent J. Schiavone, registered 4,500 names that started with

"4," including 4babies.com, 4wine.com, and 4soccer.com. The company built miniature Web portals, but they never caught on. It fired most of its work force in 2001 and later transformed itself into an online voice and video chat community.[29]

During the heady days of the dot-com era, the clear route to success in domain investing was to adhere to the K.I.S.S. system ("keep it simple, stupid"). That meant buying common, easy-to-remember words. Picking commercially relevant words—terms that people could use to promote a business or build one—was important, too. Garry Chernoff, the electrician in British Columbia, began to thrive by adhering to that doctrine. He had stretches in which he sold two or three names a week. Ten he sold at the peak of Internet mania were:

Garry Chernoff Sales

antacid.com	boatbuilder.com
displays.com	exchange-rates.com
furnishing.com	garments.com
junk-bonds.com	mortgagebroker.com
papers.com	proofreading.com

Antacid.com and mortgagebroker.com each sold for less than $10,000, Chernoff said. The other domains were part of a group he sold to one company; he declined to disclose the price. Chernoff's life became extremely busy as he began to rack up sales. He was still working full-time at the local hospital, driving his son to and from daycare, and watching him on nights and weekends. He started to lose track of which names he'd bought and which he'd sold. One day he was cleaning his desk, and he picked up his printer so that he could wipe off the dust beneath it. Lying there was a check for $5,000. He'd completely forgotten about it. At that point, "I figured it was time to quit the hospital," he said.

Chapter Three

Name Dropping

When the Internet bubble burst, the domain market ruptured, too.

The pain for domain speculators wasn't as great, typically, as it was for those who built Internet companies, because the amount of money at stake typically wasn't as large. However, the volume of domain sales—and prices—plunged. For the first time since the Web's inception, the number of registered names declined, as many investors and entrepreneurs let their names expire. They figured it wasn't worth paying annual registration fees ranging from $9 to $35 for addresses that might not be worth anything. After all, in many cases, domain owners had made little or no money off their addresses. Some also feared that Icann's introduction of new extensions, such as .biz and .info, would dilute the value of .com and .net addresses. It also became clear that, just as there'd been irrational exuberance for Internet stocks, there'd been unreasonable enthusiasm in name selection. Many people had picked domains that drew little to no traffic, and that had scant appeal to businesses seeking a memorable name.

But even short, generic addresses took a hit during the dot-com meltdown. A big reason was that many companies that had been built around such names, including pets.com, furniture.com, mortgage.com, and garden.com, failed in spectacular fashion. Pets.com, which sold pet supplies, shut down in November 2000, only nine months after going public on the Nasdaq with great fanfare. Garden.com, a publicly traded seller of gardening supplies, closed a month later. The flops, which received extensive media coverage, raised serious doubts about the value of generic domains.

"No matter how catchy or simple or all-inclusive their names are, a mere dot-com address is not worth much without brand support," Scott Kraft of marketing consultancy Sterling Group argued in November 2000. "People thought they were buying incredibly valuable real estate on the Web with these one-word, generic names, but they forgot about the need to build real brands first."[1]

Others were even more cynical. "People are beginning to understand that generic domains are not valuable," Mark Radcliffe, an intellectual-property lawyer in Palo Alto, California, said in December 2000.[2]

Amid the tumult, some large domain owners tried to unload their generic addresses. In June 2000, consumer-products giant Procter & Gamble decided to list for sale on GreatDomains.com about one hundred of the names it had registered in 1995, including beautiful.com, scent.com, and thirst.com. The company decided after reviewing the names that they were "not strategic for selling P&G-related brands." But for six months, the company failed to sell any of them. In December 2000, it finally sold one: flu.com. Neither the price nor the buyer was disclosed (the site is now owned by MedImmune Vaccines, which makes FluMist, a nasal flu vaccine). Procter & Gamble said the sale more than paid for the approximately $350,000 it spent maintaining its more than two thousand names in the prior five years, but its timing for selling its names was less than ideal.[3]

As Internet addresses lost their luster, the number of .com, .net, and .org names, which accounted for the vast majority of registrations, slid for the first time. From September 2001 to June 2002, registrations in those extensions dropped 11 percent to 27.1 million, according to State of the Domain, an industry newsletter. "The dot-com land grab is done," C. Eugene Munster, a senior research analyst with U.S. Bancorp Piper Jaffray, declared in July 2002.[4]

But despite all the doom and gloom, and the more than $1 trillion lost in the stock market thanks to the Internet bust, the Web was still growing, providing reason for optimism about the future of virtual land. The number of Internet users worldwide rose to 581 million in May 2002 from 463 million a year earlier, according to Internet research firm Nua.com. U.S. e-commerce sales grew to $32.6 billion in 2001 from $27.3 billion in 2000, according to the U.S. Department of Commerce. But spending on online advertising in the U.S. dropped to $7.1 billion in 2001 from $8.1 billion a year earlier, according to the Interactive Advertising Bureau, a trade group for Web marketers; it was the first decline in Web history.

Domain brokers tried to persuade consumers to buy Internet addresses, arguing they'd be valuable in the long run. "People thought the dot-com bust meant domain bust, but it really didn't," said Monte Cahn, who ran HitDomains.com, the domain broker. "It meant Internet-company bust . . . When people started liquidating their domain names, the smart folks said, 'I am going to buy these, because the Internet is here to stay.'"

Cahn said his company had faith in a strong market recovery. The company gained confidence, he said, when it and other firms were hired by many of the failed dot-coms to find a buyer for their names to pay off creditors, and managed to get some good prices.

In one of the more notable deals, Mortgage.com, the failed online lender, sold mortgage.com and hipoteca.com—Spanish for "mortgage"—to a unit of the Dutch banking giant ABN Amro for $1.8 million in 2000.

Still, the downturn tested Cahn's company and other brokers. Before the crash, "we were doing a couple hundred domain appraisals a week," Cahn said. "It went down to maybe five or six." To deal with the slump, HitDomains. com merged in the summer of 2000 with another broker, SolutionHome.com. They changed the company's name to DomainSystems, and pared their work force to seven from twenty-eight. DomainSystems' major rivals, meanwhile, were acquired by public companies in cash-and-stock deals in late 2000. Register.com, a domain registrar, paid about $50 million for Afternic.com. Internet-services firm VeriSign, which earlier in 2000 had paid $15 billion to acquire Network Solutions for its prosperous registry business, forked over about $85 million for GreatDomains.com.[5] Both marketplaces became shadows of their former selves under their new owners, as the dot-com bust and the 2001 U.S. recession took its toll on the companies. Register.com shuttered Afternic.com to cut costs in 2002, saying it had failed to meet expectations. Florida entrepreneur Roger Collins and his wife bought the Afternic.com name with a home equity line of credit for an undisclosed price, and Roger and his brother Michael relaunched it as a domain broker.

Sales of domains in the secondary market stayed in the doldrums from about March 2000, when the Nasdaq tanked, to the fall of 2003. But during that period, a savvy group of speculators quietly snatched up huge numbers of addresses, betting they'd be valuable in the long run. They did it by playing the drop. Their approach was similar to that of the watermelon farmer Scott Day and the electrician Garry Chernoff in the late 1990s—grabbing names that people had failed to pay for or let go on purpose—but this time the game of chasing expired domains exploded and became far more sophisticated. As domain owners chucked their sites in massive quantities in the Internet downturn, the hawks in the drop market enjoyed a feast.

One windfall came from tens of thousands of domains that were registered in 1999 and 2000, when new registrars were created, and were later abandoned by their owners. Registrars such as Register.com had offered big promotions to try to lure customers and build market share, offering names at discounts. Also, in 2000, users were for the first time able to register new domains in one-year increments, which made an initial purchase less expensive. By 2001, when all these addresses came up for renewal, the timing was bad for the domain holders. They had to decide whether to keep the names in a lousy climate. Many addresses were discarded, and the good ones often flowed right into the hands of drop catchers.

Drop catching had begun to get more sophisticated in the late 1990s. One of the main changes was it began attracting more computer programmers. People who could write good computer code had an advantage because they could automate the process of both identifying soon-to-expire names and requesting them from a registrar. Speculators who lacked such skills sometimes teamed up with someone who had them. Until 1999, Network Solutions was the lone registrar for coveted .com and .net addresses, so it bore the brunt of speculators' early forays into using so-called computer scripts, or "bots" (short for robots), to rapidly request names. Network Solutions even banned some applicants when it found out they were bombarding its system with requests.

The drop game became more complicated when new registrars were introduced. Companies such as Register.com, Enom, and Dotster began offering customers the opportunity to register a name using an interface on their Web site. Now, instead of firing off scores of e-mails to Network Solutions, some drop catchers wrote programs that repeatedly queried these registrars' Web sites. In essence, these programs asked: Is this name available? If so, register it to me.

Chasing Names

Among the people writing such programs was a computer junkie in his early twenties named Jay Westerdal. Westerdal, who studied computer science at Central Washington University and worked for a Web-hosting company, spent hours on his computer at his parents' house in the Seattle suburbs, attempting to register valuable domains. Westerdal wrote a computer program that did two basic things: It asked a registrar to register a name on his behalf, and it created another version of itself. The second version also asked the registrar to register the name on his behalf, and it, too, cloned itself. "I thought I was pretty clever," Westerdal said. "I had 16,000 programs, all asking the same question."

Westerdal competed with people such as Anthony Peppler of Fort Wayne, Indiana, who'd been a contract computer programmer and once ran computer stores. At Peppler's Internet company, Realtime Internet, which offered Web hosting and other services, Peppler and other employees regularly sought domains in the drop using computer programs.

In early 2001, drop catchers caught on that VeriSign, Network Solutions' parent, had begun releasing newly expired .com, .net, and .org domains in an orderly fashion. It released names starting at roughly 6:30 a.m. Eastern Time each day, weekends and holidays included. The release lasted about fifteen minutes. For Westerdal, living on the West Coast, that was 3:30 a.m. So he would stay up until that late hour, or set his alarm clock, and try to acquire a couple of names each morning.

The people playing the drop game shared few of their secrets with other people they encountered online. Generally, participants didn't know who else was playing, and what kind of information they had. Even the 6:30 a.m. drop time was a closely guarded secret. If you knew about it, you didn't let on that you did. At Afternic.com, a popular hangout for domain speculators, "people would discuss the buying and selling of names, and also talk about the drop, but no one would ever really say what time it was or how it worked," Westerdal said.

One of the challenges was figuring out which names would be a released on a given day. VeriSign, based in Mountain View, California, didn't want to telegraph that information, in part to deter speculators from hammering the registry with requests for domains through the registrars. "It was this art," Westerdal said. "No one knew how a domain went from active to inactive to deleted and active again." If speculators had that information, they could go into each morning with a thorough list of names they knew would drop, then decide which ones to pursue. Eventually, earnest speculators began to piece together VeriSign's general process of releasing names by closely monitoring changes to Whois records.

In February 2001, Lee Hodgson, a domain expert apparently looking to help casual investors and neophytes, wrote an article on Sitepoint.com, an Internet-information site, which explained the lifecycle of .com, .net, and .org domains. His description generally went like this:

1. If the owner fails to pay to renew the name by the expiration date, it is put "on hold." The owner typically is given a grace period of up to sixty days to renew the name.
2. If the owner fails to renew in that period, the name moves into soon-to-drop status, a five-day period when no one can register it.
3. On the sixth day, at about 6:30 a.m. ET, the name drops, and anyone can grab it.

Hodgson also demonstrated how to decipher from a Whois record when a domain was about to drop. If the record of a name that had not been renewed by its expiration date said "local whois DB must be out of date," that indicated a drop was imminent. To figure out which day it would drop, he said, investors needed to look at the "updated date" listed on the Whois record and add six days to it.

Hodgson's article, published Feb. 19, 2001, was entitled "Domain Name Goldrush Part 1—The Rules of Play."[6] It was an important article in the world of domain speculation because it revealed the nuances of a portion of the market that was little understood, even among some veteran speculators. Some investors were furious when Hodgson published the article, because it invited new competition into their little fiefdom. Hodgson, who ran his own domain-information site, DomainGuru.com, wrote six other articles in his series on the expired-name market, the last in September 2002.

Several companies emerged to offer services to the drop-catching crowd. They did the dirty work of building lists of soon-to-drop names, and sold them. One of the first, DomainsBot.com, formed in 2000, charged users $19.95 a month to receive a daily e-mail showing names that would drop the next day.[7] The service also let users search an online database of names that recently expired or were about to expire.

Some players in the drop game compiled their own lists of soon-to-expire names, including Anthony Peppler, the Indiana investor. They either didn't want to pay for a service or found their own systems more effective. Each day they would download from VeriSign an enormous file listing all registered domains, known as the root zone file, which could take hours. They then compared the list to the previous day's version using a computer program. If a name that had appeared in the first day's file was absent from the second day's, that indicated its owner had let it expire, and it would soon be released for anyone to grab. All such names were deposited into a third file, which investors then spent hours analyzing to decide which names to pursue.

About twenty thousand names in the .com, .net, and .org extensions dropped each day in 2001, about twenty times the number a year earlier. The vast majority were considered junk by experienced investors; however, tens or hundreds each day were considered valuable. Because investors didn't want to overlook any good names, the craft required that they spend a lot of time sitting alone, meticulously reviewing the lists. It was a highly antisocial—but potentially lucrative—pursuit. It's not clear how many people were involved in the expired domain market at the time. Participants estimate there were a few hundred serious players, and a few thousand who caught names periodically. The game was by no means limited to Americans. It was an international competition. According to several investors, Korean computer programmers were among the most active players.

Plenty of good names dropped in those days. Among the better names Westerdal snagged were fg.com, kg.com, babyproof.com, and bandcompetition.com. Two-letter names were coveted because they were short; users could type them with little effort. In addition, they appealed to businesses that used the letters in their names. Three-letter names also were prized for the same reason; some that dropped in the period were jcw.com, sfi.com, and bsb.com. And many generic, two-word domains fell, like winterbreak.com, fantasyhoops.com, and insidebaseball.com. Peppler bagged names such as dvdusa.com and tradingcards.com.

For individuals and companies that wanted to register a Web address and were not familiar with the drop-catching crowd, it was often surprising and disconcerting to learn that a name they wanted had been grabbed by a speculator. Consider Michael Pastore of Ithaca, N.Y, a huge fan of the novel *Zorba the Greek*, who wanted to register Zorba.com.[8] In late 2000, he found out it had expired; after the sixty-day waiting period elapsed, he kept checking for the name each morning at about 6:30.[9] But one day, to Pastore's surprise, it was grabbed by BuyDomains.com, a Washington, D.C.—area company whose business was to acquire prodigious numbers of domains and resell them. Pastore found the name listed on BuyDomains.com for $4,688.[10] "That is a lot more than the $10 I hoped to pay," he said.[11] The system of releasing domains seemed to favor insiders, something VeriSign claimed it was trying to avoid by not giving more precise notice of when names would be released.[12]

With deft computer programmers in the expired-domain market, it became more difficult for less technically skilled investors, like Garry Chernoff, the British Columbian electrician, to acquire names. "The guys that first started, none us were programmers," he said. "Scott [Day] was a watermelon farmer; Roy Messer sold carpet; I was an electrician. Once the programmers got wind of this, then it was really difficult. We'd flown by the seat of our pants."

"We weren't that sophisticated," Day said of himself and his business partner. "At that time, we kind of faded out. We are kind of a dinosaur in the industry. We wanted to play; we just couldn't play. We had our window."

Chernoff tried to keep at it. In 1998, he lost his access to lists of names in "on hold" status from SAEGIS. He said the company booted him because he used too much of its bandwidth and didn't spend money on its site. One fall day in 1998, at a high point of frustration, he posted a message in an online newsgroup, offering to pay $2,000 to anyone who would tell him how to make lists of soon-to-expire names. A programmer e-mailed him to say he knew how to do it. Chernoff was so thrilled that he paid the man about $500 a month to make lists for him. "I was back in the game. I was going to give up, and I figured out a way to keep going," Chernoff said.

Two valuable names Chernoff garnered through drops after that were jet. com and virus.com.

Chernoff continued to keep tabs on who the best drop catchers were by checking Whois reports. Instead of Scott Day, a new name kept popping up. It was Yun Ye.

Mystery Man

When domain investors talk about their idols, their lists inevitably include Yun Ye. But few know much about Ye the person, as his story is shrouded in mystery. And it may remain that way for years to come. Ye doesn't talk to the media, and his friends are reluctant to talk about him, respecting his fierce desire to remain private.

Ye was born in China in the early 1970s. He attended FuXing High School in Shanghai before moving to the United States. He was an excellent student. He earned a bachelor's degree in computer science and economics from Brandeis University, near Boston, in 1995. He made the Dean's List each semester, graduated magna cum laude, and was elected to Phi Beta Kappa. He then attended the University of Maryland in College Park, earning a master's degree in computer science in the spring of 1998. While at Maryland, Ye created his own Web page hosted on the university's site. He posted his resume and listed about a hundred sites he'd bookmarked, including five videogame sites and an eclectic list of news sites including the Far Eastern Economic Review, Fortune magazine, and PC Week.

After graduate school, public records show, Ye lived in the San Francisco Bay Area suburb of Fremont with his wife, Jin Lu. It was there that he began building an enormous collection of domains.

Ye became a legend in the drop market. He snared thousands of expired names, capitalizing on years of computer-programming experience and talent. He often seized names that the previous owners had spent years developing but failed to renew, either by mistake or because they went out of business. When domain owners discovered Ye had grabbed their name, many were mortified. Ye racked up scores of enemies who thought his actions were despicable, along with an army of admirers in the name trade.

Ye knew how to compile accurate lists of soon-to-drop domains using root zone files long before others figured out how. And he was just as skilled at writing computer programs that enabled him to nab names within milliseconds of their release.

Ye was a hard worker, a trait he'd demonstrated while at the University of Maryland, according to a former colleague. Besides taking classes, Ye worked as an assistant lab manager on the UNIX computer operating system for an interdisciplinary research institute. Linda Moniz, a fellow student who inherited Ye's job, said he was extremely knowledgeable. He went out of his way to help Moniz learn the system, working well past his last official day so that she and her boss would be up to speed, she recalled. "I sent him quite a few harried e-mails when I first took over, and he always took the time to give me not only a prompt solution to the problem, but also a way to avoid it," she said.

Chad Folkening, the domain investor from Indianapolis, said he predicted that "somebody was going to come in here and figure out this drop market, and it was just going to be huge." That person turned out to be Ye, he said.

Ironically, Folkening became a primary victim of Ye's success. Folkening registered thousands of addresses in the early days of the Web, but failed to set up a system to keep track of his names and their expiration dates. "Organization is not my strong point," he said. Hundreds of his addresses fell into Ye's lap.

Ye was so good at catching names that Folkening and other domain investors speculated that he had a contact on the inside at Network Solutions, the keeper of the master list of .com addresses, aiding his efforts. This was never proven, and several investors say it was merely a rumor.

Ye and his wife formed a domain business called NoName.com. They registered the company in their California county, Alameda, in October 1998 and incorporated it with the state in May 2000, public records show. The address they listed was a box at a Mail Boxes Etc. store at a Fremont shopping center. Ye was in charge of acquiring domains, while Lu ran the day-to-day business operations, according to people familiar with the couple.

NoName.com's business plan called for acquiring a slate of domains, and then offering Web users the chance to sign up for vanity e-mail addresses—hypothetically, that meant offering users addresses like john@smith.com (assuming NoName.com owned smith.com). The plan also called for other domain services. Besides NoName.com, Ye and Lu registered the business names Bettermail.com, Hottermail.com, and Betterdomains.com in Alameda County in 1998. It's not clear how much progress the couple made in developing their various California companies. What is clear is that by 2000, they owned hundreds of domains, including many generic terms of potentially significant value, such as consultants.com, gourmetcooking.com, and bridalstore.com. They also owned some non-generic terms that rankled trademark holders, prompting legal challenges against NoName.com.

NoName.com won at least two disputes handled by arbitrators under Icann's dispute policy. In 2000, John Berryhill, one of the leading lawyers representing domain holders, helped NoName.com defeat book publisher Macmillan USA. The publisher, which produced the "Complete Idiot's Guide" series of how-to books, sought to take away idiotsguide.com from NoName.com. An arbitration panel ruled that Macmillan failed to show that NoName.com registered the address in bad faith. (Berryhill asserted that NoName.com planned to make the name available for customers to use.) In addition, the panel said, Macmillan failed to establish that it had exclusive rights to the term "idiot's guide," which had been used by other businesses before Macmillan used it. Meanwhile, when a California company, Interactive Television, attempted to wrest interactivetelevision.com and interactivetv.com from NoName.com, an arbitration panel found that Interactive Television hadn't established trademark rights to the term "interactive television."

Also in 2000, hotel giant Marriott International sent Ye a cease-and-desist letter regarding his use of marriot.com, a misspelling of the hotelier's name. Following the letter, the domain mysteriously was transferred to someone named John Marriot. Marriott International then filed a complaint against John Marriot. John Marriot didn't respond, and an arbitrator ordered that the name be transferred to Marriott. In another 2000 case, a Denver company, Columbine JDS Systems, was awarded adserve.com after it filed a complaint against Ye's wife, Jin Lu, who'd registered the name in January 1999. The panel ruled that she hadn't made any legitimate use of it.

In 2000, Ye and Lu began using another corporate name, Ultimate Search. It was under this name that Ye's legend grew to mythical proportions. Ultimate Search listed a Hong Kong address but was incorporated in the tax haven of the British Virgin Islands on July 19, 2000. Ye and Lu sold their three-bedroom condominium in Fremont in the summer of 2001, public records show. Around that time, Zooknic.com, an Internet research site run by geographer Matthew Zook, estimated that Ultimate Search owned about 33,000 domains, making it one of the eight largest portfolio owners in the world by its count. According to Zook, now a professor at the University of Kentucky, Ultimate Search's portfolio at that time included wedding.org, mylyrics.com, ashtray.com, usapassport.com, and gambleusa.com.

Ultimate Search was also fond of adult-oriented domains. It acquired adultentertainers.com, asianplaymate.com, and sexualzone.com, among others. Like NoName.com, Ultimate Search became embroiled in legal fisticuffs. Most of the time, the company, represented by Berryhill, prevailed. Berryhill, who's based near Philadelphia and has a doctorate in electrical engineering, is a tenacious lawyer with a keen eye for details. He's "pit-bull-smart," said Michael Froomkin, a law professor at the University of Miami who specializes in Internet law. "If I ever wanted to beat the hell out of somebody, which is not my style usually, he'd be one of the people I'd think of."

From 2001 through 2005, Ultimate Search won at least eleven disputes in arbitration, while losing a half-dozen. Among the names it lost was dswshoewarehouse.com. Cincinnati-based DSW Shoe Warehouse said in its complaint that it had obtained trademark rights to its corporate name from the U.S. Patent and Trademark Office in 1995. Ultimate Search, which registered the address in 2003, didn't respond to the shoe retailer's complaint, and easily lost the case.

Ultimate Search's penchant for garnering expired names confounded companies in a wide range of industries. In 2001, a Florida collections agency, Williams, Babbit & Weisman, noticed that wbw.com was going to expire. A company called Windsurf Bicycle Warehouse had used the name but was no longer in business. Williams, Babbit & Weisman tried to grab wbw.com when it became available, but Ultimate Search snagged it. The collections agency then filed a complaint, claiming that the domain was confusingly similar to its service mark. An arbitration panel ruled that the collections agency failed to meet each of the three requirements to win the case.

PwC Business Trust, part of PricewaterhouseCoopers, the accounting and consulting giant, also lost a dispute to Ultimate Search over a three-letter name—pwc.com. It only established that the domain was confusingly similar to its trademark, failing to show that Ultimate Search lacked legitimate interest in the name, and that Ultimate Search had used it in bad faith, arbitrators ruled.

Ultimate Search became a hot topic on online message boards for domain investors. Rumors flew about who was behind the mysterious company. Some people who'd heard of the name Yun Ye weren't convinced it was a real name. Some believed Ultimate Search was comprised of several brilliant domain investors. Others speculated that Ultimate Search was run by a former Network Solutions engineer with keen insight into the domain-name system.

One investor who lost to Ultimate Search in an effort to grab several expired names wrote on DNForum.com, a popular forum for domain investors: "UltSearch must know someone in high places . . . ehhhh????? . . . How does he do it???"

Those who lost domains they'd owned to Ultimate Search warned others to pay heed to their renewal notices. In various forums, members marveled at Ultimate Search's talents. Some complained that Ultimate Search didn't respond to e-mails and phone calls about names they wanted to buy or sell. One DNForum.com member wrote, "Instead of just ignoring e-mails, why doesn't Yun provide an auto-reply that says 'our domains are not for sale, so don't expect a reply'? I'm sure the thousands of people who inquire would appreciate this." Others found that with determination, they could reach the company, and, in some cases, purchase a name.

Ye piqued the curiosity of Chad Folkening, the Indianapolis investor. Folkening sent him e-mails but never heard back. In 2001, Folkening was in California and decided to try to find Ye. He traveled to Fremont, to an address listed on Whois records for some of Ye's domains. To Folkening's surprise, it was a Mail Boxes Etc. store. Folkening left a note on Ye's box, asking him to call. That same week, Folkening recalled, he visited some friends in Los Angeles. He couldn't get Ye off his mind, because Ye had grabbed several more of his names, including moviecentre.com, studentcentre.com, and careercentre.com. "I was just like, 'Jiminy Christmas.' I was very emotional," Folkening said.

One of Folkening's friends told him he knew Ye, that he lived in Los Angeles, and that he could set up a meeting. Folkening went to a bar to meet him, but soon realized he wasn't speaking to the right Yun Ye. "He didn't really say much about domain names," said Folkening. "I was doing most of the talking." Folkening left the bar shortly thereafter feeling even more frustrated.

Some of Ye's choices in domains puzzled other investors. In 2003, Adam Strong, a speculator in Springfield, Illinois, let onskis.com expire. Strong had tried to develop the site as a portal for skiers, spending about $5,000 on software and odds and ends like business cards and T-shirts. But he didn't have much success attracting visitors to the site, so he didn't play close attention to his renewal notices and let the registration lapse. He realized quickly that Ye had snared it. "Ah sh—," he recalled thinking.

Strong decided he wanted the name back. He sent Ye an e-mail, telling him he'd invested a lot of money in building the site. He asked Ye to sell it back to him at a reasonable price. Strong recalled that Ye offered to sell it back for about $500. Strong turned it down. "I wasn't making any money on it, and I could buy twenty more domains somewhere else for that $500 that were probably better than this domain, because it wasn't really a good name," Strong said. "It was just a brand I was building. At the time, I was like, 'Why in the hell would this guy want that domain?'"

Ye collected a lot of two-word addresses that appeared to be of little value. "I remember Yun Ye registering all these crappy names," said Canadian investor Garry Chernoff. "I thought, 'Who is this Yun Ye guy?' I used to think, 'What a dummy.' I don't remember what the names were, but they were names I wasn't interested in. But looking back, the guy was a genius, because I think he understood the value of traffic. He was picking up anything and everything that might have gotten any sort of traffic. It was me that didn't understand the game. He was the genius."

Many investors operated in secrecy, but Ye and Lu were particularly quiet. However, in one unusual case, in May 2001, the Denver Business Journal interviewed Lu. The article discussed how a Denver-based nonprofit, Colorado Christian Home Tennyson Center for Children and Families, used Web sites to increase awareness about child abuse. The organization contacted Ye and Lu about acquiring childabuse.org. Although they could have offered to sell the name, the couple simply donated it. "We originally wanted to develop a Web site as a side project," Lu said. But when the center "contacted us to purchase the domain name, we thought that they had more resources and experience in the field than we do, so we decided to donate the name."[13] She added, "Domain names are valuable only when they are put to good use. When we donate a domain name for a worthy cause, we feel that the value of the domain has been maximized."[14]

Ye and Lu learned a lot about maximizing the value of their Web addresses over the next several years. They did it through a burgeoning revenue stream called pay-per-click advertising.

Chapter Four

Click, Click, Click

For years, domain investors had few options for making money off their holdings unless they sold them. Developing content on their sites and selling banner ads was one option, but it was laborious and not often worth the returns. Some investors, like Garry Chernoff, leased their domains to small businesses. Others had some success with affiliate marketing programs, particularly in adult entertainment. But with few exceptions, investing in Web addresses was a game of wait-and-see. Many investors let their names lay dormant, with no Web site of any kind. And it was easy for them to get impatient, particularly when the renewal bill arrived.

But in 1998, an Internet start-up was launched that would radically reshape the domain market. It was called GoTo.com.

GoTo was created by Bill Gross, a charismatic entrepreneur who ran business incubator Idealab. Gross formed Idealab in the early stages of the Internet boom, wanting to give entrepreneurs money and resources they could use to build businesses based on their ideas. Idealab, based in Pasadena, California, invested a maximum of $250,000 in each company and helped it find other investors.[1] The idea was that a few big hits could keep Idealab rolling for years, funding the innovations of tomorrow. Idealab funded many Internet companies, including eToys, PetSmart.com, Eve.com, and Blastoff. com. For a while, it was one of the darlings of the Internet economy. But when the bubble popped, many of Idealab's companies cratered. Idealab was sued by a long list of its high-profile investors. But it endured, and one of its signature companies that thrived during the tumult was GoTo.

GoTo was a new breed of Internet search engine. It grew out of Gross's frustrations with the search engines of the mid-1990s, such as AltaVista and Lycos. By late 1997, when GoTo was incorporated, those search engines were beset with problems. They used simple algorithms that made them vulnerable to being exploited by porn sites and others. The results they displayed often failed to provide relevant content for Web searchers. "At the time, search was horrendous," Gross said. "If you typed 'books' on Lycos, half of the top ten results were porn, and four of the rest weren't about books."[2]

Gross came up with a radically different approach to search. When users entered keywords into the GoTo search engine, they were shown a list of relevant links. But the links weren't selected using search technology. Instead, advertisers paid for each listing. And the more an advertiser paid, the higher it ranked. It was a commercial search engine, akin to the Yellow Pages. The idea was controversial. When Gross unveiled GoTo in early 1998, it was roundly criticized by journalists and search-engine purists, who believed search engines should display results based on the quality and relevance of Web-site content, not advertising dollars.[3]

But Gross stuck to his plan. He was convinced advertisers would be willing to pay for "qualified traffic": Web users searching on specific terms related to a product or service. Those searches had a direct, inherent value to marketers. They were leads. To make the system attractive to marketers, Gross came up with the bold idea of charging them only when a visitor clicked on their ad and landed on their site. In traditional Web advertising, marketers were charged a rate based on how many times their ads were viewed (the rate was known as CPM, or the cost per one thousand ad impressions), and it didn't matter whether anyone clicked.

Advertisers opened accounts on GoTo's site with a minimum of $25 and placed bids for words or phrases in ongoing, automated auctions. The highest bidder's ad was listed first, followed by the second-highest bidder's ad, and so forth. (Initially GoTo displayed the price paid for each listing next to the text of the ad, seeking to show transparency and blunt criticism from the purists.) GoTo struggled to attract advertisers at first. But by 2000, it had signed up more than twenty thousand—many of them small, budget-conscious Web-site owners. Gross understood the need for Internet businesses to acquire qualified traffic in part because Idealab had funded its own set of e-commerce companies that craved qualified leads.[4]

Gross gave birth to paid-search advertising. In a few years, it drew more money from marketers than traditional banner advertising and played a critical role in reviving the Internet economy. GoTo, which went public in 1999 and was renamed Overture Services in 2001, prospered even during the dot-com meltdown, in part because it offered Web companies a way out of the slump. Marketers paid only a few cents to a few dollars per click, and the small text ads were highly targeted. It was a stark contrast to the freewheeling, anything-goes dot-com heyday, when marketers were charged thousands of dollars for flashy banner ads that often delivered little in return in the way of sales. Now, marketers could more reliably track the return on their marketing investment, and, they hoped, survive the economic downturn. And for Web users, the small text ads were much less annoying than the pop-up ads, pop-under ads, and gaudy banner ads that had ruled the day. "Born out of these dark days was a willingness to test this new concept," said Jeff Lanctot, a vice president for Avenue A, a Seattle online advertising agency.[5]

A major initial challenge for GoTo was attracting users. By the time it launched, many Web surfers already had a favorite search portal, such as Yahoo, Lycos, or Excite. For GoTo, it became critical to drive traffic to its site through partnerships with other sites. One of its key strategies was to offer small Web-site owners the opportunity to place its search box on their sites—and receive a few pennies for every Web searcher they delivered to GoTo.com. To participate, site owners signed up for GoTo's affiliate program, which was managed by a third party, Be Free Inc. Affiliates inserted the search box next to whatever content they displayed on their sites. Each time a Web surfer entered a keyword into the GoTo box, he was redirected to GoTo.com and shown a list of relevant advertising links. GoTo paid Web-site owners two or three cents per search for the referrals. On its Web site, GoTo touted its "Search-in-a-Box" program to Web publishers by saying, "This is a terrific way to earn extra revenue with very little effort."

Domain speculators were among the thousands of Web-site owners who participated in the program. It was a no-brainer. And GoTo's statement that site owners could earn revenue with little effort was a harbinger of the great things to come—with relatively little effort—for domain investors who owned lots of popular words.

Garry Chernoff was among the investors using the program. He displayed the search box on the roughly six hundred sites he owned in 2000, such as dirtbikes.com and backcountry.com. The box ran atop the page, followed by a list of Chernoff's "favorite links"—ten affiliate links to other sites, such as takeout-ordering site Food.com and comparison-shopping site mySimon.com. Chernoff earned a flat fee for each Web user he delivered to those sites. The affiliate payments ranged from about three cents to 11 cents a click, he recalled. After quitting his job as an electrician, Chernoff didn't know what kind of money he could make by concentrating on domains. But he quickly realized he'd made the right decision. In 2000, he said, he began earning about $300 U.S. per day from the GoTo search box and the other affiliate links. That worked out to about $110,000 a year. Chernoff credited the power of type-in traffic. He owned many commercially relevant, generic names. Some

Web surfers simply typed them into the address bar of their browsers, seeking specific information, rather than using a search engine, and landed on his sites. The payments accumulated while Chernoff went about doing other things, such as hunting down more domains.

The GoTo search-box program was abused by some Web-site owners. "I can safely say that click fraud [the practice of fraudulently clicking on ads to drive up revenue for the owners of Web sites] was born shortly after GoTo began sending healthy checks to small Webmaster partners," author and search-engine marketing expert Andrew Goodman wrote in *Winning Results with Google AdWords.*[6]

Some domain owners, meanwhile, registered names that were variations of famous trademarks and earned revenue from the GoTo search box, a practice that drew scrutiny from some technology journalists and potentially violated the 1999 federal anticybersquatting law. "We can't always monitor each member of our affiliate program to make sure they're using it correctly," Kasey Byrne, GoTo's chief communications officer, said in 2000.[7]

That year, GoTo expanded its relationships with large domain holders who delivered steady traffic to its site. Instead of merely having the domain owners display search boxes, GoTo began syndicating its advertising listings directly onto their sites. The move—pivotal to domain investors—was part of a wider effort by GoTo to expand its distribution. In 2000, more than 90 percent of GoTo's traffic came from other Web sites. Eventually, in late 2001, the company stopped marketing GoTo.com and focused on earning money from ads published on other sites. At that time, it changed its name to Overture Services; "overture" referred to the introductions it made between advertisers and Web surfers. The company racked up many major distribution partners, including AOL (its most significant alliance), Yahoo, Ask Jeeves, Netscape, and MSN Search. Individual domain speculators didn't supply anything close to the level of traffic provided by AOL or MSN, but in the aggregate, their traffic was significant. Increased distribution meant GoTo could show more ads, which increased the number of clicks, and, therefore, revenue. And as advertisers gained more leads, they tended to increase their spending. New advertisers came into the fold as they learned of others' success. In the fourth quarter of 2002, the average price paid per click by advertisers on GoTo rose to 35 cents from 23 cents a year earlier.

GoTo signed revenue-sharing agreements with domain investors. At the time, it typically kept a majority of the revenue from each click for itself. For investors able to land deals with GoTo, the ad revenue was far superior to what they'd received from the search-in-a-box program. Investors' ad-laden Web pages became known as "parked pages." An investor was "domain parking" if, rather than developing a full-fledged Web site, he erected a page of nothing but pay-per-click advertising links.

In May 2000, a GoTo executive contacted Chernoff about placing ad listings on his domains. He was happy to oblige. Chernoff began displaying a generic directory of topics, such as "computers," "travel," and "shopping." When users clicked on a category, they were shown another Web page with ads related to the category. If they clicked on one of those ads, they were redirected to the advertiser's Web page, and Chernoff and GoTo divided the revenue.

For Chernoff, the results were stunning. Almost immediately, "I was making about $1,400 [U.S.] a day," he said. That worked out to more than $500,000 a year. He'd entered the salary range of an executive at a major publicly traded company. He wondered how long it could last. "I couldn't believe it," he said.

Other investors ran similar pages of sponsored links from GoTo. Roy Messer, the former carpet dealer in Tallahassee, Florida, said he contacted two GoTo executives in 1998 and told them he had type-in traffic from his domains that amounted to about ninety thousand unique visitors per day. He said they agreed to run a "beta," or test, with him for several months to see how much revenue could be generated from syndicating ads on his sites. They paid eight cents per unique visitor in the test. They liked what they saw, and then switched to a revenue-sharing agreement. In October 2000, Messer's vodka.com, razors.com, and furniturestore.com all featured a list of links for "finance" and "home" identical to the list on Chernoff's sites.

Yun Ye, the Chinese-born investor, on the other hand, reached a deal with FindWhat.com, a GoTo rival that began in 1999 and immediately began aligning itself with domain holders to gain distribution. Ye's sites, such as xky.com, contained generic directories of links such as "gambling," "finance," and "Internet." His huge portfolio became a significant source of traffic for FindWhat.

Scott Day, the watermelon farmer, was introduced to GoTo by Messer, who'd become his friend over the years. Some of Day's 1,700 sites in 2000 contained a list of ads that were directly related to the domain name, rather than a generic directory. For example, in late 2000, shampoo.com ran ads from several dozen hair-product companies. Their bids for the keyword "shampoo" ranged from a penny to 58 cents per click.

Day won't discuss the financial performance of his company, DigiMedia, but if you consider that his portfolio is superior to Chernoff's—and is considered one of the highest-quality lists in the world—it follows that it generated significant revenue from pay-per-click ads in the same period. For domain investors with descriptive generic names, the GoTo and FindWhat deals secured in the early 2000s marked only the beginnings of an ever-reliable cash cow that transformed many of the investors from average income-earners into millionaires. Revenue from paid-search advertising across the Web grew rapidly over the next several years. The number of advertisers participating in the system grew, which raised prices bid for keywords. And as more people flocked to the Internet, the number of users who clicked on the ads grew, too. U.S. spending on paid-search advertising surged to about $2.5 billion in 2003 from about $80 million in 2000, according to the Interactive Advertising Bureau, the marketing trade group.

The ad-bloated "parked" sites, however, weren't attractive. They looked like newspapers known as "shoppers" that mostly contain long lists of ads for cars or other products. While the design of the pages would improve in the ensuing years, they would come to represent a controversial component of online advertising. Some Web marketers, journalists, and consumers argued the sites, which would number in the millions, offered little value to Web users and made the Internet ugly. Domain investors and the paid-search giants, on the other hand, contended that the pages helped users find information relevant to their interests, similar to what a search engine did. And some sites generated large numbers of leads for marketers.

Oingo Changes the Domain Game

In the fall of 1998, just as Google was being hatched in Silicon Valley, a search-engine company called Oingo took root in Los Angeles. The founders, Gil Elbaz and Adam Weissman, both graduates of the California Institute of Technology, formed a "meaning-based" search engine. The way it worked is complicated, but in essence it analyzed Web pages by looking at the meanings of words on them, as well as the relationships between those words, and yielded relevant search results. Search engines traditionally had focused on matching search queries with the text found on Web sites, failing to account for the fact that some text had multiple meanings. A searcher who typed "genesis," for example, could be looking for any number of things, ranging from the first book in the Bible to the rock band Genesis.

Oingo, renamed Applied Semantics in 2001, didn't gain much notoriety as a search engine. But it built a profitable business by licensing its meaning-based search technology to domain registrars and online advertising companies. In

2000, it began selling a tool to registrars called DomainSense. The device helped the companies register more domains by displaying alternatives to the names users requested on their sites; if, for example, shoes.com wasn't available, the registrar might suggest runningshoes.com. Applied Semantics received less than a penny for every domain registered that way—a tiny sum, particularly considering that some of the names registered with the tool are now worth tens of thousands of dollars. "It never occurred to us to register any names with this tool," said Eytan Elbaz, who was a senior executive at Applied Semantics with his brother Gil. "I guarantee you that we spun names that are $50,000 or $100,000 names today."

The company generated more revenue from its next major service for the domain market. It figured out how to automatically generate a list of relevant ads for any domain name. So when a user typed an address into his browser, the technology would examine the word or phrase and then display an appropriate set of ads. For, say, beds.com, it would display ads from bed manufacturers, rather than only a generic list of advertising links. Previously, domain holders who wanted to display ads relevant to each of their addresses had to insert special computer code on each site by hand. Applied Semantics didn't sell ads, but instead acted as a middleman, distributing ads sold by Overture and FindWhat.

Applied Semantics inked deals with major registrars, including Network Solutions, Register.com, and eNom, to sprinkle pay-per-click ads on domains that people had registered but weren't using. It called the service DomainPark. Historically registrars had served up "coming soon" or "under construction" notices on those pages, which sometimes featured banner ads. The registrars earned money on the ads and didn't share it with their customers. Some Web users found the practice distasteful, and in February 2001, a customer sued Register.com in New York state court for breach of contract and deceptive trade practices for pointing his unused name to a "coming soon" page containing ads for Register.com and other marketers. Despite the pending suit, Applied Semantics managed to sign up several customers for DomainPark in 2001, including Register.com. "It was unclear whether registrars could do this at all, but the more aggressive ones did it anyway," Eytan Elbaz said. Register.com received a favorable court ruling in 2001, but an appeals court reversed part of that decision in 2003. It denied plaintiff Michael Zurakov's claim of unjust enrichment, but reinstated his claim of breach of contract and deceptive trade practices. Ultimately Register.com reached a class-action settlement in the case. It and other registrars inserted clear provisions in their terms of service allowing them to point customers' unused domains to pages loaded with ads.

In 2001, Applied Semantics also was tapped by Overture to serve up targeted ads on the sites owned by Overture clients such as Scott Day, CES Marketing, and Garry Chernoff. Applied Semantics also solved a vexing problem for Overture. Some Overture clients were taking advantage of the company and its roster of advertisers by running shady arbitrage schemes. (To engage in arbitrage is to buy an asset in one market, then immediately resell it in another market in order to profit from a price discrepancy.) For example, some owners of adult-oriented domains would place bids of about 20 cents for adult keywords in the bidding systems of Overture, FindWhat, 7Search, and other pay-for-placement search engines. Then, when that traffic came to their site, they would show the visitors online-gambling ads syndicated by Overture. At that time, gambling ads went for as much as $25 a click. The arbitrageurs were profiting on the differences in the cost of traffic between adult ads and gambling ads. Advertisers were dismayed with the quality of the traffic they were getting because few users clicked on the gambling ads, and those who did rarely signed up to wager online. Advertisers in other industries were also disappointed with the quality of the traffic they drew from some ad-laden sites. Applied Semantics' technology restored a measure of control to Overture, ensuring that the ads were relevant to the Web address. Therefore, an adult-oriented domain showed ads for adult products and services, and a gambling-oriented domain showed gambling ads.

Applied Semantics also served the growing domain market in another way. Smaller investors who didn't draw enough traffic to land a revenue-sharing deal with Overture could sign up for Applied Semantics' DomainPark service and make money off pay-per-click ads. Just like the larger investors, the smaller ones displayed ads sold by Overture, but Applied Semantics relieved Overture of having to handle a bunch of smaller accounts.

Applied Semantics' technology helped investors and Overture make more money because the ads on the sites were better targeted than a generic list of ads. Part of Applied Semantics' success was that it had hired more than a half-dozen linguists, who helped it refine its technology. "It turns out if you use a targeted page, the amount of money you could make over one of these generic pages was like two- or three-fold," said Eytan Elbaz.

On occasion the ads weren't relevant to the domain, however. Furthermore, the pages didn't look very good. Many featured a long list of blue text links against a white background. It was "an awful-looking landing page," said Christopher Wall of CES Marketing.

By late 2002, Applied Semantics was serving up ads on more than 5 million domains and had become profitable. Most of its revenue came from domain parking, but it also was making inroads with a contextual-advertising technology known as AdSense. The system enabled news sites to display relevant pay-per-click ads next to articles. For example, ads for mutual-fund companies could appear alongside articles about personal finance. Applied Semantics scored a big win in this nascent market when it landed a deal to display ads sold by Overture on the pages of USAToday.com.

Despite its triumphs, Applied Semantics' team was burned out from a frenetic four years of trying to build a viable business. Its senior management desperately wanted to be acquired. The company repeatedly tried to persuade Overture to buy it. But despite the close relationship between the companies—Applied Semantics was one of Overture's ten largest distribution partners by revenue generated—Overture wasn't interested, according to a person familiar with both companies.

In early 2003, Applied Semantics found its savior: Google.

Google was the world's most popular search engine. And it had become a major financial success in just a few years by refining the paid-search business model pioneered by Overture. Google, based in Mountain View, California, sold relevant text ads alongside its organic search results. However, unlike Overture, it didn't simply rank the ads in the order of the prices bid by marketers. Instead, it created a formula that also considered how often users clicked on each ad—the "clickthrough rate." As a result, ads that generated the most revenue rose to the top, and less-popular, less-profitable ads slid to the bottom. This brilliant wrinkle helped fuel Google's hypergrowth, and gave it a long-term advantage over Overture. (In April 2002, Overture sued Google for allegedly infringing its patent on a paid-search advertising system. The case was settled prior to Google's initial public stock offering in 2004.)

Sergey Brin, who co-founded Google with Stanford graduate-school classmate Larry Page, was a good friend of Applied Semantics' Gil Elbaz. When Google was raising money in its early days, it referred some of the investors it didn't need to Applied Semantics. Google was impressed with Applied Semantics' AdSense product. Google had just launched a content-targeting program itself, and saw an opportunity to enhance it using AdSense. Google also saw a chance to establish a presence in Southern California, improving its chances of recruiting top job prospects. A deal came together quickly. Google announced the purchase of Applied Semantics on April 23, 2003. Brin called the forty-employee company a "proven innovator."[8] Terms weren't disclosed, but when Google went public in 2004, it said in regulatory filings that it paid $102.4 million. It was Google's biggest acquisition prior to becoming a public company. Google chose the name AdSense for its contextual advertising network, which allowed Web publishers of all sizes to display relevant text ads next to their content and share the revenue with Google. The name became a household word on the Internet.

The deal was a blow to Google's archrival, Overture, because it lost a key distribution partner in Applied Semantics. The same day the deal was announced, Overture issued lower-than-expected guidance for earnings for the rest of the year. The two events prompted Overture shares to decline about 30 percent that week.

For domain investors, the Google-Applied Semantics deal was pivotal because it shook up the status quo. Through the transaction, Google inherited Applied Semantics' partnerships with investors and registrars, costing Overture significant traffic. Google, which had just a couple of domain clients prior to buying Applied Semantics, also represented a new viable alternative to investors who'd worked with Overture or FindWhat. Google tapped Eytan Elbaz to manage its alliances in the market, and dubbed its domain-parking program Google AdSense for domains. "I think what they really wanted [when buying] Applied Semantics was its language-analysis technology; then they realized the cash cow was AdSense for domains," said Matt Bentley, chief strategy officer of Sedo, a name broker and Google client.

In response to the Google-Applied Semantics deal, Overture stepped up its efforts to retain large domain clients and to sign new ones. In some cases, it increased the percentage of revenue it shared.

In October 2003, Internet giant Yahoo bought Overture for more than $1.6 billion. Under Yahoo's wing, Overture continued to work hard to garner domain investors as clients. And in December 2003, it scored a big coup. Yun Ye reached an agreement to run Overture ads on his sites, dumping his longtime partner FindWhat, a second-tier search network that had a smaller advertiser base and generated less revenue per click. It proved to be a smart move. From July 2002 through June 2003, a period when Ye teamed with FindWhat, his company, Ultimate Search, earned $2.7 million in net income on $3.5 million in revenue. From July 2003 through June 2004—the latter half of which Ye's company teamed with Yahoo's Overture unit—it earned $11.5 million in net income on $12.5 million in revenue. Overture gave Ultimate Search, which owned more than 100,000 sites by 2004, a higher percentage of its revenue than FindWhat did, in addition to running a network that was more popular with marketers.

Both Google and Yahoo/Overture deepened their ties with domain investors. It wasn't long before young, well-educated employees of the two Web titans turned up at trade shows about domains, bumping elbows with the motley contingent of people who ruled the domain market. Sometimes executives from the companies paid visits to the investors' home turf to discuss business. One day, an Overture manager was in Oklahoma visiting Scott Day. Day had been pressing for a more rewarding revenue-sharing agreement with the company, but he wasn't getting anywhere. Day took the manager to a roadside restaurant near Terral called Doug's Peach Orchard, founded in 1948. Day ordered a dish called "calf fries," and his guest ate several of the breaded, deep-fried goodies without asking what was inside them. Day asked, "Are you going to give me a better deal?" The manager said "no." Then Day asked, "Do you know what you're eating?" Again, he said "no." So Day explained: "Those are testicles." They were bull-calf testicles, a down-home Oklahoma favorite. The manager was stunned. Day still didn't get a better deal, but he got a good laugh.

Mining Data

The opportunity to milk paid-search advertising revenue from undeveloped domains sparked sweeping changes in the speculative market. Investors began to think of domains as keywords, and vice versa. If a particular word or phrase was popular among both Web searchers and marketers, investors tried to snap up the Web-address version of that term. For instance, in the case of the word *mortgages*, investors would try to obtain mortgages.com. But if that wasn't available (and it surely wasn't except at a high price), they might seek the less popular but still valuable reversemortgages.com, based on the search phrase "reverse mortgages." They even might settle for reversemortgages.net, reversemortgages.org, or reverse-mortgages.com. It also became common to register misspellings of generic terms. Morgages.com, for example, might draw similar levels of type-in traffic as mortgages.com, and the domain investor still could place ads for mortgages on the site.

This revolutionary way of thinking about domains resulted in massive speculation in keyword-style names. Many addresses that for years had been ignored by investors were rapidly acquired. They were obtained in the drop market, in private deals, and, in many cases, by simply visiting a registrar's site and paying the registration price. The dramatic shift in the market pleased registrars, as well as VeriSign, which ran the registry of .com and .net addresses, because it meant more fees flowed into their coffers.

In order to decide whether a keyword-style domain was worth having, investors needed to estimate how much type-in traffic it would receive on a regular basis. If negotiating with a seller, the seller often would disclose that information to try to close a deal. (Investors typically wanted to know the number of daily unique visitors.) But more often than not, there was no direct source for the information, so speculators used every tool they could find to estimate the traffic.

If the address turned up in Google's search-engine results, that was an indication that it had attracted visitors in the past and might continue to do so. The site might attract visitors who came across it in Google, as well as people who'd visited it in the past and bookmarked it. (Some of the latter users, however, might be disappointed to see a revamped site and might never return.) A high Google ranking also suggested the domain would attract users from links on other sites; Google based its ranking of a site in part on how many other sites linked to it. This was one reason Yun Ye sought expired domains—such as Illinois investor Adam Strong's onskis.com—that previously were built into businesses. Over time, however, the site's so-called link popularity could fade if other sites determined there was no longer relevant content on the site and removed their "outbound" links. The Google ranking, therefore, would slide.

But in many cases investors were deciding whether to acquire domains that never had been developed into Web sites, and thus didn't show up in any search-engine results. That's one reason why many investors came to rely on another tool—one offered by Overture, Google's nemesis. The free device, known as the Keyword Selector Tool, wasn't designed to help domain investors, but rather to help advertisers decide which words or phrases to buy in Overture's paid-search advertising system. By typing a term related to their line of business into the online tool, advertisers could see how often that term, as well as related terms, were searched by Web users in the Overture network in the previous month. (Yahoo continued to offer the tool after it acquired Overture, and it encompassed searches on Yahoo's network.)

Investors surmised that the volume of searches on a particular keyword in Overture—say, two thousand searches a month for "wedding cakes"—would provide at least a rough indication of the frequency by which Web surfers would type that term into the address bar of their Web browser, along with the popular .com suffix. (They also knew that, depending on the user's Web browser and its settings, simply typing the search term into the address bar could result in the user being sent to the .com address for that term, by default.) When investors ran studies using the Overture tool, they also found, somewhat to their amazement, that a significant number of Web searchers actually searched on entire domain names. So investors would estimate a domain's potential type-in traffic by looking both at how often the full domain name was searched in Overture and how often the word preceding the domain extension was searched. It was hardly scientific, but it was one of the few options investors had. Running tests on terms in Overture was valuable because it helped investors gauge Web users' interests and searching habits. Following is a list of twenty-five domains entered into the Yahoo search engine in December 2006. Note that recipes.com received more than 42,000 searches, showing how common it is for people to use the Web to hunt for information about how to prepare a meal. The name was owned by Scott Day's DigiMedia. Recipes.com drew a few more searches than porno. com, Rick Schwartz's domain.

Also note that the misspellings of several terms receive a relatively high number of searches. Lirics.com (a misspelling of lyrics.com) received 892 searches. And morgages.com received more searches than the correctly spelled mortgages.com.

Searches in Yahoo, December 2006

Search Term	Number of Searches
Antarctica.com	55
Babyshowers.com	147
Bath.com	149
Beijing.com	82
Bra.com	384
Chairs.com	367
Chicago.com	2,522
Chocolates.com	274
Computer.com	2,102
Computergames.com	522
Computers.com	1,307
Cook.com	4,923
Eatingdisorders.com	50
Foreclosures.com	2,346
Freemaps.com	117
Holtels.com (misspelling)	132
Lirics.com (misspelling)	892
Morgages.com (misspelling)	309
Mortgages.com	248
Moviereviews.com	121
Penpals.com	1,906
Porno.com	40,482
Recipes.com	42,699
Tattoos.com	7,763
Virus.com	550

Investors so revered the Overture tool that domain-appraisal services incorporated a name's "Overture Score" into their analysis. An "Overture Score + Ext" of one hundred meant that one hundred searches were conducted on the term, including the extension, in the previous month. The services also usually took into account the score without the extension. Sellers of domains began to routinely list Overture scores when peddling their wares in online forums or when negotiating in private.

It's hard to draw precise conclusions about the relationship between an Overture score and the actual traffic to a site. For the most part, investors say they use the Overture tool simply as a guide. I typed "bra.com" into the tool one day. Data for the previous month showed 384 searches. Bra.com was among a list of ad-laden sites owned by Dotzup.com. The company, which owned about fifty thousand names, said on its site that bra.com attracted about twenty-five thousand visits a month. That was about sixty-five times the number of searches conducted on "bra.com" in Overture. I did the same comparison for airlineticket.com, another site owned by Dotzup.com. It said the site drew about 2,400 visits a month. That amounted to only five times the 482 searches on "airlineticket.com" shown in the Overture tool. Revenue from ads varies by site, too. Not only are click-through rates inconsistent across domains, but keyword prices differ.

In the early 2000s, some investors treated the Overture tool virtually as gospel. They registered scores of names almost solely based on Overture statistics. This came to be known as "domain mining," a term later used more broadly to describe the registration of large numbers of Web addresses using statistical analysis. Some enterprising people in the industry even wrote computer programs that produced voluminous lists of domains showing how many searches each received in Overture the previous month. The lists were updated monthly to take into account new searching behavior by Web users. Adam Strong, the Illinois investor, said he was among several people who sold such lists to other investors. He said passion for the information was so high that "a lot of guys would buy my reject lists"—lists of names he decided didn't have enough traffic to warrant acquiring himself.

Strong mined names on a small scale. Others did it on a large scale. One of the first major miners was Dark Blue Sea, a publicly traded company in Brisbane, Australia. It registered addresses based on analyses of search data from providers like Overture, as well as statistics on advertisers' bid prices for keywords. By combining the two, it got a proxy for how much revenue a name might generate. Between May and November 2002, Dark Blue Sea acquired about 120,000 domains for $1.1 million U.S., or about $9 per domain, according to regulatory filings. That quickly made it one of the world's largest domain owners. The company's portfolio earned $1,200 in advertising revenue per day in November 2002. Seven months later, Dark Blue Sea boosted the figure to $3,500 a day, which worked out to $1.3 million a year. But the company said a third of the domains accounted for 90 percent of its revenue. That statement was important. It reflected what for many domain portfolios became a truism: 10 or 20 percent of the names produced 80 or 90 percent of the revenue. "I've never seen a portfolio that didn't adhere almost religiously to [the business-school maxim known as the] 80/20 rule," said Ari Bayme, a former investment banker who worked on a number of deals in the domain market. By the end of 2005, Dark Blue Sea owned 500,000 Web addresses. Only about eighty thousand, or 16 percent, were profitable, the company said.

The Drop Game Intensifies

Battles for expired names intensified as investors recognized the opportunity to generate cash from text ads. But to understand how the drop market evolved, it's first necessary to step back a bit.

Activity in the market began to pick up in 2001, when most investors still focused on grabbing names in hopes of reselling them for a profit. Each day at 6:30 a.m. ET, registrars pummeled the registry of .com, .net, and .org addresses—managed by VeriSign—with electronic requests to snag names on behalf of their customers, some of whom used computer programs to rapidly submit their requests to the registrars. "Everyone was starting to notice the schedule" by which VeriSign released domains, said Jay Westerdal, the Seattle investor, and people were "hammering" the system.

VeriSign had given each registrar an equal number of electronic "connections" to the registry's computer system. The connections allowed the registrar to ping the registry with requests to acquire names, which were released in milliseconds. The drop game intensified in part because some investors began paying registrars for preferred access to their connections to increase their odds of grabbing coveted names. The more connections one had, the more "get-this-name" requests one could send when a desired name dropped. The system of paying for preferential treatment didn't escape criticism, though it wasn't widely known and received scarce media attention. One critic was Lee Hodgson, the writer who ran DomainGuru.com. "If you are a 'normal' customer of one of the registrars who offer these services, and you attempt to register a name during the drop, it's very simple: you won't be able to," he wrote in his series on the expired-domain market on Sitepoint. com. "All the bandwidth will have been allocated to VIP customers. Bear in mind that registrars were accredited by Icann [the Internet regulatory body] precisely for the purpose of democratically serving all customers."[9]

Initially, registrars rented out their connections for a few thousand dollars a month. Later, as competition for expired domains increased, they leased them to the highest bidder for as much as $30,000 a month. Many of the registrars that leased their connections—particularly smaller ones—were struggling in their traditional business lines and were eager to draw a new revenue stream. For some, it became their largest revenue source.

Another important new wrinkle in the drop market was the arrival of SnapNames.com, a Portland, Oregon-based start-up company. SnapNames allowed Internet users to place back orders for already-registered domains on a first-come, first-served basis. If the name's current owner let it expire, and SnapNames grabbed it in the drop, the customer got it. SnapNames charged $35 for three years for its back-ordering service, known as SnapBack, which included periodic updates on the domain's status. If the name never expired, or if SnapNames failed to get it when it was released, the user still was out $35. (SnapNames later raised the price to $49 for one year, then $69.) SnapNames wasn't a registrar, so in order to snag expired names, the company, which had raised millions of dollars from venture capitalists and angel (or early-stage) investors, inked deals with large registrars, including VeriSign's Network Solutions, eNom, and BulkRegister. Initially, SnapNames thought its audience would be intellectual-property lawyers eager to acquire names on behalf of corporations, including trademark-related addresses. But soon after launching its SnapBack service in January 2001, SnapNames realized its real potential for success was to cater to domain investors. SnapBack became critical to the activities of major speculators, including Yun Ye. Its service also allowed smaller investors to compete on a more equal playing field with the big players.

About six months after its launch, SnapNames faced some new competition. Dotster, a registrar in Vancouver, Washington, launched a back-ordering service called NameWinner. Instead of offering expired names on a first-come, first-served basis, NameWinner auctioned them off. Users had to bid a minimum of $25. If NameWinner was able to obtain the name in the drop, it would hand it to the winning bidder. If there was only one bidder, the price was $25. All bidding happened before NameWinner pursued the domain. NameWinner didn't charge a customer if it failed to acquire the name. Because its parent company was a registrar, NameWinner had direct connections to the registry to compete in the drop. Another registrar, eNom, also started a drop-catching service in 2001. Called ClubDrop, the service catered to resellers of eNom's services.

In the summer of 2001, the fevered competition to acquire expired domains became problematic. A few registrars pounded VeriSign with requests for names so aggressively that they severely disrupted the normal name-registration activity of other registrars throughout the world during the early morning hours on the East Coast. For twenty days, VeriSign halted the release of expired names until it found a remedy. Drop catchers had to sit and wait. In an e-mail to registrars, VeriSign said "the abuse" of the registration system included certain registrars submitting as many as 1,500 requests per second for a name. Also, it said, some registrars appeared to be hoarding connections to the registry in "an apparent attempt to deny others" from grabbing expired addresses.[10] The registrars involved weren't identified.

One of the domain investors behind this activity was a Canadian named Kevin Ham, who'd paid registrars for preferential access and was racking up scores of expired names. "There were a lot of people doing this," he said. "Was I the best at doing this? Probably. But it was the collective force" that crippled the domain-registration system.

To fix the problem, VeriSign essentially created separate, distinct pipelines for normal registrar activity and for the registration of expired names. VeriSign also changed the time it released names to 2 p.m. ET each day, which in turn changed the sleeping habits of scores of investors. Each day's batch was released within fifteen minutes. VeriSign also outlined a harsh set of penalties if registrars broke any rules.

Things settled down. But a few months later, VeriSign ignited a firestorm in the industry when it proposed a new format for releasing expired names, called a wait-listing service. The idea was to centralize the distribution of the names, bringing more transparency and order to what had become a chaotic market. VeriSign tapped SnapNames to offer the service under a five-year contract. VeriSign initially proposed that it would charge a one-year, non-refundable subscription fee of $40 to registrars to back-order an address on behalf of a customer. Registrars would then mark up that price for customers. Domains would be distributed on a first-come, first-served basis, just like SnapNames' SnapBack service. "This is a huge deal," Ron Weiner, SnapNames' CEO, said at the time.[11] He estimated the contract would be worth as much as $150 million over five years for his company.[12]

VeriSign said the service would benefit consumers by offering a "simple, fair, low-cost, and easy-to-understand procedure," in contrast to an existing system that was impractical for the average consumer.[13]

But SnapNames' rival drop-catching services, many registrars, and a lot of speculators were furious. They said the service would destroy a cottage market developed through innovation, unfairly handing VeriSign a monopoly on expired domains. VeriSign, they pointed out, already enjoyed a lucrative monopoly as the registry for the popular .com suffix, receiving $6 per address per year. Throughout 2002, VeriSign's proposal was tied up in rancorous debate. VeriSign sought to appease registrars by dropping the proposed wholesale cost for a wait-list subscription to $24 from $40.

While the debate raged, Icann decided to address another controversy involving expired names.

Many of the names falling into investors' hands had only expired because their prior owners inadvertently failed to renew them. Often, they didn't receive renewal notices because they moved or changed e-mail addresses and failed to give their registrar their new contact information. Icann found that domain owners frequently didn't understand the consequences of not renewing their names on time. Some were stunned when their name was snared by a speculator or entrepreneur. A few were horrified. It wasn't uncommon, for example, for a church group to lose its domain and suddenly find its Web site redirected to a porn site.

Saying it faced "a rising tide of problems and complaints," Icann proposed in February 2002 that domain holders be given an extra thirty days to renew their names.[14] "The public interest would be served by reform of the current system, which operates to allow a few well-informed and well-connected profiteers to prosper from others' mistakes," Icann said in a discussion paper in February 2002.[15] Its proposal enjoyed broad support among Icann constituents, and Icann's board approved it in June 2002. VeriSign implemented the policy, known as the redemption grace period, in January 2003. The new system worked like this:

1. If a domain holder failed to pay to renew his name by the expiration date, VeriSign nonetheless automatically renewed it for the *registrar*, and the registrar was charged the $6 annual wholesale fee for the name.
2. The registrar then had one to forty-five days to contact the customer and get him to pay for the name. It could decide at any time within that period to delete the name, and recoup the $6 fee from the registry. It had to delete the name if the customer didn't pay for it.
3. If the domain was deleted, it triggered the new thirty-day redemption grace period approved by Icann. During this period, the Web site

associated with the name would become inactive. The idea was that an inactive Web site would alert the domain holder that there was a problem, even if renewal notices weren't reaching him.

4. The domain holder had thirty days to renew the name. VeriSign charged the registrar an extra fee for such renewals, and registrars could mark up the price.

5. If the name wasn't renewed, it entered a five-day period known as "pending delete." No one could register the name during that period. On the sixth day, VeriSign released the name at about 2 p.m. ET.

The new system was heralded for giving new protections to domain owners. However, Icann failed to make it mandatory for registrars. Most generally adhered to it—but only at first.

Lawsuits Fly

In August 2002, Icann's board gave conditional approval to VeriSign's controversial proposal to implement a wait-listing service. More than a half-dozen conditions had to be met. As VeriSign worked to address those, lawsuits over the service began flying.

Pool.com, a rival of SnapNames and NameWinner based in Ottawa, sued Icann in a Canadian court in July 2003, seeking to block implementation of the service, which it called "monopolistic." The same month, the Domain Justice Coalition, which included eNom, Go Daddy, and Pool.com, filed suit to block the service in a Los Angeles federal court. Also that month, Paul Stahura, CEO of eNom, criticized the service at a U.S. Senate subcommittee hearing on communications on Capitol Hill. "Since WLS is a monopoly service, to be only offered by VeriSign, it completely destroys today's competitive marketplace," he said.[16]

Acrimony in the name trade escalated two months later, in mid-September, when VeriSign introduced a service called SiteFinder. It steered Internet users who attempted to reach nonexistent or inactive Web addresses to VeriSign's site, where it ran pay-per-click ads sold by Overture and offered a "Did You Mean?" listing of similar domains. Critics of SiteFinder said it allowed VeriSign to unfairly profit from its control of the master directory of .com and .net addresses. Previously, some makers of Web browsers, including Microsoft and AOL, funneled such traffic to their search-engine listings. But those services raised far fewer hackles because the companies weren't in charge of the .com and . net list, and consumers could choose whether to use their products. Bickering over SiteFinder erupted into a debate over how the Internet should be governed. At least three lawsuits were filed against VeriSign. Ultimately, about three weeks after SiteFinder launched, Icann forced VeriSign to shut down the service. Icann said the service disrupted many Internet applications, including some spam filters, and violated VeriSign's obligation to act as a neutral registry.

Though SiteFinder was short-lived, the traffic it generated illustrated that large numbers of Web surfers typed names directly into the address bar of their browser in search of information. In September 2003, VeriSign's Web site was the 11th-most visited site on the Internet, up from 135th the previous month, according to research firm ComScore Media Metrix. The number of unique visitors soared to 30.8 million from 4.8 million. And SiteFinder only operated in the last two weeks of September. It was a testament to the power of type-in traffic. Although no firm data existed, analysts estimated that 10 to 15 percent of Internet searches consisted of users typing domains into the address bar, a behavior known as "direct navigation."

In 2004, the legal battles grew even uglier. VeriSign filed an antitrust lawsuit against Icann in federal court in Los Angeles. It accused Icann of overstepping its authority by blocking services such as SiteFinder and delaying the launch of the wait-listing service. SnapNames sued Icann in state court in Los Angeles, claiming unlawful interference with its agreement with VeriSign to run the wait-listing service. The battles underscored deep animosity among some of the key companies and groups that managed how the Internet operated. Eventually, all the suits were either dropped, dismissed, or settled. The wait-listing service never was implemented.

Delays in implementing the service, and responses to them, ended up having profound repercussions for domain owners.

A key instigator of changes in the market was Pool.com. Pool, a unit of Momentous.ca, an Ottawa-based registrar, launched its back-ordering service in June 2003, about two years behind other major drop-catching services.

Pool quickly became a powerhouse. Like Dotster's NameWinner, it used an auction system. However, instead of running an auction before a name was released, it held one only if it was able to grab the name in the drop. Users bid a minimum of $60, and paid nothing if they failed to get the address. In 2004, auction sales at Pool included carfinancing.com ($46,000) and gourmetcoffee.com ($23,000).

Pool's business model was ideal for investors, and the company quickly became the biggest drop-catching service. Meanwhile, SnapNames, which had been No. 1, was in a tough spot. It continued to offer names on a first-come, first-served basis for a nonrefundable fee of $69 a year. It couldn't simply switch business models, because it had signed a deal with VeriSign to offer the pending wait-listing service, modeled after SnapBack. "They'd gone out and told the world how great their model was, they couldn't change to ours, and they were really handcuffed," said Rob Hall, chairman of Pool and CEO of Momentous.ca.

SnapNames nearly went out of business, said Ray King, former CEO of the company. Pool "really ate our lunch there for a while, and the whole time we're sitting there holding our breath for" the wait-listing service. "We had thought of the auction system, but it was counter to what we were thinking and counter to our message. Pool was making more money, they were able to pay partners more, and get more connections that way and get more names." Icann dragged its feet many times on the wait-listing service, King said. It approved it on several occasions, but then introduced new hurdles that had to be cleared, he said.

Besides its superior auction model, Pool also figured out a new way to get more connections to the registry for the drop. Like SnapNames, it had been leasing connections from other registrars. Then Pool saw that the operator of the registrar NameSecure.com had quietly formed another fifteen Icann-accredited registrars whose sole activity was to grab names in the drop, rather than offering traditional registration services. Icann didn't bar the practice, Hall said, so Pool decided it needed to create a bunch of its own new registrars, too, for competitive reasons. It created about one hundred new Icann-accredited registrars. The cost of being an accredited registrar is a minimum of $4,000 a year. But it was easy to justify the cost, because the new registrars helped Pool grab more names that it could sell to the highest bidder. Enom followed suit, creating more than one hundred such registrars for its ClubDrop service. Within a few years, there were more than eight hundred Icann-accredited registrars. But at least three hundred offered no registration services to the public; all they did was help their parent companies grab expired domains.

Hall said Icann didn't block the practice because the accreditations gave the organization substantial revenue. King agreed. "They were benefiting from their own disorganization" in overseeing the Internet, he said.

Initially, SnapNames complained about its competitors' use of what it called "shell registrars" and avoided creating its own. "We didn't want to compete with our [registrar] partners," said King. "And for a long time we believed registrars couldn't be involved in 'frontrunning' domain names, and that Icann would do something about it, and that turned out not to be true. Icann was saying, 'Maybe it is a legit business model,' which I just found crazy."

In an e-mailed statement, Tim Cole, Icann's chief registrar liaison, said the approval of numerous registrars resulted from a "consistent application" of its registrar-accreditation policy. The policy, he said, was adopted in the late 1990s, a time when Icann was striving to increase the number of registrars to enhance competition. He added that the approval of hundreds of drop-catching registrars "had nothing to do with the collection of funds."

SnapNames eventually decided to follow the principle of "if you can't beat 'em, join 'em." It created more than eighty Icann-accredited registrars for the drop, which had names such as DomainHysteria.com and DomainsAreForever.net.

As the drop-catching companies sparred, investors tried to improve their odds of getting a name by placing back orders through multiple companies. That way, if SnapNames failed to get a name, but Pool succeeded, the investor could participate in an auction at Pool and have a shot.

One such investor was a powerful firm called BuyDomains.

Playing to Win

In the fall of 1998, Mike Mann pulled one of his many all-nighters. Mann, hunched over a computer in his basement, wanted to know if he could find combinations of words that domain speculators had failed to think of registering. These were still the halcyon days of the Web, when online businesses were sprouting up like wildflowers. Each of those businesses needed a domain. Perhaps, Mann thought, some of the terms he strung together would have value to somebody. But he really had no idea where his search would take him. He was bored, he was curious, and he had time to burn. Barely into his thirties, Mann already had built and sold several successful businesses, including a courier service and an Internet service provider, and had banked several million dollars. The son of a labor lawyer and small businesswoman, he excelled in business despite little formal education; he had an associate's degree in business management from Santa Barbara City College in California. Mann was taking it easy for a few months at his modest house in Bethesda, Maryland, near the nation's capital. He lived frugally for a young millionaire, so he figured he didn't need to work for a while.

Mann thought of generic word combinations and typed them into a Whois site to see if they'd been taken. He'd sold a few domains for a profit, including menus.com, which fetched $25,000 and made Mann think there may be some potential in domain speculation. But Mann wondered if there were long lists of word combinations that speculators had completely overlooked. Many one-word generics like menus.com were long gone, but Mann wondered if perhaps scores of two- or three-word combinations remained up for grabs.

That night, he discovered that many were. But as intrigued as he was, he didn't enjoy typing names over and over to see if they'd been claimed. He also knew that, although he had a good imagination, he was incapable of conceiving every possible word combination that might appeal to businesses. Mann figured there had to be a more efficient way to do the job. He realized that he could find valuable names a lot faster if he could write a computer program that automatically generated word pairs and scoured the Whois database to see if they were available. He called a friend and programming whiz, Ronald Fitzherbert. Fitzherbert wrote a simple program that allowed Mann to quickly pull up lists of unclaimed Web addresses featuring common subjects inside them, like "cars," "food," or "movies." With the aid of the program, Mann began registering dozens of names, including adventurevacations.com, certifiedmortgage.com, caribbeanfinancial.com, and justenvelopes.com. They weren't the types of names that human beings would intuitively think of, but a computer could generate names like them by the thousands. At the time, you could register an address for two years for $70, and for $35 a year thereafter. Mann figured the names were worth more than the registration cost, and that he could profit by selling them to businesses and speculators.

Mann and Fitzherbert patented their simple name-searching program, which they called NameFind, and later licensed it to several registrars. (It also was licensed to Applied Semantics for its popular DomainSense name-spinning tool.) Mann created a company to buy and sell names. For the next seven years he did just that, working almost nonstop, much to his wife's chagrin. He initially called the company RareDomains.com, but it later primarily went by the name BuyDomains.com. Mann found that there was a big appetite for many of the names he registered. Some sold for one hundred times the cost of registration—a $70 investment yielded $7,000. "As long as we sold five out of every one hundred, we were in the black," Mann said. "We sold a lot more than that, but that was all that was required to have good economics."

Mann and his employees concentrated on the expired-domain market to grab potentially fruitful names. They garnered some premium generic terms, but they mostly collected middle-of-the-pack names because the company's primary focus was to sell addresses to small and midsize businesses. In the company's first ten months, 90 percent of its sales were priced from $488 to $1,088.

Mann and his team became fierce and formidable players in the drop game in the late 1990s and early 2000s. Mann and two lieutenants, Chip Yamasaki and Alex Ikenson, played the drop nearly every day of the year. The company was "virtual," so everyone worked from their own home offices. They often grabbed 500 domains a day in the drop. "It was a lot of hard, contentious work," Mann said. BuyDomains leased connections to the registry from about a dozen registrars. BuyDomains also back-ordered domains through SnapNames to help it garner as many good ones as possible. Ikenson built software to help BuyDomains quickly weed through lists of soon-to-expire names and choose which ones to pursue. The software assigned a ranking to each name; a name rated a ten, for example, would be at the top of the list for the company to seek on a given day. "We knew what names we wanted, and we were very good at grabbing them," said Michelle Miller, who served as chief operating officer, among other roles, at BuyDomains.

Miller ran the company's sales division, peddling the thousands of names that it acquired each week. She was one of the few prominent women in the industry. Mann hired her in 2000 when she was about a year out of college, and he told her at the time that the plan was to spend less than a year acquiring a bunch of domains and reselling them at a fat profit. "We had no intention of building a real company," she said. Miller had attended the University of Maryland in College Park, earning a bachelor's degree in finance and marketing. She also played on the women's basketball team for two seasons.

Mann wasn't easy to work with, Miller said. He expected people to work as hard as he did. And he had a temper. When things didn't go right, he often flew off the handle, screaming at employees.

"Mike's a character," Miller said. "It's funny. One of the reasons I think we connected really well is I came from an athletic background, and at Maryland, we had probably one of the toughest coaches in the NCAA: Chris Weller. She ran us into the concrete . . . She spit in your face. She was just unbelievable. The joke with Mike was that, 'As long as you don't spit in my face and make me run stairs, you can't do anything. I'm pretty tough.'"

Mann admitted that he was a difficult boss. "I'm impossible," he said. "I have to hire people like [Miller] because most people can't handle my personality."

BuyDomains ranked among a handful of the best drop catchers, regularly going head to head with Yun Ye. Just as some of Ye's choices confounded other investors, so did some of BuyDomains'. "People in the drop game would often ask Chip Yamasaki, 'What are you thinking, going after these names?'" Miller said. "We were picking up two-word generics, and most were so focused on the one-worders. It was sort of a strategic play for us. We'd go after a lot of names [others weren't interested in] and then I'd sell it the next week for $2,000."

Mann punished his body with his schedule. When he slept, it was usually in the realm of 4 a.m. to 11 a.m. But he thrived on the competition. He was obsessed with making money, not because he liked material things, he said, but because it was a way of keeping score. BuyDomains amassed one of the largest portfolios of domains in the world, totaling about 500,000 monikers by 2005. It enjoyed high profit margins because it exploited discrepancies between the cost of acquiring the names in the drop and the price at which it sold them to businesses and investors. The closely held company also had low overhead; it had about fifteen employees, who dealt with customers by e-mail and phone. The game was simple: buy low and sell high, again and again. And the company was a shrewd and brutal competitor. Some rivals speculated that BuyDomains was doing something underhanded to grab so many names. But Mann said the company played by the rules and simply outworked and outsmarted many of its foes. "I would never have recommended anyone to compete with BuyDomains because our whole business plan was to screw them," Mann said. "That is how we got 500,000 names in the first place. We weren't big on sharing."

The drop game became more difficult for the company when Pool.com launched in 2003. Pool corralled scores of names for its clients. BuyDomains went from getting as many as five out of every six names it sought in the drop to as little as one out of six, Miller said. The company decided it would be better to work with Pool than compete with it, so it began back-ordering names at Pool's Web site and battling in the auctions to acquire the names after they dropped. "Mike loved these names," Miller said. "He had this attachment, and when a name came up to drop, he wholeheartedly had to have that name. I had no problem flipping these and moving on. When he saw Pool getting all these names that he had to have, he said, 'We've got to work with Pool.'"

Said Mann: "I didn't care about the names themselves. But I cared about the market. People were stealing our market share, and I needed the profits that the names brought."

In the summer of 2004, SnapNames came up with a strong competitive response to Pool and soon dethroned it as the leading drop-catching service. SnapNames began striking deals with registrars such as Network Solutions to do what was known as "transfer fulfillment." (Network Solutions was independent of VeriSign by then, having been sold to a private-equity firm in

2003.) If a back order had been placed at SnapNames on a name belonging to a customer of one of the registrars, and the name expired, the registrar would transfer it to SnapNames within as little as a few days, rather than letting it go through the normal deletion process which gave everyone a chance to vie for the name. SnapNames would auction off the name, and share the revenue with the registrar. The process completely circumvented the redemption-grace period policy Icann had put in place to protect domain holders who inadvertently let their names expire. That policy provided for at least thirty days after the expiration date for owners to get their names back.

But Icann rules didn't require registrars to adhere to the grace-period policy, and when they recognized that by abandoning it, they could collect a share of the revenue from expired domains, many did. Network Solutions, Go Daddy, eNom and other major registrars created provisions in their lengthy (and rarely read) terms-of-service agreements with registrants allowing them within days of the expiration date to transfer a name to an auction service like SnapNames or auction it off themselves. The time frames varied. Go Daddy said in its terms of service that it offered a 12-day grace period, but that it could be subject to change. Network Solutions and eNom said they might, but were not obligated to, offer a grace period. On the bright side, a few registrars, including Network Solutions, shared a portion of the revenue they received from selling an expired name with the previous owner.

The rapid transfer of expired names to auction services baffled many consumers who lost their names, and some in the registrar community thought it unseemly. But none of Icann's constituents formally proposed a policy change requiring registrars to adhere to the redemption-grace period—a system created a mere two years earlier, in Icann's words, due to "a rising tide of problems and complaints." Ross Rader, an executive with the registrar Tucows, said he tried to initiate a proposal within Icann to address the issue. However, he dropped the idea because other registrars adamantly opposed him even raising the topic.

An Icann spokesman said the organization is built on "a bottom-up consensus" process, so it would take no action unless someone thought it necessary and made a proposal. Even then, the spokesman said, "grace periods are not an entitlement." In fact, he added, "a registrant's rights cease upon expiration of their domain name."

Expired names were rapidly building wealth for shrewd speculators like Mike Mann and his BuyDomains team. But a man who was late to drop-catching helped transform the domain game for everyone.

Chapter Five

Better Late Than Never

Frank Schilling woke up in paradise, literally, in the spring of 2002. He and his wife, Michele, lived on Grand Cayman Island, a flat, low-lying slice of land in the Caribbean, about 150 miles south of Cuba. Despite their exotic surroundings, things weren't going all that smoothly. The Schillings had just uprooted from their home in Vancouver, British Columbia, so that Frank could start an online gambling business. They'd emptied their retirement accounts and sold off their house and several others Frank had built and rented, leaving Frank with about $200,000 to start the business. They set up shop in the Caribbean, rather than Canada, because of uncertainty about the legality of running an online gambling concern from Canada. Dozens of offshore casinos had sprung up in the Caribbean, and Frank had designs on joining them in reaping millions of dollars from the many Americans who wagered online despite the U.S. government's contention that online gambling was illegal. Grand Cayman offered the Schillings a tax haven, too. There was no income or property tax, and no controls on foreign ownership of property and land. On the other hand, the cost of living was high because most goods had to be imported.

Schilling, thirty-two years old, didn't plan to start an online casino right away. Instead, he aimed to earn revenue as an affiliate for casinos. He'd begun acquiring domain names, such as sportsworld.com, and placing ads on the sites linking users to gambling sites. In return for delivering customers who opened wagering accounts, he earned a commission. At the time, gambling sites paid hundreds of dollars for referrals. "I thought, *Wow, my ship has come in*," Schilling recalled. "I thought Internet gambling was the big thing. We [his wife assisted him in the business] were going to operate a network of feeder sites, like a tour bus dropping visitors off at the casino door. And if we were successful, we had grand designs to run a casino ourselves."

But things got off to a rough start, and the Schillings feared they'd made a big mistake. By April 2002, it dawned on Frank that perhaps he hadn't done enough homework on the gambling sector, and that perhaps he should explore other ways to make a living. Not many people were clicking on his links to casinos and sports-betting parlors. He'd also learned it was actually illegal to run a gambling operation from the Cayman Islands, even though many other Caribbean islands allowed it. And he'd begun to observe unfavorable industry dynamics. Major U.S. credit-card issuers such as Bank of America had begun blocking transactions to online casinos. And on Internet message boards for gambling operators, users expressed concern that the U.S. government would ultimately impose a formal, unequivocal ban on online wagers. Schilling wanted to strike it big with his Web venture, but the prospect of easy riches suddenly seemed remote. He and his wife began to seriously consider going back to Canada. "By April, we're scared," he said. "We just realized it was going to be a tough road to hoe."

Finding a Focus

Frank Schilling was born in Stuttgart, Germany, in 1969, while his father, Ray Schilling, was in medical school. When Frank was three years old, the family left their native Germany for Canada. They lived in Hamilton, Ontario, for a few years before moving to Langley, a suburb of Vancouver. Ray ran a family medical practice, and his wife, Tina, a former schoolteacher, helped him manage it. Frank's parents were well-educated, hardworking people who built the houses they lived in. Frank also was hardworking, but his education was more informal than formal. At D. W. Poppy Secondary School in Langley, Frank showed an affinity for English and geography but was poor at math. On graduation day in 1987, he celebrated with his fellow students, but was actually two credits shy of a diploma. He had to make up the credits—in math and earth science—the next year.

Schilling was intrigued by film, so he enrolled in the Vancouver Film School, which offered a two-year postsecondary program. He graduated near the bottom of his class. Also attending the school around that time was Kevin Smith, who never finished but went on to fame directing movies such as "Clerks" and "Jersey Girl." Schilling wrote a couple of screenplays and enjoyed the creative challenge. But he feared it would be brutal to try to make a living in the movie business. "I saw too many guys twenty-eight to thirty who were in it and thought their big break was right around the corner, and it wasn't going to happen," he said. "I didn't want to be that guy."

He enrolled at the University of British Columbia to pursue a degree in economics. But that wasn't for him either, and he dropped out. In the meantime, he'd begun building houses for a living, taking advantage of skills he'd picked up from his parents. In the 1990s, western Canada was enjoying a mini-boom in real estate, and it was easy for Schilling to make good money building houses. He did that work part-time, and took various sales jobs. In the mid- to late 1990s, he served as senior manager of sales and marketing for Act Labs, a maker of videogame accessories in Vancouver. In that role, he regularly did business with executives at the headquarters of major U.S. retailers, such as Wal-Mart and Best Buy.

Schilling had always liked computers. He played a lot of videogames and killed time on online bulletin boards, even before the emergence of the World Wide Web. During the dot-com craze, he read a newspaper article about a few big sales of domains. He figured that he could boost his income by assisting domain investors with administrative tasks, such as finding Web-hosting providers and keeping track of their renewal notices. He also was interested in being a domain broker. So he launched his own Internet business.

In 2000, Schilling was trying to help a client acquire fastener.com. The person who owned it was Garry Chernoff. Schilling cold-called him. The buyer wanted to pay $80,000 or $100,000 for the domain, but Chernoff wanted more, because "fastener" represented an entire industry. Every screw, nut, and bolt is a fastener. They weren't able to reach a deal, but Schilling made a friend in Chernoff, who was laid back and willing to share a little of his expertise about domains. Like Schilling, Chernoff had been raised in British Columbia, albeit in a small town 250 miles from Vancouver.

Schilling asked Chernoff how he earned a living. At the time, Chernoff had about 600 domains, and made money from the GoTo search box and his list of "favorite links." So Chernoff explained that he earned revenue from visitors who typed his addresses into their Web browsers, landed on his pages, and clicked on links. Schilling was in awe. "He said, 'You're kidding,'" Chernoff recalled. "It was like a lightning bolt hit him in the head. You could just hear the gears turning after that." At one point, Schilling was looking at one of Chernoff's sites, and asked him, "Why are those your favorite links, Garry?" Chernoff replied, "Frank, those are my favorite links because they make me money."

Schilling couldn't stop asking questions, Chernoff remembered. "He said, 'You can make money doing nothing? You just put up a page, and you make money?' I said, 'Yeah,' and he said, 'Oh, my God. That's amazing.'"

Chernoff's revenue from affiliate links and the GoTo search box was what prompted Schilling to launch a gambling-affiliate business. "When I talked to Garry, a light bulb went off," he said.

But when that plan began looking bleak in the spring of 2002, Schilling began mulling a backup strategy. In preparation for starting his gambling business, he'd scooped up several thousand generic Web addresses. Many had been unclaimed, so he paid merely the registration fees to obtain them. "Many were crappy," Schilling conceded. Some were gambling-related, but others had nothing to do with it. Schilling registered a bunch of non-gambling names thinking he could still place ads on them for casinos. A certain percentage of the population is predisposed to gamble on a Friday night, he figured, so some fraction of visitors to his sites would be interested in clicking on an ad that delivered them to a gambling portal. As he steadily acquired domains, Schilling signed up for various affiliate programs, including the GoTo search box, and tried some pay-per-click advertising programs. In 2001, he signed a revenue-sharing agreement with Overture. In the summer of 2002, he did some math and determined that even though his gambling-affiliate business was foundering, he was earning about $300 in revenue per day in affiliate and pay-per-click revenue across all his sites. It was a decent amount of money, and he had mediocre names. He began to consider scotching his gambling business in favor of building a large domain portfolio. One name might not make much money, but in the aggregate, a big list of names could flourish. Plus, he surmised, as Internet usage increased and more advertisers sought to pitch their products online, the increased competition to bid on keywords would prompt higher pay-per-click rates. That would help generate more revenue for each site he owned.

The cost of registering domains was no longer a major drawback to owning thousands of them. Registration fees were less than $10 a year. Earlier in the industry, few people owned thousands of domains because the fees were relatively high, and it was difficult to produce cash flow. "The big players were these guys like Garry [Chernoff] with 400 or 600 names," Schilling said. "Early on, I was like, 'How can you afford the renewals? $30 a year? That's $18,000 a year. That's like property taxes on a mansion!'"

Like others before him, Schilling stumbled into being a domain investor while focusing on other business ideas. "Nobody in this business woke up, I don't think, and said, 'I'm going to be a big domainer,'" he said. "It was all kind of conceptual: How am I going to get enough traffic to run my Internet business?"

In late 2002, Schilling got down to business in a big way. He decided
he was going to stake his family's future on Web addresses by acquiring
commercially relevant, generic words that would draw type-in traffic. It
was another form of search. And though he was late to the game of domain
investing, he found an ideal window of time to slip into the market. The
Internet economy had not yet rebounded from the dot-com meltdown.
Thousands of the domains acquired in the boom were being relinquished.
"We saw all these names start to expire," Schilling said. "We are like, 'These
are really good names.' That is what gave us our huge leg up."

Schilling began acquiring expired domains in an impassioned shopping
spree. He formed a company called Name Administration to own and operate
the domains; like Yun Ye, he incorporated his company in the tax-friendly
British Virgin Islands. He used the family's nest egg of about $200,000 to
sweep up names. As that money ran out, he paid a visit to a banker on Grand
Cayman Island and requested a personal loan of $50,000. When he candidly
explained how he'd use the money, the banker looked at him as if he were
insane, Schilling said. "He said, 'You're going to buy what?'" So Schilling
turned to credit cards.

Michele Schilling was terrified. She thought her husband was taking a
huge risk. At one point, she was so scared that she called Frank's parents,
saying, "I don't know what he's doing," and that she was worried something
might be wrong with him. But Frank remained calm: "I just had this idea that
I can't be wrong." The approach was a bit out of character, he said, because
he'd long been conservative with money. As an investor in stocks and bonds,
for instance, he tended to buy low-risk mutual funds.

One of the first moves Schilling made was to open an account with
SnapNames. SnapNames ended up helping Schilling become very wealthy;
in turn, he helped it make a lot of money.

"We put hundreds of thousands of domain names into their system to
try to get them, knowing they wouldn't get them all, but if they did, we'd be
rich, because these are such good names," said Schilling, who went by the
names "Cuervo" and "Ben Franklin" in the SnapNames auctions. Schilling
initially funded his SnapNames account with credit cards. Later, it gave him
a line of credit because he was such a big customer. But many of his early
wire transfers to SnapNames were funded with several credit cards. He later
used other drop-catching services, including Pool.com, where he was a major
customer spending as much as $500,000 a month on domains.

Most desirable one-word names were in the hands of investors or
corporations when Schilling made his big foray into the market. So he focused

on acquiring compound phrases that were popular among Web searchers. One of his favorites was eatingdisorders.com, which he bought for $1,100 in a private auction in December 2002. It was a classic keyword-style domain. Schilling thought of his network of sites as a reverse search engine. Instead of running one search site that got millions of searches each day, he could run thousands of sites that drew a handful of highly targeted visits each day. In the aggregate, the traffic added up to millions of Web surfers.

"Megadic"

Schilling entered the drop game long after Yun Ye and others had already staked their claim there. But despite being late to the party, he managed to acquire legions of addresses by working almost around the clock. He pored over lists of soon-to-expire names he bought from Exody.com, a service run by a Georgia farmer and computer expert, Dwayne Rowland. Schilling estimated domains' potential traffic using several "keyword tools," including the popular Overture Keyword Selector Tool. His favorite source of keyword data was Wordtracker, a London firm that charged users for statistics. Schilling learned some basic computer programming and built a huge database of hundreds of thousands of words and phrases, including terms in Spanish, German, and other languages. It even featured lists of the most popular boys' and girls' first names downloaded from the U.S. Census Web site. He incorporated the keyword-search statistics from Wordtracker and others. He called his database the "megadic," which was short for "mega dictionary." It didn't feature definitions of the words, but rather the words and their projected type-in traffic. Using a computer program, he'd compare lists of soon-to-expire names against the megadic. If an expiring name wasn't in the megadic, he typically didn't pursue it.

To come up with ideas for names that might be valuable, Schilling also looked around his house and thought of basic things that people make and sell, such as wooden spoons. And he placed a lot of bets on names that other investors, using conventional thinking, didn't immediately see as having value. "We stuck our necks out," Schilling said, again acknowledging his wife's support. "We decided we'll take everything that looks good and, if they don't work, we'll let them expire."

Schilling garnered many domains through SnapNames at bargain-basement prices. In January 2003, he acquired more than one thousand names through SnapNames at a flat rate of $39.33 each. SnapNames had given him that discounted price—the normal rate was $69—because he was its biggest customer in terms of volume, he said. At that time, SnapNames charged users even if it didn't snag the back-ordered names for them in the drop. The domains from the January 2003 haul included chapter11. com, apartmentlisting.com, and gasolineprice.com. Many were two-word names that were relevant to advertisers on the Web. But he also landed some single-word names, such as fettucine.com.

For the next two years, Schilling continued to acquire thousands of names that were valuable as sources of advertising revenue. "The dot-com bust fell right into my hands," he said.

Schilling grabbed antarctica.com, one of his favorites, in 2003. It's not a name that one would presume gets a lot of traffic. But it draws about one hundred visitors a day. "Any name that gets fifty visits today will get fifty tomorrow, and if it's three hundred, it will get 296 or 289 tomorrow," he said. "That's just the way it is."

In the early days, the expired-name auctions would close at a set time, similar to auctions on eBay.com, even if there was more interest in bidding. Later, the auction services realized they were leaving money on the table, so they started extending the closing time with each additional bid. But before the change, Schilling garnered several valuable names by "sniping," or placing a very high last-minute bid for a name. In 2003, he nabbed eshopping.com on Dotster's NameWinner service for $8,000, a high price for such a name at the time.

In the month of May 2003 alone—less than a year after Schilling began concentrating on domains—he earned $550,000 in revenue from ads sold by Overture. At that point, he had more than seventy thousand domains drawing 11.4 million unique visitors a month. He'd begun driving a silver Mercedes-Benz E320. Later that year, two executives from FindWhat. com, the second-tier search engine, paid Schilling a visit. Over dinner at an Italian restaurant, Pete Neumann, FindWhat's vice president of business development, asked Schilling if he'd consider selling his domains to FindWhat. They discussed a potential price of $30 million to $40 million. But Schilling rejected the idea. "Not that it wasn't a lot of money," he said, but his company was growing fast and he felt he'd be selling prematurely.

During his two-year domain-shopping spree, Schilling slept little. He worked on domains about twenty hours a day, nearly every day of the year, nursing as many as ten double espressos a day to stay alert. The family didn't take any vacations. Schilling holed himself up in an office in the back of his two-story house. Houses on Grand Cayman Island are built of cement block, with high walls. It was cool in Schilling's office, and he kept the drapes drawn to keep out the sunlight. He wore T-shirts and lightweight surfer shorts. He went through a fairly dramatic physical transformation. When he arrived on the island, his light-brown hair was clipped short, and his five-foot-nine-inch frame was a bit flabby. But while sitting all day in front of a computer and rarely eating, his hair grew to his shoulders and he became very thin. "All I would do is sleep and do this," he said. "We're in the Caribbean, and I'd literally be out at night, and I hadn't seen daylight. I was the whitest man in Grand Cayman . . . People would mistake me for a tourist."

In barely two years, Schilling inhaled huge swaths of Internet real estate. In 2004, his company, Name Administration, owned about 260,000 domains, making it one of the ten largest portfolio owners in the world. And it was a profit machine. Its annual revenue topped $10 million, and its profit margins were about 90 percent. At the time, Name Administration's revenue-sharing agreement with Yahoo, an old contract inherited from Overture, provided Yahoo with the majority of the revenue earned on his sites. Later, they renegotiated terms.

Schilling didn't have a dazzling array of premium one-word generic domains like Scott Day, the watermelon farmer, whose company owned about 1,700 sites. But Schilling had many keyword-style domains with dependable type-in traffic. "Scott's portfolio was far better than mine; mine was just larger," Schilling said. "He has more multimillion-dollar names than anyone I know."

Among Schilling's most profitable names were chapter11.com, antarctica. com, eatingdisorders.com, and reversemortgages.com. Some marketers bid more than $2 a click on the term "reverse mortgages."

"The guy is so smart and creative," said Chernoff, who became pals with Schilling. "He started late, and he just voraciously learned things from everybody very quickly. He came up with some creative ideas no one had thought of, and he just took it to a whole new level."

Chernoff said Schilling inspired him to remain active in the market. "He may credit me for getting him started, but I credit him for keeping me in the game because he did so well," said Chernoff, who owns about 3,200 names. "I kept thinking it's going to end any day."

Schilling's focus on generic names kept him out of legal trouble. If a company notified him that it had a trademark associated with one of his addresses, which was relatively rare, he usually promptly transferred the name to it, avoiding a dispute. "I tried my guts out to steer clear of trademarks," he said.

Pursuing trademark-related names was wrong, and wasn't a sustainable business model, Schilling said. From 2002 through 2006, ten companies filed complaints under Icann's arbitration policy against Name Administration. John Berryhill, who was Yun Ye's lawyer, represented Name Administration, and in each of the ten cases, it won. The names included meterman.com, cheaphotels.net, and oilchanger.com.

Schilling rarely sold any names. There was too much money in pay-per-click advertising, he said, and selling names took a lot of time. The seller had to evaluate the offer, and for Schilling that meant breaking his concentration. His priority was snagging expiring names in what he considered a unique period of opportunity in the history of the Internet to acquire quality names relatively inexpensively. Sell names "over and over, and you'll make some money, but it takes a lot of effort; you need an office full of people," he said. "With paid-search advertising, it's all automated."

With all the money he was making, Schilling splurged on a few toys. He bought his second Mercedes with cash. And he took part-ownership of a Gulfstream IV corporate jet.

Small World

On the night in 1987 when seventeen-year-old Frank Schilling celebrated his high school graduation (albeit two credits shy of the diploma), he needed help commandeering some beer for his party. He turned to his friend Vern Jurovich, who had a fake i.d. given to him by his buddy Skid Lenihan. That night, Jurovich got Schilling an ample supply of beer. And as it so happened, more than fifteen years later, both Jurovich and alcohol were involved in a confluence of events that would have powerful repercussions for Schilling and the entire domain market.

In August 2003, Jurovich, who ran an Internet consultancy in Vancouver, British Columbia, celebrated his bachelor-party weekend in Seattle at the home of his brother-in-law, Dean Jones, who ran a Seattle real-estate marketing firm. They were drinking and carousing at Jones's house when Jones mentioned that a friend was having a house party on Lake Washington, just east of Seattle. They took a taxi cab to the party, and hung out well into the night. In the wee hours, Jurovich was introduced to the owner of the spacious abode. He was John Keister, co-founder and president of Marchex, a fledgling online marketing company. Keister and several other Marchex founders, including CEO Russell Horowitz, Keister's high-school chum from Seattle, made millions of dollars near the height of the Internet bubble by selling their company, Go2Net, to InfoSpace, an online marketing company. InfoSpace wound up becoming one of the most spectacular disasters of the dot-com era. Much of the $1.5 billion in stock it paid for Go2Net, which owned the Dogpile and MetaCrawler search engines, plummeted in value.

Keister asked Jurovich how he wound up at the party and what he did for a living. Jurovich said he ran his own consulting firm, and mentioned that one of his clients was Name Administration, an owner of a domain portfolio in the Cayman Islands. Marchex, it turned out, was researching the domain market for potential acquisitions. The company, founded in January 2003, primarily was a middleman in the online advertising industry, helping merchants place targeted ads on search engines, shopping directories, and other sites. Marchex was exploring acquiring domains so it would have its own source of traffic. Keister didn't immediately make the connection when he met Jurovich, but Name Administration was on the list of companies Marchex wanted to meet. A few weeks later, Keister connected the dots, and Jurovich helped Keister get in touch with Schilling.

At first, Schilling blew off the e-mails. One reason was that he fielded many inquiries from companies wanting to talk to him. Another was that Marchex owned Enhance Interactive, a pay-for-placement search engine formerly known as Ah-ha.com. Schilling was angry with Ah-ha because it had failed for months to pay him money it owed him for paid-search traffic. He mistakenly assumed that the team running Marchex was the same one that had run Ah-ha, but Ah-ha management had changed in March 2003, when Marchex bought Ah-ha in the first of what would be many acquisitions. "I thought, 'I never want to meet these guys,'" Schilling said of the initial inquiries from Marchex. But Jurovich liked Keister, and he and Schilling agreed that it would be worthwhile to talk with Marchex. "Vern kind of got the ice broken," Schilling said.

Schilling suggested a meeting in Las Vegas in May 2004. Schilling flew in from the Caymans, and Jurovich from Vancouver. Present from Marchex were three of its founding officers: Horowitz, Keister, and Chief Strategy Officer Peter Christothoulou, a former Go2Net executive and investment banker. Marchex was a newly public company, having begun trading on the Nasdaq in March 2004. The men met at the Mandalay Bay Resort and Casino on the Las Vegas Strip. Over a couple of meals, Schilling described his view of the domain market. The Marchex team already had some insight into the business from their days at Go2Net. Also, in 2003, the company had spoken with other large portfolio owners, according to Christothoulou.

Schilling said he and Jurovich "filled in a lot of the things that Marchex couldn't have known without being an active participant in the business." Horowitz, the CEO, "was really enthused, really engaged, and excited about the space," he remembered.

Before their second meal—a dinner at famed New York chef Charlie Palmer's Aureole—the men gathered at the Mandalay Bay Casino. Schilling said he was awed by the vision of the three Marchex executives, all in their thirties, leaning back in front of the twenty-five-cent slot machines, waiting to meet "a long-haired domainer from the Caymans."

The encounters felt dreamlike to Schilling because he saw himself as a boy who'd never grown up, and here he was talking business with polished men who'd already been successful in corporate America. Eight years earlier, Schilling had gotten married in Las Vegas in a brief ceremony that cost all of $500; he and Michele were two broke kids in love.

"Having them be at all interested in what we do was just so surreal," Schilling recounted. "You've got these guys who can basically do whatever they want, and they want to talk about this. These guys do not need to do this. For that matter, they do not need to start Marchex. But they are sitting there enthralled with what we do in the domain space, and they're like, 'This is awesome.'"

Horowitz had spent about two years considering new business opportunities before starting Marchex. He'd become president of InfoSpace in 2000 after it acquired Go2Net. But he left in January 2001 after only four months amid turmoil in the executive suite. He sold his InfoSpace stock for more than $30 million.[1]

Schilling stuck to the high points of the market in the conversations with Marchex; he didn't give away trade secrets. "We didn't touch on a lot of the subtleties and nuances about what we do day to day," he said. "And at that point, in early 2004, anyway, secrets were already evaporating quickly. The space had become a lot more mature.

"It was a good open discussion. They were trying to figure out who's who, and said they'd really like to potentially make a big splash. What they thought they wanted to do, and what I think to this day would have been the *coup de grace*, is buy out all the big portfolio owners. After the dinner, we went home, and I think they thought to themselves, *This might be too big a bite. Let's buy one or two.*"

Schilling told the Marchex executives that he believed Yun Ye had the world's best portfolio. But he strongly encouraged them to acquire BuyDomains. Mike Mann, the founder of BuyDomains, had told Schilling his company was for sale, and that he was looking for $50 million to $70 million, Schilling recalled. Marchex could get a good deal, Schilling told the executives, because Mann was underestimating the value of his company. BuyDomains had focused on selling names, but it owned many that could generate significant ad revenue if it held onto them. "What he'd built was quite a good enterprise," said Schilling. "I told Marchex the business is cheap." Marchex, it turned out, had already taken a look at BuyDomains. Marchex told him, "we don't like the culture," and Mann "is a difficult chap to get a handle on as a personality," Schilling said.

Though Schilling refrained from touting his own portfolio, the idea of Marchex acquiring his company's domains was also discussed.

Before they parted ways, the Marchex executives told Schilling they'd been unable to make contact with Ye, who was living in Vancouver, British Columbia, despite extensive efforts. Schilling had been friendly with Ye for several years, though he hadn't met him in person, and offered to contact Ye and urge him to speak with Marchex. Soon after the Las Vegas meeting, Schilling called Ye and told him, "If you're at all interested in a potential merger, these guys really have their 'A' game on. These are not your average guys." Ye agreed to meet with Marchex.

Said Schilling: "I thought that these are the sharpest, smartest guys I've ever seen interested in this space, and I want to help them out."

Schilling talked to Marchex's senior executives several times in the next few months. He met the team for a second time in person while in Vancouver on vacation. Near the end of July 2004, Horowitz sent Schilling an e-mail offering to buy his portfolio for a price north of $100 million. Schilling was surprised and flattered. "There'd been some jawboning about potential deal structures, but this made it real," he said.

Schilling agreed to do the deal without negotiating on the price. "I was naïve," he said. "I was like, 'Wow, oh my God, that's amazing.' We thought we'd try to engage them and work with them on it."

Schilling needed to go through a number of steps to complete the sale. One was to have his company's books audited. That wasn't a simple matter. There was little precedent for the auditing of domain portfolios. And Schilling didn't even have an accountant. His wife, Michele, kept records for Name Administration in a Microsoft Excel spreadsheet, but they weren't extensive. Frank hired a financial consultant in Seattle to help them get their books in order so they could then a hire a large auditing firm, such as Ernst & Young or KPMG.

That summer, Schilling met Ye for the first time in Vancouver for dinner. Also that summer, while Schilling was in the midst of discussions with Marchex, he and Ye attended a barbecue at the Vancouver home of Richard

Lau, another successful investor. Kevin Ham, the drop-catcher, who owned one of the industry's richest portfolios, was on hand, too. Ye attended with his wife and children.

Schilling knew Ye had met with Marchex, but he wasn't privy to the details. At the barbecue and during other conversations that summer, Ye said little to Schilling about Marchex. The Marchex executives also told Schilling little about any discussions they had with other portfolio owners. They said "we're talking to all kinds of people," Schilling said, and "we want to do this right."

For Lau, the 2004 barbecue was a special moment. He had deep respect for both Schilling and Ye. Lau had only recently met Ye. And, up until then, he was not convinced Ye was a real person. Lau, like others, thought "Yun Ye" might be an alias for a coterie of sophisticated speculators.

Lau found Ye to be a shy and modest man. He was uninterested in discussing his accomplishments or his wealth. "The guy is so down to earth," Lau said. At the barbecue "he didn't even have a watch, let alone a flashy watch. If I was to describe him in one word, it would be 'humble.'"

Did Ye strike him as brilliant? "Not really," Lau said. "He just seems like an average guy. I think he sees himself as lucky."

A Devastating Storm

About six weeks after Marchex offered to buy Schilling's domains, the weather, of all things, intervened.

Hurricane Ivan formed in the Atlantic Ocean in early September. As it barreled toward the Caribbean Sea, the Schillings quickly made plans to leave Grand Cayman Island. They left their dog with a friend and evacuated on a Delta Air Lines flight to Atlanta, the last commercial flight available. The Schillings had a young child, and Michele was pregnant with their second. When the Schillings arrived in Atlanta, they went to the Hertz counter to rent a car. In line with them was a middle-aged man who'd also occupied a seat near them in first class on their flight. Michele struck up a conversation with him while Frank went to get their car. His name was Bill Messer. He was a fellow Canadian who worked in the Caymans for the private-banking arm of Rothschild, the global banking empire. He asked Michele what the Schillings did for a living, and Michele told him Frank managed a domain portfolio and earned revenue from paid-search advertising. To Michele's surprise, Messer said he was familiar with the industry. In fact, he told her, he had a client who was very active in it. Messer didn't name the client, but Michele thought it could only be one person: Yun Ye.

When they left the Caymans, the Schillings weren't all that worried about the hurricane. They thought it might change course or weaken by the time it arrived in the area. But on the afternoon of Sept. 12, 2004, Ivan packed a withering punch when it hit the islands. Labeled a Category 4 storm—the second-highest level—it contained wind gusts of 150 to 175 miles per hour. It caused a devastating storm surge that submerged most of Grand Cayman Island. Thousands of homes and other buildings were destroyed. The Schillings, watching the news from a Ritz-Carlton hotel in Atlanta's trendy Buckhead neighborhood, were certain their house and belongings lay in ruins. Two days later, they boarded Frank's Gulfstream IV at Dekalb Peachtree Airport, a general-aviation airport in Atlanta, and flew to Miami so they could be closer to the Caymans and begin loading relief supplies for a flight home. They invited Messer, who'd also stayed at the Ritz-Carlton, to join them on the flight.

Three days after the hurricane, Schilling was able to fly to Grand Cayman Island on the Gulfstream to survey the damage. He took Messer, who would have had to wait days to get a commercial flight home. He also brought a bunch of relief supplies, including generators and all-weather tarps. Schilling's family stayed behind. The men were on one of the first airplanes cleared to land in the aftermath of the hurricane. When they touched ground, Schilling was stunned by what he saw. Power poles had snapped, airplanes and trees lay on their side, and the ground reeked from dead fish caked in salt that had been deposited on the land. Roofs of houses were blown off. "It was the weirdest experience," Schilling said.

Schilling couldn't get to his house because the roads were impassable. But he received word from friends still on the island that the house was destroyed, along with just about everything inside it. The storm surge had sucked the Schillings' furniture and other belongings, including their Hewlett-Packard and Compaq desktop computers, into a canal. Schilling flew back to Miami the same day, towing his dog, as well as several friends from his neighborhood who'd endured the storm. Messer remained on the island.

The Schillings made plans to lease a house in the Bahamas for six months while the island recovered. But they'd lost their computers, which contained critical information for the audit of Frank's portfolio. They also lost all their paper records related to the company. Schilling didn't even have a copy of Marchex's letter of intent to purchase the domains. It would be weeks, if not months, before an audit could be completed, because Schilling had to figure out how to piece together records of his business—purchases of names and other key information—without easy access to his electronic files. At the time

Ivan hit, said Schilling, the financial consultant in Seattle had completed about 60 percent of the work he needed to do to compile the company's books prior to the hiring of an auditor. "He just kind of stopped where he was at that point," Schilling said. "The whole thing just ground to a halt." But Schilling thought he still could get the audit done in a few months and complete the sale.

While the Schillings waited to be able to start leasing a house in the Bahamas, they stayed at a Ritz-Carlton in Naples, on Florida's Gulf Coast, for a few weeks. On the evening of Oct. 5, 2004, Schilling was unwinding with a glass of red wine in his room, thinking about the family's plans to move to the Bahamas, and wondering how to complete an audit. Meanwhile, in Cleveland, U.S. Vice President Dick Cheney was sparring with his election-year challenger, U.S. Senator John Edwards, in a televised debate. Halfway into the debate, Cheney referred to a Web site that he said would refute allegations Edwards had made regarding Cheney's former company, Halliburton.[2] Cheney told viewers they could visit "factcheck.com." But that was a mistake. He should have said "factcheck.org," run by the Annenberg Public Policy Center at the University of Pennsylvania. Schilling owned factcheck.com. Soon after Cheney's gaffe, Schilling noticed on his laptop that traffic to his company's servers was surging. He realized he needed to act quickly to prevent the servers from crashing. He could turn them off, but then he'd forgo thousands of dollars in ad revenue on his other sites. A few days earlier, he'd read an anti-Bush ad in The Wall Street Journal by billionaire financier George Soros. Schilling had no preference for either George W. Bush or his foe, John Kerry, but he agreed with Soros's contention that some of Bush's decisions had damaged the country's reputation. So Schilling quickly decided to redirect factcheck.com to georgesoros.com, which centered on the subject of "why we must not re-elect President Bush." It was just "a reflex," Schilling said. "It felt like the right thing to do." As a result, thousands of Web surfers landed on Soros's site. The number of visits to factcheck.com surged to more than fifty thousand in the two hours after the debate, from 854 the previous day.[3]

For a few days, the story received widespread media coverage. Schilling's lawyer, John Berryhill, based in Media, Pennsylvania, fielded a host of calls from reporters. He helped put to rest speculation that Soros had been involved in some kind of stunt to harm Bush, explaining that the move was done simply to protect an Internet business from crashing. "It was an effort to deal with a technical problem and do it in a whimsical way," said Berryhill, who declined to tell reporters who ran Name Administration.[4]

The incident prompted Schilling to question whether he wanted to sell all his domains because it demonstrated the sheer power of Internet traffic. But the sale to Marchex appeared to be in jeopardy anyway. Without access to his files, Schilling couldn't get the information he needed to complete an audit. As weeks went by, and he shuffled between Florida, the Caymans, and the Bahamas trying to get his family's life in order, he felt the Marchex deal slipping away. At one point, he said, someone from Marchex intimated that the company was looking "at other people" and couldn't "wait forever" for him to get the audit done. However, Schilling said, "part of me always thought there's still hope. I was never resigned that this wasn't going to work."

On Nov. 23, 2004, a Marchex press release hit the news wires.[5] Marchex had agreed to acquire Yun Ye's portfolio for $164 million—$155 million in cash and $9 million in stock. It was stunning news for domain investors, and it came as a shock to Schilling. Though he'd gotten the impression that Marchex might be close to acquiring another's portfolio, he didn't think it would be Ye's. He just didn't think they would come to terms.

Marchex didn't formally tell Schilling that its deal with him was off, but it was clear the company was going in another direction, and Schilling wouldn't be part of the first major financial maneuver in the domain market. Schilling felt Ivan was largely to blame. "The hurricane was more than 50 percent of it," he said. "There were still some contractual issues that had to be resolved. Ultimately, we might have gotten past all that. But the hurricane was the nail in the coffin, for sure. We just couldn't get an audit done. We couldn't get our records; it was just nightmarish."

There was a "pragmatic understanding [with Marchex] that the time had sort of run out on our letter of intent," he continued. "We couldn't come to terms, and it just sort of went away. Now when we discuss it, we both understand that we tried to make a deal that didn't work."

Ethan Caldwell, Marchex's general counsel, declined to discuss in detail why the deal fell through. "I'm certain the hurricane had an impact, but there are lots of different reasons why certain deals go forward and others don't," he said.

A tantalizing question is whether Marchex had planned to buy both Schilling's and Ye's portfolio simultaneously. Caldwell declined to directly address that question. Marchex was "looking at pretty much everybody" in the market, he said. "We knew we were going to make a significant play into this market. And so as a result of that, we needed to look at every significant portfolio."

Marchex's acquisition shook up the domain market. A mostly underground industry was about to attract a lot more attention—and money.

Chapter Six

Big Money

For diehard domain investors, Marchex's acquisition of Yun Ye's portfolio marked a huge breakthrough. Never before had a speculator sold so many names at such a high price. In the previous twelve months, a few big sales had signaled the revival of the market—Rick Schwartz sold men.com for $1.3 million, and Internet Real Estate Group, run by veteran investors Mike Zapolin and Andrew Miller, sold creditcards.com for $2.75 million. But Marchex's announcement was stupefying. It was the boldest statement yet that generic domains were valuable, long-term investments. It cemented direct navigation—industry parlance for traffic that came from users typing in a domain name, rather than using a search engine—as an Internet business model. It also represented a public company's stamp of approval to the concept of investing in Web addresses in huge quantities. And it ushered in a new era in the market. Before Marchex, most investors were mavericks who worked out of their homes. After Marchex's audacious leap, private-equity investors, wealthy families, and other public companies jumped into the fray. The business suits helped improve the image of domain speculators, a group that for years had been described in broad brushstrokes as cybersquatters, even though a significant number focused on generic names and didn't run afoul of the law. The professional investors also offered the wildcatters something very important: a way to cash in their chips.

But as big a deal as Marchex's acquisition was for domain junkies, the news media barely took notice. Both of Seattle's large daily newspapers covered the news, but most national publications and wire services ignored it. One reason was that Marchex was little known, even though it had one of the most successful initial public stock offerings of 2004. Also, unlike other major domain purchases that drew lots of media coverage, this deal wasn't a simple transaction in which one Web address fetched a mind-boggling price. But there was another big reason: Marchex didn't go out of its way to sell the story. There was a truly fascinating tale behind the deal, but that was the story of the seller: a Chinese-born man who'd moved to the U.S., mastered computer programming, and become a multimillionaire at a young age scooping up expired names. The thirty-two-year-old Ye didn't want any attention, and Marchex's executives said nothing about him in discussions with the media. Marchex's news release not only lacked the obligatory quote from the CEO of the selling company—usually extolling the virtues of the buyer—but Ye's name wasn't even mentioned. The driving force behind the more than 100,000 domains being sold got zero credit in print.

The release didn't mention Ultimate Search, either. Instead, it said Marchex was buying certain assets owned by Name Development. Ultimate Search had formally changed its name in the British Virgin Islands to Name Development a mere six days before the announcement of the deal. It appears the reclusive Ye wanted to use a different company name partly so people wouldn't catch on that he was selling his sites for a huge sum of money.

Because the new corporate name looked similar to Name Administration—Schilling's company—some domain investors called Schilling to congratulate him on selling his portfolio.

"I was really surprised they called it Name Development," Schilling said. "I don't know why the name switched, but I have a hunch. Yun is a very private guy. He didn't want a lot of attention as a result of this deal, and I think he thought that this would be a nice quiet way to do it." Within twenty-four hours of Marchex's news release, domain investors figured it out. On a chat forum, someone mentioned that a site previously registered to Ultimate Search now was sitting on Marchex's servers.

In a Securities and Exchange Commission filing accompanying the announcement, Marchex said a trust, The SSV Trust, was the sole stockholder of Name Development. That trust's administrator, or trustee, was Rothschild Trust Cayman Ltd. That was Bill Messer's firm. It turned out that Schilling had twice escorted on his corporate jet a man representing Ye—his friend and business rival and the man whose blockbuster deal had all but ensured that Schilling's deal wouldn't happen.

Name Development's corporate structure seemed clearly aimed at protecting Ye's privacy. But it also limited his tax bill. As a registered international business in the British Virgin Islands, Name Development didn't have to pay income tax there. It thus avoided a hefty bill on the sale of its domains to Marchex. Before the sale, Ye's company did make provisions for some income-tax expenses related to Internet-business dealings in several other countries, according to SEC filings. Name Development, whose books were audited by KPMG, set aside $1.2 million in the fiscal year ended June 30, 2004, for taxes.

In SEC documents, Marchex also indicated it had some concerns about a legal risk to buying Ye's portfolio, which contained a number of names resembling corporate trademarks. Marchex disclosed that it was putting $25 million of the purchase price into escrow. The money would remain in escrow for eighteen months, until a determination was made as to whether Name Development had to pay anything to indemnify Marchex for legal liabilities.

On the morning of the deal's announcement, Marchex invited investors and the media to listen to an online presentation. Marchex said Name Development's sites were expected to generate more than $19 million in revenue in calendar year 2004, with astounding operating profit margins topping 80 percent. The domains, including debts.com, videocamera.com, and lasvegasvacations.com, attracted about 17 million unique visitors each month.

The company disclosed little about Name Development besides its assets. "This transaction gives Marchex a broad footprint in one of the most rapidly developing categories of Internet user traffic," Horowitz said in the Webcast.[1]

Marchex didn't comment to reporters beyond the Webcast, and neither Seattle paper was able to determine who was behind Name Development. "Attempts to reach Name Development and the Caribbean Island trusts that make up the corporation were unsuccessful," wrote the Seattle Post-Intelligencer. "The company's management and employee headcount were not disclosed."[2]

Alan Davis, a securities analyst with McAdams Wright Ragen, told the Post-Intelligencer the deal was unusual because the seller was obscure. Marchex is "being pretty private about it, that is interesting," Davis said.[3]

Domain investors who caught on to the fact that Ye was behind Name Development celebrated on message boards. A member of DNForum.com wrote the morning after the deal was announced: "Clearly the market is still hot and the cashflow superb, otherwise why would this firm pay ONE HUNDRED AND FIFTY FIVE MILLION DOLLARS in CASH for a bunch of domains?"

Some remained skeptical, astonished at the price. "I am seriously starting to think something is not quite right. Maybe he's ot [sic] really getting this much or MCHX is just feeling the deal out and will then later pay the break-up fee and walk. Just food for thought but could this deal have some other unpublished elements at play?"

To finance the purchase, Marchex conducted a secondary public offering of stock in February 2005. The company, whose stock price had leaped 223 percent the previous year, raised $229 million in the secondary offering. That compared with just $27 million in its IPO. On the day of the secondary offering, Marchex also completed the purchase of Ye's domains. In addition, it reached a long-term deal with Yahoo's Overture unit to share revenue from ads listed on the newly acquired sites.

According to Marchex's federal filings, Name Development wound up earning $17 million in net income on about $21 million in revenue in 2004. The purchase price of $164 million meant that Marchex paid roughly eight times Name Development's 2004 revenue. This became a significant metric in the domain market. If Marchex achieved the same revenue each year in subsequent years, it would take the company eight years to recoup its investment. It had been very difficult for investors to assign values to their portfolios, so many seized on the Marchex multiple. "8x" became a baseline for establishing a valuation. Investors considered Ye a hero in part because he demonstrated that portfolio owners could command an attractive multiple. Investors who owned, say, one thousand names earning $100 a year, on average, might expect to sell their portfolio for $800,000. But there was much debate about whether 8x was a reasonable multiple. Some considered it too high—particularly buyers seeking the best deal they could get. Some considered it too low. After all, not all names in a portfolio are alike. Some garner more traffic, and thus advertising revenue, than others. Some may not have a lot of traffic, but may appeal to a small-business owner who would spend much more than eight-times-revenue to own the name.

Marchex had about 200,000 domains after gobbling up Ye's portfolio. The company had quietly acquired about 100,000 before buying Ye's because it believed the announcement of the deal "would change the playing field in the industry and create more competition for high-quality names," said Christothoulou, the chief strategy officer.[4] Marchex snapped up thousands of keyword-style names. The company had access to data on user behavior and traffic through its search-advertising businesses, and used some of that information to decide which names to buy.

In the first quarter of 2005, when the Name Development deal closed, Marchex said it paid about $4 million for other addresses. The company padded its portfolio, which grew to more than 220,000 domains by 2007, by registering unclaimed names, buying domains in expired-name auctions (its nickname in SnapNames auctions was "mangas," which is Greek for *macho*), and purchasing domains from smaller investors, such as Chad Wright of Fresno, California. Wright sold names including matchmaking.com and monstertrucks.com to Marchex; he said he was prohibited from disclosing prices under a non-disclosure agreement.

Marchex bought domains with a careful strategy in mind. It wanted to own addresses that fit into vertical categories such as travel, health, autos, insurance, and personals. It also wanted to own names that were geographical in nature. The company believed that "local search" was an untapped market that would grow significantly in the coming years. In local search, Web users seek services in their area, such as searching in Google for "Seattle lawyers." Some users also seek local information by typing domains like SeattleLawyers.com—owned by Marchex—into the address field of their browser. Local search-ad revenue will grow to $13 billion in 2010 from $3.4 billion in 2005, estimated research firm Kelsey Group. For years, consumers have used the yellow pages—a roughly $15 billion business in the U.S.—to search for local information. But increasingly, they will seek that information on the Web. It's simply faster and easier. And Marchex is one of the companies working to get more local businesses to place their ads online.

Marchex believed it could drive more users to its sites and increase ad revenue by adding an assortment of content to the pages. It strongly believed it was important to improve the user experience. Instead of running stagnant one-page sites filled with advertising links, it built sites with multiple pages that included relevant information. On bayareahotels.com, for example, it added user reviews of San Francisco-area hotels, and allowed users to click buttons to take them to pages that contained reviews and ads for hotels in a specific neighborhood, such as San Francisco's Nob Hill. Users also could search hotels by price, and see where hotels were located on a map. By adding content, Marchex aimed to draw more repeat visitors to the sites. Building content also meant the sites were more likely to show up in organic search-engine results, so the sites wouldn't completely rely on type-in traffic. In 2006, Marchex paid $13 million to acquire Open List—a search and content engine that aggregated user reviews, professional reviews, and other content from across the Web—and deployed its technology to sprinkle relevant information on many of its sites. Because much of the site content was generated in an automated fashion, Marchex's overhead wasn't as high as a traditional media company's.

"If you want to be a high-growth company and be unique, you need to create destinations out of these sites," Christothoulou said. "To use a real estate analogy, we're taking parking lots and we're building skyscrapers."

As part of its move into local search, Marchex acquired about seventy-five thousand ZIP Code names, such as 90210.net, separate from its deal with Ye. It also created MyZip.com, where users could search for information in their local area. Marchex's ZIP Code-oriented sites featured information about local hotels, restaurants, and sightseeing. One user review of a Denver hotel on 80204.com featured some colorful commentary. "This is a terrible place to stay, from the smelly Mexican Resturant [sic] that shares the lobby to the falling down & torn drapes," it said. "The smoke detector was hanging down the wall by its cords."

Christothoulou said he was amazed by the level of traffic some sites received. An average of 107 people a day visited 91899.com (a ZIP Code for Alhambra, California). "That's why we think if you can get search traffic on top of the type-in traffic, you have something that's pretty powerful," he said.

Marchex believed it nabbed the best portfolio in the world when it bought Ye's. It also felt it enjoyed an advantage as the first big corporate player in the market. "The beauty of this space," Christothoulou said, "is once you own a name, you own it and others can't come in and compete with it. For instance, no one can go in and buy Beijing.com because we own it."

In addition to serving up ads sold by Yahoo, Marchex offered advertisers an opportunity to buy ads directly through its own pay-for-placement search engine, which it built through its acquisition of Enhance Interactive. That way it didn't have to share the ad revenue. By 2007, analysts estimated that ads sold directly by Marchex accounted for about 30 percent of the ad revenue on its sites.

Marchex drew about 31 million unique visitors on its roughly 220,000 sites in December 2006, up 15 percent from year-earlier levels. The company was still trying to persuade Wall Street that its direct-navigation business would succeed. The company's own traffic accounted for roughly a third of its revenue. In 2006, it posted net income of $2.8 million on $127.8 million in revenue. The company's stock price traded around $14 in mid-March 2007, about 40 percent off a 52-week high of $23.24 in April 2006.

The outlook of equity analysts was mixed. A near-term downside was that Yahoo was revamping its advertising system to compete better with Google's. The change, which included listing ads based on relevancy, rather than just bid prices, was resulting in lower revenue for site owners such as Marchex. "I like companies that have real estate on the Internet, and these guys have a lot of real estate," said Bill Morrison, an analyst with JMP Securities in San Francisco, who didn't own Marchex shares. "The key to me is: Can they continue to grow their audience base and deliver quality leads to advertisers?

Can they create sites that provide value to users? I believe they can, but it's a work in progress."

Venture Capitalists Jump In

When Marchex was planning its incursion into the market, another veteran of online media was quietly scouting the industry.

Jeff Bennett had been a vice president at Lycos, an early Web portal and search engine. Lycos was sold to Spanish phone giant Telefonica for $12.5 billion in 2000, near the height of Internet mania, but plummeted in value afterwards, eventually getting resold for only $95 million to Korea's Daum Communications.

Bennett left Lycos in 2002, and wanted to get back into the Internet game. He was an outside advisor to Highland Capital Partners, a venture-capital firm in Waltham, Massachusetts, near Boston, and began working closely with several of its partners to invest in a new business. The partners included Bob Davis, the founder and former CEO of Lycos, who'd engineered its sale to Telefonica. Davis had been a mentor to Bennett for nearly two decades.

Bennett wanted to build a Web-media venture that started with a base of robust traffic. "One of the places we were drawn to was the domain channel, because of the fact that people do search through the browser," said Bennett, a Boston native who began his career at Wang Laboratories, an early personal-computer maker. "If someone has a large portfolio that mimics search terms, then you're going to be able to own a beachhead" of traffic.

Bennett talked to several large domain holders about a potential acquisition, including BuyDomains. Mike Mann, BuyDomains' founder, had hired Ari Bayme, then a vice president with Milbank Roy, the boutique investment-banking firm in New York, to find a buyer for the company. It had not been an easy task. Bayme approached a variety of companies, including major e-commerce sites. "The first challenge was to explain to people why this was something they should look at," Bayme recalled. "To this day, it's still a frustrating aspect of doing transactions in the direct-navigation space." He explained to e-commerce companies that they would get their own source of traffic if they owned BuyDomains' huge portfolio of more than 500,000 sites. That would reduce their paid-search advertising costs. And they could offer names for sale just like BuyDomains did. "No one even understood it," said Bayme. "The perception was that this traffic would go away. The feeling was that people typing in domains were idiots." Another perception, he said, was that there wasn't much demand from businesses and consumers for buying Web addresses in the secondary market.

As Bayme worked with BuyDomains executives to sell the company, he was amazed at how hard they worked. "Mike Mann seemed to work twenty-four hours a day," he said. "I would e-mail him when I'd be leaving at 1 a.m., and he'd be responding to me at 4:30 in the morning. And I would get back to him, and he'd come back to me at 6 a.m. And [Chief Operating Officer] Michelle Miller was a dynamo. How they ever got that much done in one day, I'll never know."

Though Bayme couldn't entice big e-commerce sites to bid for BuyDomains, the company drew interest from the Bennett-led Highland Capital Partners group and several other companies. BuyDomains chose Highland, which was joined in the deal by Summit Partners, another Boston-area venture-capital firm. In February 2005, the same month that Marchex closed its purchase of Yun Ye's sites, the Boston group bought a majority stake in BuyDomains, which was owned by Mann and a few other investors. Some say the buyers got a steal, paying about $80 million, according to people familiar with the deal. Mann kept a minority stake in the company, later renamed NameMedia, of less than 15 percent.

Miller said she was disappointed that Mann didn't negotiate a higher price. Bennett's team "acquired a cash cow," she said. "It was really ridiculous. If it was up to me, it would have sold for $180 million. Mike didn't get it . . . It was an absolute steal. I sat at the table negotiating with these guys and I had to bite my tongue ten times over, and I could have squeezed out more, but I wasn't authorized." (Though Miller didn't own a stake in BuyDomains, she said she'd arranged a deal with Mann to receive a certain fee if the company was sold. Miller stayed on after the acquisition as vice president of sales. But she left after about eight months, saying she didn't get to have much input in the new company, and the people running the show weren't her "cup of tea.")

For his part, Mann said he was "a motivated seller," and agreed the company sold for "too little." However, he said, "nobody offered more at the time." Also, he said, he had the potential to make a lot more money because he kept a stake in the business. "Now it's a lot bigger company, and a serious, professionally managed company, whereas we were hustling," he said.

Bayme said it's inappropriate, as some people have done, to directly compare BuyDomains' sale price to Ye's sale to Marchex. Ye's company drew all its revenue from paid-search ads, whereas most of BuyDomains' revenue came from selling names. Thus, one couldn't make an apples-to-apples comparison. Generally speaking, Bayme said, it is hard to compare domain-portfolio deals.

"Every deal is very different because the underlying assets—the domain names themselves—are very different," he said.

When asked if BuyDomains was a steal, Bennett said, "We were interested in buying the company at the best possible price we could. But in doing so, we took a leap of faith that this asset would be the targeted [traffic source] it has proven to be. It was a good deal for us, and I think a good deal for the former owners."

For about a year after the acquisition, the buyers said little publicly about their plans. They moved BuyDomains to Waltham from its traditional home in the Washington, D.C., area. While in stealth mode, the new company went by the name YesDirect, reflecting its participation in what it called the direct-search market. In June 2006, the company unveiled itself as NameMedia to reporters. It announced the hiring of Kelly Conlin, a veteran media executive, as CEO. Conlin began his career at CNN in New York, where he helped assign news stories. He also worked in editorial at the New York Times before switching to the business side of publishing. He'd run Primedia, a magazine publisher, and had an MBA from Harvard.

"Our objective is to build the largest portfolio of undeveloped real estate on the Internet," Conlin said. "It's a content-light, user-friendly way for people to find what they want."[5] Like Marchex, the company planned to build content on the best of that real estate, which he called waterfront property. It planned to resell other sites. Added Highland Capital's Davis, a director of the new company: "You hate to predict the future, but I think a business like this can be a multibillion-dollar franchise."[6]

NameMedia built a diverse business, though it emphasized it was by and large a media company. It bought Afternic, the domain broker, as well as many small collections of Web addresses owned by individuals and small businesses. NameMedia had about 115 employees by 2007, whereas BuyDomains had about fifteen at the time of the acquisition.

About 95 percent of BuyDomains' revenue had been from selling domains, said Bennett, NameMedia's president. By the fourth quarter of 2006, NameMedia drew a majority of its revenue from pay-per-click advertising, Bennett said. (Like many domain investors, its sites also earned some revenue from annoying pop-under ads.)

NameMedia's sites include biking.com, cats.com, photography.com, jobfinder.com, and myfinance.com. The number of sites it owned ballooned to more than 700,000 in 2007.

NameMedia used the term "direct search"—Web searches conducted by entering terms into the address bar of the browser—to describe its business.

It was a better term for describing the industry than "direct navigation." Those who came up with the latter had included traffic from people who'd bookmarked a particular site or arrived from a link on another site; that was too broad to describe a field largely dependent on type-ins.

Like Marchex, NameMedia tried to create useful content on its sites. Myfinance.com contained information on how to pick a mortgage lender, the importance of having good credit, and the pros and cons of payday loans. WonderfulWeddings.com featured photographs and links for wedding products for sale on other sites, as well as pay-per-click ads. "We want to give [Web users] a good experience visually, but also in the depth of information that's there," Bennett said. The company had a revenue-sharing deal with Google, but like Marchex, it also began selling ads directly to marketers for sites in specific commercial categories, like photography, jobs, and mortgages.

In late 2007, NameMedia announced plans to go public. It intended to raise $172.5 million and list its shares on the Nasdaq under the symbol "NAME." For the nine months ended Sept. 30, 2007, the company reported net income of $160,000, compared with $2.2 million in the same period a year earlier. Revenue jumped to $58.3 million from $42.1 million. It had been nine years since Mike Mann had started the company in his basement in Bethesda.

Back in the Game

In late 2004, Marc Ostrofsky, the serial entrepreneur who was famous for selling business.com for $7.5 million, was prowling for new business ideas. He met a merchant banker in his late twenties, Bob Martin, through the Houston Angel Network, a nonprofit whose members explored early-stage investment opportunities. Martin was friends with an Austin, Texas, domain investor, Andrew Allemann. Martin thought it would be a good idea to introduce Allemann to Ostrofsky. In December 2004, the three men gathered at a Starbucks in Houston and afterwards at Ostrofsky's home. Ostrofsky still owned a lot of generic names, but he wasn't using them. Allemann showed the men how he was making as much as $100 a day from pay-per-click ads on certain domains. "Marc's getting excited because I'm telling him about parking and how he can make money at these," Allemann recounted.

Over the next few months, the trio met several more times and made plans to invest in names together. "We talked about creating content, not just parking," Allemann said. They drew up formal papers to start a partnership, but Allemann ultimately decided to back out. He wasn't confident the three would make a good team because of differing "work styles," he said.

Ostrofsky and Martin plowed ahead. They were convinced there was a big opportunity to buy inactive or poorly developed sites and turn them into cash machines. They co-founded Internet REIT, a name inspired by the concept of a real-estate investment trust, or REIT—a company that buys, sells, and runs properties. iREIT, as it became known, initially was an angel (or early stage) investment for Ostrofsky and Martin. They saw domains as a side business that wouldn't require a staff. Each invested about $100,000 to buy a few portfolios from speculators. "We believed that domain names were similar to [house rentals] and that with a $100,000 investment, we could generate approximately $20,000 to $40,000 in annual cash flow that had better characteristics" than rentals, Martin said. Unlike renting houses, they didn't have to bother with tenants or worry about repairs and other hassles.

After buying a few portfolios and studying the market more closely, they decided the opportunities were even greater than they'd envisioned. The market was highly fragmented—they counted about 13,000 participants at various stages of activity—and ripe for consolidation, Martin said. Ostrofsky and Martin believed they could raise $100 million to $250 million from private-equity investors to buy names and generate high rates of return.

The men made an odd pair. Ostrofsky, who was named president of Houston-based iREIT, talked fast, and his mind danced from one idea to the next. He had strong convictions and could be candid with criticism, which rubbed some people the wrong way. In contrast, Martin, the CEO, an economics major at Harvard, was extremely polished and diplomatic. "I'm the marketing and creative side," Ostrofsky said in 2006. "Bob is the intellectual. He's the brains to get investors to own the proposition. He's really financially savvy."

One of Martin's first moves was to bring Stuart Rabin into the fold as iREIT's chairman. Rabin had a glossy resume. He ran Jacobson Family Investments, the investment arm of a wealthy New York family, and had worked for Wall Street firms Morgan Stanley and Bear Stearns. He also had an MBA from the prestigious Wharton School at the University of Pennsylvania.

Rabin was impressed by Martin and Ostrofsky's business plan, and Jacobson Family Investments became iREIT's first outside investor. Rabin then lined up two other top-tier investors: Perot Investments, a Dallas investment company founded by former presidential candidate and billionaire Ross Perot, and Maveron LLC, a venture-capital firm co-founded by Starbucks Chairman Howard Schultz and former investment banker Dan Levitan. At a gathering at Starbucks headquarters in Seattle in 2006, Howard Schultz met with a group of about fifty domain investors who were in town for an industry conference. Schultz asserted that he was bullish on Web addresses as long-term investments, and espoused the virtues of type-in traffic, according to several people who were there.

iREIT also tapped Adam Dicker, a Toronto investor, as an executive vice president. Dicker, a college dropout, owned about 200,000 sites of his own, including penpals.com, planets.com, and download.net. He retained his domains, rather than sell them to iREIT. Dicker, who began investing in names in 2002, also owned DNForum.com, the most popular domain user forum. Dicker said he bought the forum from longtime domain investor Greg Ricks in 2003 for only $75,000. By 2006, he was fielding offers of more than $1 million for it.

iREIT raised more than $125 million to acquire domains.[7] The company went on a buying binge, snapping up about 400,000 addresses in about eighteen months. By early 2007, it had completed more than ninety deals. According to Martin, the company's most profitable names included creditreports.com, recipe.com, officesupply.com, and shows.com. Its traffic amounted to about forty million unique visitors a month. That equaled about one hundred unique visitors per month per domain, compared with about 140 at Marchex.

iREIT inked a deal with Google to display pay-per-click ads on its domains. But iREIT, like Marchex, also created content. It planned to develop its sites into ten major commercial verticals. The company also was exploring many different forms of advertising revenue. Martin said he believed the industry's primary form of generating revenue would shift from the pay-per-click model to a blend of cost-per-impression (CPM) and cost-per-action (CPA) models. In a CPM model (typically used in online banner advertising), advertisers pay each time their ad is shown, not just when someone clicks on it. It is the traditional form of brand advertising on the Internet. The CPA model is a form of affiliate marketing in which an advertiser only pays when a customer buys something or takes another specified action, like signing up for a newsletter. iREIT also was exploring pay-per-call, a nascent form of performance-based online advertising in which marketers list a phone number in their ads and only pay when users call it.

iREIT began running user-generated content on some sites through a partnership with Associated Content, a Denver company that drafted Web users to submit articles in a wide range of categories, including arts and entertainment, business, and health. Associated Content's contributors earned only $3 to $20 upfront for each article, but they could earn bonuses depending on how much traffic their articles drew.

"Step one in the development of this industry was the realization of the value of the traffic and the aggregation of names and portfolios," said Maveron's Levitan, who sat on iREIT's board. The second step is creating "a relevance, so instead of just landing on these pages, there's some compelling reason to stay and perhaps come back."[8]

In February 2006, iREIT paid an undisclosed price to acquire Netster. com, a Knoxville, Tennessee-based search portal, as well as many of its more than 100,000 domains. Several investment-banking firms had expressed interest in making major investments in Netster, and possibly taking it public, prior to iREIT's purchase.[9] Netster's portfolio included domains that were misspellings of various English words, as well as misspellings of corporate trademarks. Buying and holding such names put iREIT at some legal risk. Typos were part of Netster's heritage. Co-founder Blake Bookstaff had owned and profited from typos of 1-800 telephone numbers, such as 1-800-CCAL-LAT, a typo of 1-800-CALL-ATT.[10] In 2002, The Kansas City Star reported that collect calls placed using Bookstaff's typo phone numbers—a mistake known as "fat finger dialing"—cost consumers at least three times as much as those placed with 1-800-CALL-ATT.[11]

Martin said iREIT paid "six figures" in 2005 for officesupply.com, which was owned by Brian Null, a Columbia, Missouri, investor. iREIT scrapped a planned purchase of another generic name—a $4.5 million deal to acquire cellphones.com, owned by Michael Bahlitzanakis, a New York investor, and a business partner. The parties had signed a letter of intent, but iREIT backed out. Cellphones.com at times earned pay-per-click ad revenue of $2,500 a day, said Bahlitzanakis. That works out to the staggering figure of more than $900,000 a year. Bahlitzanakis paid about $100 for the name in 1996.

Ostrofsky left his position as president of iREIT in 2006 but remained on the board. He also was writing a book on how to make money online, and continued to own and manage more than 300 domains of his own, such as mutualfunds.com and consulting.com. Ostrofsky said he was proud to have coined the statement "domain names are the real estate of the Internet." iREIT even took the trouble to get that phrase trademarked.

The Media Catches On

It took a while, but eventually the mainstream media began to recognize that a new boom in domains was under way. Newsweek, The Wall Street Journal, Business 2.0, USA Today, and a few other news outlets published lengthy articles in 2005 and 2006 documenting how the market had been transformed since the late 1990s. The attention was welcomed by a few players in the industry. In particular, name brokers like Sedo, Moniker, and Afternic relished the coverage, because it helped increase awareness about the market, which brought more domain buyers into the fold. Indeed, those companies routinely pitched story ideas to the media, which helped fuel the coverage. Sedo, a U.S.-based unit of the German advertising company AdLink Internet Media, noted happily on its Web site that "all the attention from the media elite has resulted in a surge of new interest and new offers for domains as well as a jump in the number of domains being parked."

But many investors didn't like the publicity. That was partly because they benefited from a lack of public knowledge about the vibrant market for Web addresses. If more people entered the market, the veteran investors would have more competition to acquire names, and prices would likely rise, which was good for sellers, but not buyers. Some investors also worried about the media shining a light on the unsavory aspects of the industry, such as the continued widespread acquisition of addresses corresponding to corporate trademarks (for more on that, turn to Chapter Eight). Finally, some investors—particularly those who didn't report their domain income on their tax returns—feared the media coverage might arouse interest from the Internal Revenue Service or other tax authorities.

One member of DNForum.com, the popular domain forum owned by Adam Dicker, wrote: "Will these people stop publicizing the industry!! ugh."

The author of a blog at DropWatch.com, which published information on expiring names, wrote: "Many domainers are shocked to see the mainstream coverage already beginning to creep into our secret world. We have all known that it would eventually start to happen, and like squirrels stockpiling nuts before winter, domainers have been trying to cushion their stockpile before the big storm . . . Are you ready for the secret to be unveiled?"

The most colorful and best-reported article on the market was Paul Sloan's December 2005 piece in Business 2.0, entitled "Masters of Their Domains." It featured an unforgettable ending. Sloan had attended an industry trade show known as Traffic in South Florida in October 2005. One night, a group of fourteen Yahoo executives joined several investors, including Frank Schilling, at a strip club. They sat in a VIP section of the club, and at the end of the night, an employee told them the booths cost $1,000. Sloan wrote, "In the end no one wants to submit the $1,000 tab to the expense department back at [Yahoo] headquarters. Finally, Schilling pulls out a roll of cash and pays up. Not a big deal for a guy who owns a share of a jet. But considering that

Schilling's traffic generated more than 1 percent of Yahoo's $3.6 billion in revenues last year, you'd think one of those guys could have stood up and taken one for the team."[12]

The article was the talk of domain investors for months. And it played a part in the creation of yet another new media company.

Web 2.0 Meets the Domain Market

Shortly after Frank Schilling's pivotal meeting with Marchex's founders in Las Vegas in 2004, the domain guru received an unexpected phone call. The caller was Mike Gorzynski, a young associate with Spectrum Equity Investors, a private-equity firm. Gorzynski, who worked in the firm's Boston office, was interested in learning about Schilling's business. Like many private-equity firms, Spectrum enlisted associates to cold-call businesses to find investment opportunities.

Marchex CEO Russell Horowitz had told Schilling that he was likely to be contacted by other companies that saw potential in the domain market. According to Schilling, he also said, "[Marchex will be] grateful if you don't talk about this [industry] with too many people." So when Gorzynski called, Schilling figured "this has got to be Russ testing me." So Schilling politely told Gorzynski that he couldn't speak with him.

But Gorzynski was persistent. Several months later, he called back. At that point, Schilling realized he wasn't affiliated with Marchex, so he gave him a cursory overview of the industry. Gorzynski "was very sharp," Schilling said. "He got the space right away."

That conversation preceded the announcement of Marchex's acquisition of Yun Ye's portfolio in November 2004, and the closing of that deal in February 2005. Around March 2005, Gorzynski contacted Schilling and told him he'd like for him to speak with Shawn Colo, a principal in Spectrum's office in Menlo Park, California.

Colo, thirty-two, had worked for Spectrum for nearly a decade after graduating from Princeton. He'd focused on investing in media, including cable television, radio, and print properties. In 2003, he began concentrating on Internet investments. While studying the market, he kept running across small Web-media properties, such as Trails.com, a recreational site. He began wondering if there was a way to consolidate such sites and build a successful business, similar to how firms like his had been involved in "roll ups" of print magazines. Spectrum was an investor in Apprise Media, owner of a wide array of niche magazines including Bow & Arrow Hunting, Inside Kung-Fu, and Modern Plastics Worldwide.

When Colo spoke with Schilling and learned about his business model, he realized that domains "were actually media assets," Colo said. By buying Schilling's portfolio or someone else's, he thought, Spectrum could form the Web-media company he'd envisioned. Colo began negotiations with Schilling and other portfolio owners. Spectrum offered to buy Schilling's domains in late 2005. Neither Colo nor Schilling will disclose the price, but it was "way more" than the $100-million-plus that Marchex had offered a year earlier, Schilling said.

In December 2005, Schilling met with Colo and other Spectrum executives at their office in Menlo Park to discuss the potential alliance. For moral support, Schilling brought along Vern Jurovich, his longtime friend and consultant. They drove to Menlo Park from San Francisco International Airport in a Jaguar XJ that cost Schilling $1,000 to rent, including insurance. Schilling wanted a big car because he was paranoid that he'd get into an accident and ruin his imminent deal of a lifetime.

Colo introduced Schilling to a Microsoft executive he was courting as the potential CEO of the planned venture. Afterward, Schilling told Colo he didn't think the executive was a good fit. But Colo had another candidate in mind as well. According to Schilling, Colo told him, "As hard as it is to find a [domain] portfolio as good as yours, a CEO like the one I have in mind is even harder to find. I want you to meet him."

Richard Rosenblatt was flying high in December 2005. The thirty-six-year-old serial Web entrepreneur had just clinched his biggest deal ever, engineering the sale of MySpace.com, a wildly popular social network, to media giant News Corp. for $580 million. The price topped Rosenblatt's previous megadeal—his $565 million sale of Web-shopping company iMall to Excite@Home near the peak of the Internet bubble.

Rosenblatt, who'd run MySpace.com's parent Intermix Media, had spoken with Colo several times about becoming the CEO of his new media venture. Rosenblatt liked the concept. And when Paul Sloan's article in Business 2.0 came out just prior to Rosenblatt's introduction to Schilling, he began liking it even more.

"When I saw 'Masters of Their Domains,' it struck me that" a domain is "the perfect media property," Rosenblatt said. "Why? It generates its own traffic through direct navigation. And it generates its own content: ads. And it sells its own advertising: Google or Yahoo ads." The article helped convince Rosenblatt that running Colo's business would be a wise move. But the ambitious and charismatic Rosenblatt thought the media concept should be taken a step further. He fancied sprinkling user-generated content and social-networking features on thousands of domains, borrowing a page from the MySpace playbook. His plan was akin to that of Marchex, NameMedia, and iREIT, but he was the first to place a big emphasis on social networking. Colo loved his idea.

Rosenblatt's concept was a Web 2.0 play in the domain market. Web 2.0 was a buzz word used to describe a new wave of Web businesses that leveraged social networking, user-generated content, and other forms of collaboration and information-sharing on the Internet. At the time, venture capitalists were pouring millions of dollars into a plethora of Web 2.0 start-ups in Silicon Valley and elsewhere, encouraged by the success of user-driven sites such as MySpace. "I thought that if you put [Web 2.0 features] on this kind of self-contained media property, a domain, you could really blow it up. You could really stoke its growth," said Rosenblatt, who'd been building Web businesses since 1994, when he co-founded iMall. Central to his idea was to create content inexpensively, relying to a large extent on Web users. That way, he figured, the company would enjoy high profit margins.

Schilling met with Rosenblatt and Colo at a tony Ritz-Carlton overlooking the Pacific Ocean near Laguna Niguel, California, a few days after Schilling's trip to Menlo Park. He immediately liked Rosenblatt. "He had this energy to him that's just very unique," he said. He told Colo that Rosenblatt was "the guy."

When Schilling flew back to Grand Cayman Island later that month, he was all set to sell his portfolio and be part of Colo's new media venture. But he soon received a surprise phone call from yet another company interested in buying his domains. The company, which Schilling declined to name, made a written offer before Spectrum had drawn up paperwork to formalize its offer. The price was "significantly more" than what Spectrum had proposed, Schilling said, declining to reveal details.

The bid derailed the Spectrum deal. "We weren't willing to hit what he thought was the right" price, Colo said. "There was just a big gap in terms of valuation expectations."

For months, Schilling worked on the other deal. But it, too, fell apart, for reasons he declined to discuss.

Colo and Rosenblatt had been exploring other options. One was to buy eNom, the Bellevue, Washington-based domain-name registrar, which had been building its own portfolio in addition to offering registration services. In May 2006, Rosenblatt and Colo announced the formation of Demand Media, a "next-generation" media company based in Santa Monica, California. Colo left Spectrum to be the company's president. Rosenblatt was chairman and CEO. The pair raised $220 million in two rounds of financing in 2006, led by Spectrum, Oak Investment Partners, Generation Partners, and 3i Group. Over the course of the year, Demand Media bought eNom and another registrar, BulkRegister, as well as several user-driven content companies. It bought eHow, which published numerous how-to articles; Hillclimb Media, which ran recreational sites Trails.com, GolfLink.com, and GardenGuides.com; and Answerbag, which allowed Web users to post and answer questions on any subject. The company also snapped up domains owned by small businesses and individuals. By 2007, Demand Media owned about 300,000 Web addresses drawing more than 35 million unique visitors a month. Rosenblatt said he didn't like to talk about the quantity of names, but rather the company's efforts to build quality sites. "It's more about what you actually do" with the domains, he said.

Still, Demand Media didn't plan to build content from users or professionals on every site, he said. For sites that fit into a certain category, such as recreation, Demand Media might redirect the traffic to one of the portals it had purchased, such as Trails.com. For domains that didn't clearly fit into any category, it might maintain a page of all pay-per-click ads or create a lead-generation site—a site that received commissions for sending qualified customers to mortgage lenders, insurance providers, and other types of businesses that must prequalify their customers.

Demand Media was in the early stages of creating content-driven sites at the time of this writing. One of the showcase sites it hoped to turn into a well-known Internet brand was Deals.com, a well-designed online community whose members posted links to discounts, coupons, and bargains offered for products on the Web. The deals were ranked in the order of how many favorable votes they received from the community. Deals.com was modeled in part after Digg.com, a popular news site in which members submitted links to articles and blog entries.

Demand Media's portfolio included gardening.com, maternity.com, run.com, usedcar.com, and flashgames.com—all sites it aimed to develop. For much of the company's first year, flashgames.com was merely a page of text ads with a photograph of a computer keyboard. But the site drew several hundred thousand visitors a month seeking online games that use flash-animation technology. And its ad revenue topped $150,000 a year.[13]

Rosenblatt hoped to take Demand Media public in just a few years. Around the office, he said, the bold mantra was "$2 billion in two years," referring to the market capitalization it hoped to attain in that brief time frame. In Demand Media's first six months, Rosenblatt began fielding inquiries from several major media companies interested in possible deals or alliances. He said he'd spoken to the New York Times Co. and Viacom, as well as to media legend Barry Diller, CEO of IAC/InterActiveCorp, which ran companies such as Ask.com, Ticketmaster, and LendingTree. "There's a lot of interest out there with the media companies about what we're doing," said Rosenblatt, a native of Los Angeles's San Fernando Valley. "At first blush, when someone thinks 'domains as a media company,' they first think you're kind of crazy. But then when they start to hear about it, and then they think, *You know, this guy's got a track record . . . maybe there's something there*, they're inquisitive."

Demand Media wasn't a pure media play because it owned two registrars. On the other hand, those registrars gave it a more diverse revenue stream than a media-only business. eNom alone generated annual revenue of more than $45 million; Demand Media refused to say whether that included BulkRegister's revenue. eNom had begun in founder Paul Stahura's garage in the Seattle suburbs in 1997. Stahura became Demand Media's chief strategy officer after he sold eNom in a deal in which he said he personally made in the "eight figures."

One of the top portfolio owners Demand Media acquired was Hotkeys Internet Group. The San Francisco company owned fewer than one thousand names, but many were of high caliber, such as deals.com, gardening.com, and maternity.com. Michael Blend and Thomas Kundel, co-owners of Hotkeys, joined Demand Media after the sale. Blend, thirty-nine, said he began investing in names in 2003, mostly buying them from other owners. Prior to that, Hotkeys helped other domain investors line up deals to redirect their traffic to Web sites of marketers interested in leads. For example, all visitors to hair.com might be redirected to Pantene.com. Hotkeys was in the process of transforming its sites from static, ad-laden pages to media portals when it agreed to be acquired in 2006. "We sat down with the folks at Demand," Blend said, "and we said to ourselves, 'These guys are going to do it better than us.'"

Demand Media didn't announce its purchase of Hotkeys. The reason was strategic. Blend and the Hotkeys unit pursued buying portfolios on Demand Media's behalf. By not disclosing to sellers that Demand Media was the interested buyer, the company was "less likely to get gouged," said Quinn Daly, Demand Media's vice president of marketing. Many investors had heard of Demand Media because it had raised a lot of money. The company's tactic was similar to the stealth acquisition ploys long used by large corporations in the name trade. Sometimes, for instance, intellectual-property lawyers representing big companies tapped their paralegals to buy addresses.

Several other companies joined Marchex, NameMedia, iREIT, and Demand Media in trying to build thriving companies on a pile of domains. They included Oversee.net, based in Los Angeles; InterSearch Group, a San Francisco company which traded on the American Stock Exchange; and NetShops.com of Omaha, Nebraska. Each became a suitor for names owned by smaller speculators. NetShops.com was different from the rest because it was an e-commerce company, not a media company. Backed by venture-capital firms Insight Venture Partners and Sequoia Capital (an early Google investor), NetShops.com built more than a hundred stores on domains, including Hammocks.com, DayBeds.com, CoatRacks.com, and Telescopes.com.

If you added up all the Web addresses owned by all these companies, as well as Frank Schilling's Name Administration and other large investors, they totaled at least six million names. While that represented a significant percentage of all the domains in the world—at least 5 percent—it showed that the market remained highly fragmented. There were still ample opportunities for smaller investors to sell domains at hefty prices. A frenzy of deals was yet to come.

Chapter Seven

The Domain Craze

Buoyed by new players, the domain market soared to new heights.

In 2005, about forty reported domain sales exceeded $100,000—more than double the number a year earlier—and one reached $1 million, according to DNJournal.com, the industry's main trade publication. In 2006, about seventy sales topped $100,000, and several reached the millions, including diamond.com, which fetched $7.5 million. Most sales are never publicly disclosed, so the figures only offer a sampling of market activity.

Roy Messer, a veteran investor from Tallahassee, Florida, was one of the people who benefited from the new craze over Internet addresses. The former carpet salesman, in his early sixties, decided in early 2006 to put vodka.com up for sale. "Google and Yahoo frowned on domains dealing with sex, gambling, and liquor," Messer explained, so "it was difficult to generate revenue from pay-per-click" advertising. He knew wine.com had fetched $3 million in 1999, so he felt confident that in 2006 he could land a multimillion-dollar deal. He enlisted Sedo, the Cambridge, Massachusetts-based name broker, to find a buyer.

Messer suggested that Sedo contact Roustam Tariko, a Russian billionaire who owned Russian Standard, a maker of premium vodka. Messer had read about him in BusinessWeek. When Sedo got Tariko on the phone in April 2006, he offered $1 million.[1] But Messer and the Sedo broker, Christian Kalled, were looking for $5 million, so Messer immediately turned him down.[2] About six months passed, and Messer still couldn't get the price he wanted. But in October 2006, Russian Standard was opening a new $60 million distillery, part of its efforts to hike sales and market share, and decided to contact Sedo about the name. The company invited Messer and Kalled to St. Petersburg to meet Tariko and attend the launch ceremony. They struck a deal for vodka.com for $3 million within half an hour, Messer said. It "was an exciting time."

The sale, which was covered by the Reuters news agency, Messer's hometown Tallahassee Democrat, and several blogs, ranked as one of the ten largest reported deals of all time. It showed that "domains are becoming status symbols," said Jeremiah Johnston, Sedo's chief operating officer. Russian Standard planned to use the site to market its vodka to U.S. drinkers. Before the sale, Messer ran pay-per-click ads for vodka and other liquor products on the site, along with a stock photograph of a bikini-clad woman toting a martini glass in shallow beach waters.

Sales of Web addresses increased in the mid-2000s, but it's not clear by how much. There's no central database where sales are recorded. Most deals happen privately and are never disclosed. An analysis of twenty-five thousand sales by Sedo, however, showed a sharp increase in the volume of deals and their dollar value. The analysis found that the number of sales rose 75 percent to 16,000 in 2005 from a year earlier. The total dollar value of the deals climbed 58 percent to more than $60 million. The transactions either were reported by DNJournal.com, which aggregates information from several domain marketplaces and other services, or were brokered by Sedo.

A year later, Sedo estimated that the total size of the secondary market, including unreported private transactions, was about $700 million in sales worldwide annually.

Meanwhile, Zetetic, a domain appraisal and research firm in Davis, California, reported that the median price for domain sales rose 24 percent to $900 in 2005 from $721 in 2004. Zetetic looked at a sample of about nine thousand transactions. Keith Pieper, senior analyst for the firm, cautioned that the limited information about sales made it difficult for buyers and sellers to gain a clear picture of the market. "We estimate that no more than 20 percent of the dollar volume of domain names sold are ever made public," he said. "The other 80 percent of the market value is what drives the 'irrational exuberance' and greed many domain name sellers exhibit. And with good reason—it's almost impossible to know if the guy you're negotiating with might pay $20 million for the domain name you're willing to unload for $5,000."

In many large reported deals, the sellers enjoyed a huge return on their initial investment.

Take Amy Schrier. In March 2006, the thirty-seven-year-old former magazine publisher sold blue.com for $500,000. That was more than seven times the $65,000 she paid for it about four years earlier.

Schrier's passion for blue.com began in the dot-com boom. In 1997, she formed Blue, an adventure travel magazine. Someone already owned blue.

com, but she kept an eye on the name and its various changes in ownership, thinking she might try to buy it someday. In 2001, a Canadian Internet company, Microforum, told her it would sell the name for $65,000. Schrier didn't have that kind of money. But she went to the board of directors of her company, Blue Media Ventures, and proposed that it buy it. The board thought the price "was laughably too high," she said. So she decided to find a way to acquire it on her own. She gave Microforum a down payment of about $30,000, she recalled, and paid off the rest over time for about $2,000 a month. She got a license from her company to publish its content on blue.com.

"I instinctively knew that $65,000 was a bargain price," she said. "When you have a gut instinct, you have to follow it. Most people operate in this financial-risk comfort zone. I felt it was a worthwhile investment, and that if anything were ever to go wrong [with the site], it would have a high resale value."

Blue magazine folded in 2003, she said. Afterwards, Schrier stayed home taking care of her young kids. About a year later, she began trying to sell blue. com. But it took the New Yorker a while to get the price she wanted. In 2005, she hired Sedo to sell the name for her. She set the minimum, or "reserve," price at $240,000. For five months, nobody bid even the minimum. There were interested buyers at $200,000 or less, but Schrier felt strongly that the name was worth more. So she created her own sales methodology that she believed would help her obtain a much higher price. She won't share details of her proprietary formula. Sedo agreed to use the model only to sell her name, and the plan worked. Within a month, she sold blue.com to an unidentified domain investor.

After finally clinching a deal, Schrier was considering marketing her proprietary formula to help owners of "premium" domains extract the highest price possible. The new owner of blue.com, meanwhile, displayed pay-per-click ads on the site for marketers such as JetBlue Airways and Blue Cross Blue Shield.

Some deals generated even higher returns. Garry Chernoff closed his biggest all-time deal in late 2005, selling refinance.com for $706,850 to Homebridge Mortgage Bankers, a New York mortgage company. A year later, Homebridge changed its name to Refinance.com and built a national home-refinance portal. Chernoff had grabbed the name in February 1998 after someone let it expire, and paid only the registration cost of $100 for two years.

Top Reported Domain Sales of 2006

Name	Price
Diamond.com	$7.5 million
Vodka.com	$3 million
Cameras.com	$1.5 million
Nav.no	$717,978
On.com	$635,000
Antispyware.com	$550,000
Macau.com	$550,000
Bike.com	$500,000
Blue.com	$500,000
Gays.com	$500,000
Wrestling.com	$500,000

SOURCE: DNJournal.com

Another early domain investor, Rick Schwartz, reached into his bank account to make one of the biggest purchases of 2005, buying property. com for $750,000. The man who sold the name, Ted Kraus, of Mercerville, New Jersey, said he tried to get $1 million but decided to accept the lower figure "when Rick basically said, 'take it or leave it.'" Kraus, who said he paid only $20 to register the name more than five years earlier, publishes trade magazines about commercial real estate and sells and manages properties. He'd created property.com to serve as a Web portal with news, information, and commercial real-estate listings. After selling the name to Schwartz, he began using dealmakers.net. Since then, the number of unique visitors to the portal has dropped to 1.5 million per year from nearly 3 million per year, he said, which reflects the superiority of a single-word, .com address.

Scores of other six-figure sales have been reported by DNJournal.com amid the market's new growth phase. Even misspelled generic names often command hefty prices. Consider mortage.com ($242,400) and forclosures. com ($150,000).

While .com names remain the most highly valued, the boom extends into several other extensions, such as .es for Spain and .br for Brazil, as Internet use increases around the world.[3] Many owners of overseas extensions are also seeking to profit from the online-advertising boom by displaying text ads on their sites. For example, Camisas.es, which means "shirts" in Spanish, in 2007 contained a page full of ads sold by Google, which garners nearly half of its revenue overseas. Camisas.es contained ads from sellers of clothing in the U.S. and Latin America.

Among the big deals in Spain in 2007, apartamentos.es ("apartments") fetched $40,370, while piscinas.es ("pools") drew $27,459, according to DNJournal.com.

In Germany, meanwhile, .de, the nation's suffix, is extremely popular. In 2006, blackjack.de sold for $300,000. The next year, poker.de went for a whopping $957,937, DNJournal.com says.

By 2007, the vast majority of the best domain portfolios in the world had been probed and prodded by the industry's largest players, and scores of offers had been made. In most deals, the parties sign non-disclosure agreements. Several companies, such as iREIT, offer a tool on their Web site allowing investors to submit a list of names they want to sell, as well as their asking price. The big companies also scour the Web for potential targets. "Pretty much every portfolio out there has had people interested in it," said Michael Blend of Demand Media. "There's nothing unknown. There's no buried treasure."

While a number of deals have been reached, many portfolio owners continue to hold out. Some don't like the prices they're being offered. Others have a hard time parting with names they've come to love. Rick Schwartz falls into both categories.

Schwartz, who's received a number of inquiries from buyers, said he doesn't know what he would do with himself if he sold all his domains. Besides, he said, "The value to me is probably greater than the value it has to most buyers. I look at this way: I'm in my fifties and, God willing, I'll live another thirty years, and I have oil wells that will pump oil for another thirty years and have a good chance of pumping more oil as time goes on." Schwartz said his portfolio of about five thousand names generates "several million dollars" in revenue annually, but he won't share specifics.

Marchex's purchase of Yun Ye's portfolio at a multiple of about eight times annual revenue helped establish a baseline for a revenue multiple that a buyer might pay for a portfolio. Though domain investors have debated whether the multiple was too high or too low, it at least gave them a starting point for how to evaluate an offer. "Having other people sell makes it easier for people to sell," Blend said. "Until then, you had a lot of people with portfolios of domain names where they literally had almost no idea what they're worth. The market had no idea. Things are beginning to normalize."

Still, "the best portfolios remain in independent hands, by far," said Ari Bayme, the former investment banker, who is now an executive with online-advertising company Gorilla Nation Media LLC. "And the reason why is none of the large players have really been able to offer them competitive valuations."

The new frenzy for Web addresses ensured that speculators would lock up most of the common remaining English words and other potentially profitable letter combinations. For example, each of the 676 possible two-letter combinations and each of the 17,576 possible three-letter combinations was taken by March 2006, according to an analysis by Dennis Forbes, an analyst with Vastardis Capital Services, a New York mutual-fund services company. Of the 456,976 possible four-letter sequences, 97,786 were still available, or about 21 percent. The available four-letter addresses included agjv.com and qfev.com, but they're generally not as desirable as a two- or three-letter sequence (unless they spell out real words, of course). Forbes's analysis of the .com database was featured in an article in The Wall Street Journal.[4]

Forbes discovered other interesting tidbits. The most popular length of a .com name was eleven characters. Some people were fond of registering the maximum number of characters, sixty-three. That included a person who'd registered didyouknowthatyoucanonlyhavesixty-threecharactersinadomain-name.com. Each of the one thousand most common English words was registered. And more than 250,000 names included the word "sex."

Speaking of sex, the owner of sex.com, Gary Kremen, sold the name in 2006 in a deal valued between $12 million and $14 million in cash and stock, according to news reports. That would make it one of the biggest domain sales ever. The buyer was Escom, a Boston adult-entertainment company. The domain has a complex and sordid history. In 1994, Kremen, a Web entrepreneur who founded the personals site Match.com, registered the address at no cost. The next year, Stephen Michael Cohen, a convicted felon, hacked into Network Solutions' registration system and stole it.[5] Later, in an effort to justify his control of the name, Cohen forged a letter that purported to come from Kremen's company, Online Classifieds. The letter said Kremen had been fired and that the company had no use for the name and was authorizing Cohen to take it. Cohen sent a copy of the phony letter to Network Solutions, which allowed him to keep the name. Cohen then used sex.com to build a thriving porn empire. Kremen sued Cohen and Network Solutions, and after a long battle, a federal court ruled in 2000 that the domain should be transferred back to Kremen. It also required Cohen to pay him $65 million. But Cohen fled to Mexico without paying him. Network Solutions, meanwhile, reportedly paid Kremen $15 million in a legal settlement.[6] Cohen was later extradited from Tijuana to California, where he spent more than a year in federal prison. In February 2007, Cohen asked a federal judge to erase the $65 million he owed, pleading poverty.[7]

One-syllable adult-oriented domains often land high prices. In May 2007, a closely held company, MXN Ltd., paid $9.5 million for porn.com, one of the biggest domain sales in history. "The possibilities with porn.com are limitless," the Detroit-based Internet media company asserted.

Domain Parking Lots Abound

The Internet land rush has spawned a number of sub-industries. One of the biggest is domain parking. Domain-parking companies—also known as domain-monetization services—act as middlemen in the industry. Most investors don't generate enough traffic to their sites to be able to go directly to Google or Yahoo and land a revenue-sharing agreement to have ads displayed on their sites. (Google seeks relationships with investors generating at least 750,000 unique "page views"—a single Web page viewed by a user—each month. Yahoo said it primarily seeks to team with midsize and large investors, but won't reveal exact metrics.) But investors can go to one of the many middlemen, which place ads sold by Google or Yahoo on the investors' sites in exchange for a cut of the revenue. The middlemen are able to ink revenue-sharing deals with Google or Yahoo because, in the aggregate, their clients' traffic is significant. Some middlemen also distribute ads sold by smaller search-ad networks such as Ask.com, Miva (formerly FindWhat), and Looksmart. The vast majority of the services charge nothing for domain owners to sign up.

The middlemen help explain why the Internet is filled with ad-heavy pages. In late 2006, VeriSign, which manages the list of .com and .net names, conducted a study that estimated that 15.4 million, or 23 percent, of the 66.9 million such names registered worldwide were "parked." It defined parked sites as one-page sites listing pay-per-click ads or that described themselves as "under construction." The opportunity to derive revenue from such sites also contributed to big increases in domain registrations worldwide. Registrations climbed to 120 million in the fourth quarter of 2006, up from 91 million in the year-earlier period, according to VeriSign and Zooknic. com, a research site.

Applied Semantics pioneered the middleman model when it rolled out its DomainPark service in 2001. In the early to mid-2000s, at least two-dozen similar services arose. One of the largest was DomainSponsor, a division of Oversee.net, a closely held Internet advertising company that recorded revenues of more than $100 million in 2006. Oversee.net also has its own portfolio of more than 500,000 names. Lawrence Ng, who co-founded Oversee.net in 2000 at the age of twenty-one, worked with domain owners to build a parking service that appealed to them. He corresponded with them online, often through instant messaging, asking them what worked and what didn't. DomainSponsor signed up enough site owners that it could generate traffic totaling millions of monthly unique visitors for the ad networks. In late 2003, it reached a revenue-sharing deal with Google. DomainSponsor won't disclose how revenue is divided among it, Google, and domain owners. By 2007, DomainSponsor's client list represented more than 2 million names.

DomainSponsor draws competition from TrafficZ, also based in Los Angeles; Sedo's parking service; NameDrive; and Dark Blue Sea's Fabulous.com, among others. Many registrars, such as Go Daddy, also now offer a parking service, as do several of the large portfolio owners. NameMedia bought two: GoldKey and SmartName. There are so many middlemen competing for investors' business that a shakeout is expected in the segment. People keep trying "to elbow into that space because it is very profitable," said Ron Jackson, editor and publisher of DNJournal.com.

The services aren't all alike, however. Site owners find that their advertising revenue can vary widely depending on which service they choose. The quality of the services' technology used to serve up a page of relevant ads varies, as does the quality of their customer service.

Some investors change services frequently—it generally can be done without any financial penalty—to find the best one for their domains.

Another reason it can be difficult to decide which service to use is that the services typically don't tell users how much money they'll receive for every dollar of revenue generated on their sites. Some services publish the percentage of their cut from Google or Yahoo that they're willing to share with the domain owner (it typically ranges from 50 percent to 80 percent, and may be negotiable). But that information often isn't all that helpful because the service typically is contractually forbidden by the search-ad network from telling the domain owner what kind of cut it gets from the network.

When pressed, neither Google nor Yahoo will disclose even a range of the percentage of revenue they typically share with the services and with the large domain holders with whom they have direct relationships. But industry insiders say the range usually is between 50 and 70 percent.

"It is a business that has very little transparency," said Jackson. "It's a frequent complaint. People always suspect their parking company might be shortchanging them. That is why, to me, you should go with a company that you trust."

The differences among the services prompted several entrepreneurs to create Web sites that review the quality of the services. Howard Hoffman, a former engineering consultant in Palo Alto, California, launched PPCincome.com in 2003. Leonard Holmes, a clinical psychologist in Virginia, started rival ParkQuick.com in 2004. Both have gained a following because they help users sort through the complexities of the services. Both, it should be noted, earn revenue from referring customers to the services, so they have at least the appearance of a conflict of interest.

Hoffman, who has degrees from Stanford and the Massachusetts Institute of Technology, regularly runs tests on a sample domain portfolio to determine which of the services generates the most revenue. The test list represents a diverse sample of Hoffman's 11,000 domains. Among his findings: Sedo, which originated in Germany, delivers better revenue for many foreign-language sites than do other services. He started sending all his Spanish, Portuguese, German, and Italian domains to Sedo, which decides which language to show Web users based on the user's location (typically determined by the user's IP address). Hoffman used to make a low six-figure salary as an engineering consultant. Now he's earning much more, he said, from his parking-review service and his portfolio, which includes freehotspot.com, visitidaho.com, and laketahoehotel.com.

Controversial Advertising

Although domain parking clearly has been good for investors and the ad networks, the level of value the sites offer to consumers has been hotly debated. Some critics say the proliferation of the bare-bones sites has sullied the Internet. Some liken the millions of ad-bloated sites to an endless stream of billboards along a highway, distracting drivers and ruining the scenery.

Andrew Goodman, the founder and principal of Page Zero Media, a Toronto-based online marketing agency, said the sites offer a poor user experience. They essentially dupe Web surfers into clicking on ads so the domain owners and search-ad brokers can profit, he said. Therefore, he cautions advertising clients about having their ads appear on such sites. "It's misdirection," said Goodman, author of the book *Winning Results with Google AdWords*. "The intent is usually somewhat deceptive."

The sites are devoid of editorial content by design, he said. The domain owner wants to limit the range of choices the user can make. If there's no content to read, the user's choice is to click on an ad, hit the back button on his Web browser, or close the browser. "Any pages that are devoid of content . . . clearly are optimized to get the most clicks out of people," Goodman said.

Rick Schwartz, the Florida investor, has said his Web sites are designed to maximize clicks. "I like to build sites with limited content," he said. "In other words, I have mostly crappy sites! But even that is for a reason. I don't want anyone sticking around on my sites. I want them off as quick as they came via a revenue-producing link."[8] Schwartz doesn't believe he's misleading any Web users. If a user has typed one of his domains, the user is seeking relevant information.

Goodman said he's unimpressed by efforts to spruce up static sites by adding photographs or graphics. "If the intent is to just overlay a slight cosmetic change, then it's not a fundamental change," he said.

Jon Lisbin, founder of Point It, a Seattle online ad agency, said the pages have "some value" because advertisers attract some customers through them. However, he said, "It's a link farm . . . It's making the whole Internet experience a little uglier."

Executives at Google and Yahoo argue that the sites are useful to consumers. If Web users type "kidstoys.com" into their browser, for instance, they're searching for a specific thing. If they visit the site and are shown a list of relevant ads, they're being given information that can help them find what they're looking for. They read the ad messages and determine whether to click on them; if they do, they might find a site where they can buy children's toys. In other words, it's highly qualified traffic, Google and Yahoo contend. The user is showing strong intent.

"The domain space adds value both to the advertiser and the end user," Hal Bailey, strategic partner manager for the Google AdSense for domains program, said at a Search Engine Strategies industry conference in Chicago in December 2006. "Otherwise, we wouldn't be in this business. We feel that the advertisers and end users can benefit because people are using the URL bar for search."

But neither Google nor Yahoo considers the sites valuable enough to include in their organic search-engine results. Both generally exclude sites solely featuring ads from showing up in their results. The policy helps explain why many domains depend entirely on type-in traffic.

Debates have raged online between critics of ad-choked sites and the investors who own them. In June 2006, Erick Schonfeld, an editor at-large for Business 2.0, wrote on his blog, the.next.net, that "it is the domainers who are largely responsible for gunking up the Web." He said domain investors, along with spammers and sploggers (people who create phony blogs, known as "splogs"), are the reason "that it is getting harder and harder to find what you are really looking for on the Web."

Schonfeld's dispatch prompted a torrent of criticism from investors, who posted their comments on his blog. They argued vehemently that the sites served a useful purpose. Otherwise, they said, Google and Yahoo wouldn't syndicate their ads on the sites. The investors also took offense to the headline of Schonfeld's dispatch, which read, "The New Cybersquatters."

One of the investors blasting Schonfeld's commentary was none other than Rick Schwartz. "You spew a point of view that is not consistent with reality," he wrote. "Is it just sour grapes that you and many others missed the single biggest opportunity in your lifetime? That it buzzed right by you and you were not able to grab a piece of the action? That there are many folks making millions? You compare domainers to spammers?? Are you nuts? A spammer sends something that is unwanted and unasked for. Going to a domain name is exactly the opposite."

Schwartz continued, "And I got news for ya, the parking lot business is very good and it is very good because the traffic that gets typed into the browser bar is among the most potent on the net. They convert into sales which may mean nothing to you but means everything to the folks buying the traffic."

Schwartz touched on an important matter: the issue of whether the sites were valuable to marketers. Do the ads really convert into sales? Many investors and parking services say the sites generate high conversion rates. But they're making a big generalization. The sites actually vary widely in the quality of traffic they deliver to advertisers. Some do very well, some are in the middle, and some do very poorly. And a key reason is that domains are not all alike. Hardly, in fact. Some are popular terms that many users would type into the browser, such as recipes.com. Others are filled with hyphens and three or four words—names unlikely to draw much qualified traffic.

When it comes to the performance of ads on the sites, many factors are at play, including the design of the site, and whether the advertising copy appeals to users.

Marketers measure the performance of pay-per-click ads in several ways. One measure is the click-through rate. It is defined as the percentage of Web users who, upon being shown an ad, click on the ad and arrive on the marketer's site. Another measure—typically the most important—is the conversion rate. It refers to how often a user who lands on the marketer's site takes a specific action desired by the marketer. The marketer's goal could be as simple as getting the user to sign up for a free trial of a product. Or it could be to get the user to complete a survey and enter a drawing to win a prize. So conversion rates mean different things to different marketers.

For companies that spend significant amounts of money bidding on keywords in the ad networks offered by Google, Yahoo and others, it is extremely important, of course, to see a return on their investment. On a regular basis, the marketers examine reports that tell them where on the Web their ads have been displayed. They see numbers telling them how many times those ads were shown, and what percentage of users clicked on them. They also see the ads' conversion rates.

Yahoo and Google don't share specific details about the conversion rates of ads appearing on parked sites. But Josh Meyers, general manager for the domain channel at Yahoo, said the company has found that conversion rates on average are similar to those of ads appearing alongside the search results on Yahoo.com and Google.com. (Those rates also aren't disclosed). Some domains do very poorly, while others do very well, he said.

Several marketers said they were upset to find that many of their ads were showing up on the ad-laden sites, and converting at extremely low rates. Rob Montalbine, Internet marketing manager for Churchill Corporate Services, a relocation-services company in Hawthorne, New Jersey, said he cut his advertising spending at Yahoo in part because of poor performance of such ads. "A lot of this traffic coming from Yahoo's Domain Match program is garbage," he said. In 2006, he noticed his company was getting a lot of traffic from FurnishedApartmentDirectory.com, a site displaying ads sold by Yahoo. When Montalbine looked into it, he found that there were 3,100 clicks on Churchill's ad on that site in 2006. Only 19, or 0.6 percent, converted into customers, which in Churchill's case meant they requested a reservation at one of its corporate apartments. "That's abysmal," Montalbine said. The company was paying an average of 52 cents a click for the keyword "furnished apartments," he said.

Melissa Mackey, search marketing director for Okemos, Michigan-based MagazineLine, which sells magazine subscriptions, said "we get some good traffic" from parked sites. However, many deliver "very poor traffic," and some are "absolutely terrible." The company found it received very poor conversion rates from DiscountMagazineInfo.com, she said, but declined to share specific numbers, citing competitive factors. At the same time, she said, the company enjoyed fairly high conversion rates from Seveteen.com, a misspelling of Seventeen.com, the Web site of Seventeen magazine. Mackey routinely bids on the names of magazines her company sells, including "Seventeen" and "Cosmopolitan."

"I don't really like these sites personally," said Mackey, who spends tens of thousands of dollars monthly on paid-search ads. "I mean, somebody typing this in wants to go to Seventeen magazine's Web site. They don't want to go to a page of ads." (For more on misspelled corporate names and brands and the controversy surrounding them, see Chapter Eight.)

Point It's Lisbin found that many of the ads placed on Google's search network for one of his clients, a financial-services company, appeared on parked sites, and many converted very poorly. When he warned his client about the problem, however, it said it wanted him to continue to buy ads on Google's search network because some of the ads converted well and it didn't want to throw out the baby with the bath water. "They were like, 'Well, if it's getting me any leads, I still want it,'" he said. So "it's not a non-value."

But Lisbin, Mackey, and Montalbine are all part of a large and growing camp of marketers who want to have more control over where their ads appear in the Google and Yahoo networks.

At the time of this writing, if a marketer wants to bid to have ads appear alongside the search results on Yahoo.com, their ads also will automatically appear next to search listings on other sites, as well as on sites without content. Yahoo doesn't allow marketers to exclude the domain segment, for example. Marketers also can't ask Yahoo to exclude specific sites. "With future versions of our platform, I'm sure that is something that will be considered," Yahoo's Meyers said.

Google offers more user control than Yahoo does, but not enough for some marketers. Google said marketers could exclude sites lacking content by opting out of its search-ad network. But that meant their ads only would appear on Google.com, leaving them off the sites of major partners like AOL and Ask.com.

Google does use a tool it calls "smart pricing" to analyze the quality of traffic on its partners' sites. If its data show clicks on certain ads are less likely to convert to sales, it may reduce the price the marketer bid for the click. "For example, a click on an ad for digital cameras on a Web page about photography tips may be worth less than a click on the same ad appearing next to a review of digital cameras," Google said in a 2004 blog entry on its site. At the time of this writing, Yahoo was working on a similar tool.

Danny Sullivan, a search-engine expert who runs the blog SearchEngineLand.com, has called for Google to offer marketers a separate media buy for the domain segment. "I basically have said to them, 'You've dragged your feet,'" he said.

Said Lisbin: "I don't think most advertisers are even aware that they're advertising on these sites. And I don't think there's enough transparency from the search engines to allow advertisers to remove themselves easily [from the segment] or even know which sites they should remove themselves from."

Other marketers are more bullish on the sites. Andrew Beckman, president of Denver-based SearchAd Network, an online ad agency, said one of his clients, a children's educational portal, enjoyed high conversion rates when its text ads purchased in Google's auction system appeared on several ad-filled sites, including kids.com, owned by the media company CNET. In one period he analyzed, 11 percent of users clicking on an ad on kids.com for his client became a customer. The rate was 30 percent for an ad running on toddlergames.com, owned by iREIT, the big domain investor. At the low end, funshcool.com, a misspelling of funschool.com, also owned by iREIT, converted at a rate of 2 percent. "We're definitely getting some good quality," Beckman said.

Some critics speculate the sites are often used for "click fraud." Click fraud, a major challenge for search-ad companies, occurs when a person maliciously clicks on an online ad to boost his own ad revenue or to drive up a competitor's marketing costs. Both Google and Yahoo say they have strong automated systems to filter out most suspicious clicks so marketers aren't billed. Marketers also can receive refunds if they demonstrate to the paid-search giants that they've been wrongly charged. 'We catch most invalid click activity before advertisers are affected," said Eytan Elbaz, head of the domain channel for Google.

Neither Google nor Yahoo will give specifics on the percentage of fake clicks in their ad networks. Google has said its rate is in the single digits. The Yankee Group research firm in Boston estimates the industry's rate is about 10 percent.[9] Critics claim the search engines don't have a strong incentive to stop the problem of click fraud because they earn revenue from each bogus click. Some perpetrators of click fraud use computer programs to automatically generate clicks on ads across the Web and try to remain anonymous. Others organize "pay to read" networks, enlisting Web users to click on ads in exchange for cash.

Howard Hoffman, the Palo Alto, California, domain investor, said he sees young kids naively talking in domain forums about how they could make more money by clicking on each other's ads. He routinely types a reply telling them to watch out. "The advertisements are our golden goose," Hoffman said. "You take care of your golden goose. You don't mess with it. And most people understand that. But there are some dishonest people . . . They have like five crappy domains, and they're trying to make a lot of money off that, so they look to methods that are illegal, and it hurts the whole industry."

Neither Google nor Yahoo will disclose how much revenue it receives from parked sites.

Jordan Rohan, an analyst with RBC Capital Markets in New York, estimated that about $800 million of worldwide paid-search advertising revenue in 2006 came from direct search, a term used to describe revenue from ads appearing on sites dependent on type-in traffic. He projected that the figure would rise to $1.1 billion in 2007.

For Google it seems to be a "dirty little secret" that they make money off ad-choked sites, said Sullivan. "When Google goes out and they talk about all these wonderful things that they're doing, they never mention the domaining side."

Cognizant of the flaws of domain parking, some investors and parking services have revamped the heavily formatted pages to include some editorial content. TrafficZ started letting domain holders type content onto their pages in 2005. In 2007, it upgraded its offering to allow them to automatically sprinkle content relevant to the domain name. It made the content dynamic—it changed from time to time, so users would get recent information. "The parked pages aren't bringing value right now, and you need to bring value," said Ammar Kubba, TrafficZ's chief operating officer.

New business models emerged in response to negative reactions to the sites. They included NoParking.com and WhyPark.com, which offered content-development services to domain holders who didn't want to take time to build content on their own or who couldn't easily do it on dozens of sites.

Google's Elbaz indicated that, despite the company's belief that ad-laden pages served a useful purpose, it would like to see domain holders move away from them. "We hope that the industry will focus on making the user experience the best it can be," he said. "Users are able to find relevant information quickly and easily. Advertisers get qualified leads. And domain holders make money by having relevant content and corresponding ads."

"Taking Their Masks Off"

On a warm afternoon in Hollywood, Florida, in October 2006, about 200 people gathered in a vast conference room at the posh Westin Diplomat Resort and Spa, which straddled the Atlantic Ocean. They were there for a live auction of domain names. The 300 names ranged widely in value; they included everything from cameras.com to guacamole.us. Among the more amusing names was hell.com, whose owner set a minimum price of $2.3 million.

The auction was the most anticipated event of Traffic, a conference for domain investors founded by Rick Schwartz and Howard Neu, a lawyer who'd represented Schwartz in domain disputes. For a long time, investors rarely met in person. Many knew each other only by their "handles," or user names, that they displayed in online forums. Schwartz and Neu brought them together face to face. The Traffic show was inspired by an earlier, less formal gathering of investors. In late 2002, the Australian Internet marketing company Dark Blue Sea, founded by former adult-entertainment magnate Dean Shannon, invited investors to the famed Beverly Wilshire Hotel in Los Angeles to discuss domains and view the rollout of its new registrar and domain-parking service, Fabulous.com, and its affiliate network, DarkBlue. Many of the roughly one hundred attendees of the event—dubbed "DeanFest"—were members of Schwartz's private online domain forum. Schwartz and Shannon had known each other since the mid-1990s, when Schwartz cut deals with Shannon to deliver traffic to his porn sites. DeanFest was officially a one-day show, but many of the guests arrived early and stayed around for several days afterwards.

About two years later, in October 2004, the first Traffic show took place at the Marriott in Delray Beach, Florida. It was only supposed to be a thirty-five-person gathering, said Schwartz, but as word spread, dozens more people wanted in. Ultimately, 135 people attended, and Schwartz managed to land the author, actor, and comedian Ben Stein (famous as the vapid economics teacher in *Ferris Bueller's Day Off*) as the keynote speaker. New York domain investor Michael Bahlitzanakis said the show was "really fascinating" because investors got to meet the people behind the Whois information they'd looked at for years. "It was like everybody was taking their masks off," he said. "Everybody knew what domains you had, but nobody knew who you were, and that was really cool." The next show, called Traffic West, was held in Las Vegas and drew 235 people. The numbers went up from there. But Schwartz and Neu didn't let just anyone attend. You had to be invited, although you could request an invitation on the show's Web site, TargetedTraffic.com. The show I attended, Traffic East 2006, attracted about 500 people. For most, the five-day event didn't come cheap. Standard admission was $2,000.[10] Meals were paid for, but if you added the cost of a reservation at the swanky hotel, a rental car, roundtrip airfare, and various odds and ends, you easily could drop $5,000. Several guests grumbled privately that the price of the show was outrageous, but that they felt they might glean enough valuable information to make it worthwhile.

The show's official name was T.R.A.F.F.I.C. Many people had no idea that it stood for Targeted Redirects and Financial Fulfillment Internet Conference. They just knew it dealt with Internet traffic and domains, their stock and trade. In the days leading up to the auction, investors attended panels on topics ranging from how to decide whether to sell a portfolio to click fraud. Some people skipped the sessions to negotiate deals. At night, the fun began. Parties sponsored by the likes of DomainSponsor, TrafficZ, and iREIT ran into the wee hours, and their attendees either slept in the next day or trudged with weary eyes into the panel discussions. One late night, I joined a group at the Scarlett's Gentlemans Club, the strip joint described by Paul Sloan in Business 2.0 where Frank Schilling had to foot the bill for a group of Yahoo employees. This time, Schilling was nowhere to be found, but his long-haired and eccentric lawyer, John Berryhill, was there, dressed in a Pope costume. At about 5 a.m., amid the din of the music, the clinking of glasses, and loud chatter, I leaned close to Jay Westerdal—the Seattle domain investor, who was now running a market-research firm called Name Intelligence—and asked him why Schilling wasn't there. He said Schilling decided to stay back in his hotel room and analyze a list of domains he might try to buy. Westerdal said this explained succinctly why Schilling was so successful. "He's working right now, and we're here," he said in my ear.

Schilling—who walked around the conference wearing a nametag that said "Schillings," courtesy of a typo by the show's coordinators—joined many other successful investors at the auction. Schwartz was there, of course, as were Marc Ostrofsky and Adam Dicker. So, too, was Michael Berkens, a former lawyer in his late forties who owned about fifty thousand domains. Berkens, sporting a goatee and dark glasses, sat right behind me in the middle of the room. About six months earlier, it was Berkens who'd helped inspire me to write this book. "Has anyone ever written a book about you people?" I'd asked him in so many words. "No, a lot of people have talked about it, but no one has," he said.

Seated next to me was an earnest undergraduate from Yale, Mitchell Hoffman, son of Howard Hoffman, the engineering consultant-turned-domain investor. Mitchell sat right behind his father. Mitchell, like me, was there not to bid on names but to closely follow the action. He was writing his senior-year economics essay on the domain market, a field receiving scarce study in the academic world.

The cavernous room was dominated by men. Among the fifteen women I counted was Lesli Angel, an early domain investor from North Miami. Angel, a former nurse, owned several hundred addresses, including beautytips.com and drugoverdose.com. She said she'd been obsessed with names since she became acquainted with the Web in the mid-1990s. "I never saw how the Internet could be a losing proposition," she said. Michelle Miller, formerly of BuyDomains and now running a domain consulting business, WebVerb, was in the audience, too. Miller said she was one of three women—"maybe"—at the first Traffic show in 2004. "It's definitely evolved," she said.

The four-hour auction attracted not only industry veterans, but also newcomers who hoped they weren't too late to the market. For the rookies and the veterans, there was an air of great anticipation. There were predictions from Moniker.com, the auction's organizer, that it might draw $5 million to $10 million in sales, a live-auction record for Moniker. Standing at center stage in the front of the room was Joe Langbaum, a gray-haired professional auctioneer in a beige suit. A huge blue Traffic banner hung from the ceiling behind him. Monte Cahn, who ran Moniker, stood to his left. When the audience wanted to pose a question about one of the domains—such as how much traffic it drew—Cahn, a consummate salesman, did his best to shout a response.

Bidders studied printouts of the names for sale, scrawling notes next to each name. Some used the wireless Internet connections on their laptops to download information about the domains as they came up for bid. Spectators gathered in the back of the room, nursing bottles of Heineken and soft drinks distributed at an open bar. The curious onlookers included Ari Bayme, then an investment banker, Google's Eytan Elbaz, and the ubiquitous Berryhill.

Bahlitzanakis was one of the most active bidders right out of the gate. He scooped up fixedloans.com for $10,000. Then he nabbed loanfinance.com for $8,000. On a break to visit the restroom, I bumped into him as he dashed back to the auction with a cup of coffee, grinning from ear to ear. "I had to get loanfinance.com!" the thirty-year-old shouted. "That's a steal! Opportunities, baby!" Bahlitzanakis—whose Greek last name is so tough to pronounce that he recommends people call him "Michael B."—also grabbed queens.net for $5,000, locking up the .net version of his borough in New York City.

More aggressive than Bahlitzanakis was a balding man in his mid-thirties seated behind him. His name was Scott Richter, and he happened to be one of the world's most prolific senders of junk e-mail. In 2005, Richter agreed to pay $7 million to settle a lawsuit by Microsoft over spam, admitting no wrongdoing. Richter ran several marketing companies, including OptinRealBig.com. During the auction, he snapped up a dozen domains, including trusted.com for $37,500, telephonecall.com for $20,000, So.net for $13,000, and babyoutlets.com for $7,000. In an e-mail interview a few months later, Richter said he'd bought the names for both investment and business purposes. "We are looking for premium names to continue to rise in value, as well as earn revenues from them in the short term while parking them," he wrote. He owned about fifteen thousand domains, and the number was growing daily.

Cahn and his team from Moniker had hoped that several domains would sell for more than $1 million at the auction, but only one did, and it happened in the first half hour. The name was cameras.com. Schilling joined in the bidding, competing all the way up to $1 million. But he didn't want to pay more than that. Later, he wrote on his personal blog that he was "too cheap for his own good." Sigmund Solares, a former day trader who ran several registrars in Tampa, Florida, won the name for $1.5 million, drawing a flurry of applause. The seller was E. P. Levine, a store for professional photographers in Boston that had owned the name for years. Schilling wasn't interested in any other names, so he jumped in a limousine, which took him to a private airport in ten minutes. He boarded his jet and was at his house on Grand Cayman Island within an hour, while the auction was still going on.

Schwartz was at the center of several of the most thrilling battles. He decided to take a chance on names ending in .mobi—a new extension that its founders hoped would be widely adopted for Internet browsing on mobile devices such as cellphones. When flowers.mobi came up for bid, about a half-dozen people vied for it. Schwartz didn't jump in right away, but when he did, he didn't let anyone beat him. Schwartz bid $100,000, then $120,000. When someone else topped that, he raised his bid to $150,000. Finally he claimed the domain for $200,000. A second later someone shouted, "You're f—!" Then everyone in the room rose and cheered for Schwartz. "Want to flip it, Rick?" someone yelled. It was a whopper of a sale, especially given that Moniker had placed the domain in the price category of zero to $10,000. When bisexuals.com came up for bid next, Ostrofsky rushed over to Schwartz and jokingly said, "Hey Rick, buy this one too!" But Schwartz didn't budge, and bisexuals.com went to a European company for $60,000.

With about an hour left, another .mobi name came up: fun.mobi. This time, Schwartz duked it out with one person: Larry Fischer, vice president of business development at domain-parking service SmartName.com. Fischer surprised the crowd with a bid of $67,500. Then, in rapid-fire succession, he and Schwartz traded bids all the way up to $100,000. When Fischer bid that amount, Schwartz bowed out, and everyone in the back of the room, where both men were sitting, gave a thunderous cheer for Fischer.

Hell.com came up near the end of the auction. The Wall Street Journal ran a colorful article that morning saying "the online address of the underworld" was up for grabs.[11] But the seller, BAT Flli LLC, a creative think tank, wanted far more for it—$2.3 million—than anyone in the crowd was willing to pay. "This made the news today," Cahn shouted to the bidders. "Let's make us proud." But his plea went unanswered. There was no interest whatsoever. Indianapolis investor Chad Folkening's DSL.com, priced at a minimum of $4 million, also drew no takers.

All told, about 115 of the 300 available names sold. The auction ended with about $4.5 million in total sales, at the low end of the range Moniker expected but still its highest-grossing live auction. Schwartz's flowers.mobi wound up as the second-highest sale at $200,000. The smallest sale of the event? Guacamole.us, which went to Howard Hoffman for $600, prompting a chuckle from his son.

After the show, several veteran investors told me that many sellers' expectations were too lofty. That in part reflected the hype surrounding domains. Sellers with generic terms felt they could command a high price, and weren't all that willing to budge. Several investors also told me they avoided bidding in live auctions because they were prone to pay too much in order to beat a rival bidder in front of the crowd.

"If you did the real analysis [the auction] was a flop," said the twenty-eight-year-old Westerdal, who bought cityuniversity.com for $14,000. "Basically everyone had reserve prices way too high."

Rick Latona, a thirty-four-year-old from Atlanta, had one of the most successful days of any of the sellers in the auction. DigiPawn.com, one of several companies Latona owned, sold thirteen names for about $100,000, including loanfinance.com and fixedloans.com, which went to Bahlitzanakis. DigiPawn had paid little for the thirteen domains, so the sales were almost all profit, Latona said. Meanwhile, Latona bought outsourcing.net ($11,000), raise.com ($25,000), and sumowrestling.com ($11,800). "I'm not sure what I was thinking on the last one," said Latona, a high-school dropout. Outsourcing.net fit well with one of Latona's businesses, Offshoring.com, which helped companies find inexpensive staffing overseas. Latona owns about 13,000 domains and is an executive with ConsumptionJunction.com, a well-known so-called shock Web site that shows bizarre and sometimes gruesome videos and photos of violent acts, pornography, and drunken misbehavior.

That night, the last of the Traffic show, I joined Latona, Bahlitzanakis, Folkening, and about a dozen other investors at a small party in South Beach hosted by a fledgling investor who'd apparently once worked for a hedge fund. On the drive from Hollywood, I shared a car with two young men who in many ways embodied the new frenzy over domains. The driver, Ofer Ronen, thirty-one, had recently completed the MBA program at Cornell, moved to Silicon Valley, and cofounded a start-up. His company, Sendori, offered a marketplace allowing marketers to strike deals with domain owners to have traffic redirected to the marketers' sites. In the backseat was Kevin Daste, twenty-seven, who dropped out of Louisiana State University a few years ago and only nine credits shy of his bachelor's degree, to invest in domains full-time. Daste started buying names with credit cards soon after arriving at LSU, quickly racking up about $8,000 in debt. But by his senior year, he said, he was doing so well in the market—and spending so much time at it—that he could no longer justify going to class.

The party was held at an immaculate multimillion-dollar waterfront condominium. Most guests gathered on the balcony, sipping cocktails and gazing into Biscayne Bay. I was introduced to an investor from San Francisco known as Slavic, who focused on adult names. When someone told him I was writing a book on the name trade, he said, "OK, then I'm Bob."

A few minutes later I was alone with Kevin Bordes, a stocky twenty-six-year-old from Louisiana and Daste's business partner. We both looked around the balcony. Bordes noted that there were several young millionaires in our vicinity. "It's weird," he said. "Some of the people at this conference are so young, and they're saying, 'I'm done. What do I do next?'" It was a position I couldn't fathom.

Everyone piled into taxi cabs and headed to a trendy nightclub, Mokai, where we wound up dancing next to baseball slugger Sammy Sosa and his small entourage that included two mammoth bodyguards. At nearly four in the morning, I snapped a photograph of Westerdal and a surprised-but-smiling Sosa.

Too bad Sosa wasn't at the auction: homerun.com had gone unsold.

A few months after Traffic East, the show's top sponsor, DomainSponsor, announced it was starting a new conference, DomainFest Global, to compete with Traffic. Schwartz was furious, DomainSponsor's Ron Sheridan told me. DomainSponsor believed there should be an industry conference that let everyone attend and that cost much less than Traffic did. Admission cost $395 to the first show, held in Los Angeles in February 2007.

It was a bit ironic, because at the Traffic show, Sheridan handed Schwartz an award for having the greatest influence on the industry of any single person. "If there's anybody in the business who deserves the title of domain king, it's certainly Rick Schwartz," Sheridan told me. "That said, Rick's Achilles heel is that he has a tendency to be very reactionary. And he's extremely opinionated and inflexible at times."

When I asked Schwartz how he felt about DomainSponsor starting a rival conference, he said, "It's a free country . . . Folks have been trying to copy the success of Traffic since we started, and none have succeeded. Traffic is the gold standard, and they really don't understand the chemistry that makes Traffic so successful. They think giving it away for free will make them successful. But when they do that, they allow folks in that really have no business there, and that becomes a time waster for folks that are not inclined to waste time. That is why Traffic is by invitation only. We want only qualified professionals that know how to do business and make deals on a handshake."

Needless to say, DomainSponsor wasn't the top sponsor of the next Traffic show, though it was a sponsor.

It wasn't the first time Schwartz was angry about a new domain conference. When Westerdal and his company, Name Intelligence, started a Seattle show called Domain Roundtable in 2005, Schwartz kicked Westerdal off his private online forum, adding him to a long list of people who'd gotten the boot. "He didn't say anything. He just turned off my access," said Westerdal. "That was it. He's kind of this arrogant guy who thinks he controls the universe."

Schwartz said Westerdal attended the first Traffic show in 2004 and then tried to "compete with us, so there was an obvious conflict of interest."

Schwartz is quick to agree that he has a big ego, but stresses that many successful people do. "Don't confuse ego with egocentric," he said. "My 'ego' is for the betterment of all domainers. My job was to make domain names known to businesses throughout the world."

Registrars Become Speculators

The recent success of domain investors hasn't escaped the attention of the registrars that serve them. Registrars duke it out in a highly competitive industry with thin margins. Many have long had to scratch and claw to earn a profit. So it is unsurprising that they became envious when they saw their customers thriving. Eventually, hungry for new sources of revenue and tired of watching their customers enjoy the spoils of the name game, many began speculating in thousands of domains themselves. Among the many ways registrars acquired names was by registering ones that their customers failed to renew. "Everyone is getting in everyone else's space," Marc Ostrofsky observed.

Registrars that have built portfolios—often to garner pay-per-click revenue—include DirectNIC (part of Intercosmos Media Group), Demand Media's eNom, Dotster, and Tucows. Though the practice is not barred under Icann rules, critics contend it is a conflict of interest. Registrars were created to serve individuals and institutions that wanted a Web address. Now, through their speculative efforts, they're reducing the pool of available domains, critics say. Registrars defend the practice by saying Icann doesn't ban it, and that they have a free-market right to explore new lines of business.

"It's a conflict," said Larry Seltzer, an author who pens a column for the technology trade publication eWeek and often writes about the name trade. On the other hand, he said, if Icann prohibited registrars from speculating, it might have difficulty enforcing the ban because registrars undoubtedly would set up related companies to hold the assets. It would hardly be unusual for registrars to find loopholes to get around Icann guidelines, he said.

Icann's existing "registrar accreditation agreement," which each registrar must follow, doesn't exactly give rousing support to the idea of registrars speculating on domains. A clause says registrars must "abide by any Icann adopted specifications or policies prohibiting or restricting warehousing of or speculation in domain names by registrars." No such policies have been adopted, however. (Speculating, it should be noted, is different from registering a few domains for business purposes, which all registrars, of course, must do.) Icann officials, when asked to comment on registrars' speculation in domains, said through a spokesman that it would be inappropriate to venture an opinion. "Icann's operations are dictated by policy that is developed through a bottom-up consensus driven process involving the entire Icann community," they said. "It is fair to say that Icann policy reflects the interests and concerns of the majority of members of its community. Therefore, it is both irrelevant and inappropriate for an individual staff member to express a personal opinion on Icann policy." Among the Icann constituents they referred to were registrars, many of which seemed to enjoy the freedom to speculate on domains.

One of the most active registrar speculators is Intercosmos Media Group, which runs DirectNIC and other registrars. The Tampa, Florida-based company owns hundreds of thousands of domains, according to its chief executive, Sigmund Solares, the former day trader. Solares, who also used to practice law, said the company began compiling domains in the early 2000s somewhat by happenstance. Here's how: When a person registers a name, the registrar pays the registry to get the name on the customer's behalf, and it makes money off the additional amount it charges the customer. In some cases, however, customers contact their credit-card companies after the fact and cancel payment to the registrar, leaving domains in the registrar's hands. In other cases, customers use stolen credit cards, get caught, and the domain purchases are canceled. Over time, these instances can add up to thousands of domains of mixed quality landing in a registrar's system. Of course, registrars can simply let the domains expire when they come up for renewal. But if the registrar is pleased with the pay-per-click ad revenue a particular name generates—or if it likes the resale prospects—it is tempted to keep it. And some registrars do exactly that.

Solares said his company also has registered for itself domains its customers have failed to renew. When asked if he was concerned its activities might alienate customers, he said, "Certainly you have so many different registrars out there, and so many places a customer can take their business. I can see that some customers would have problems with it and would rather have their names at a registrar that has no domains."

But he'd received few complaints. At one industry conference, he said, a customer told him, "I had some names [registered with DirectNIC] that I didn't renew, and I know you took them, and it doesn't bother me, because I know you have to make money."

And money is what talks to registrars. More than half of Intercosmos Media Group's annual revenue, which totaled more than $25 million in 2006, came from advertising, Solares said. That includes the pay-per-click ads on the sites it owns, as well as the ads served on sites its customers own but aren't using. In 2001, when the company first became an accredited registrar, about 90 percent of its revenue came from registering domains and associated services, and about 10 percent from ads.

Solares said the fact that many registrars are now speculating is a natural evolution of a competitive marketplace. In many industries, he said, businesses "want to vertically integrate. You're going to have cases where people expand . . . into areas their customers enter into, and some customers aren't going to be happy with it."

eNom began investing in domains before it was acquired by Demand Media, said John Kane, former senior vice president for Demand Media. Like Intercosmos and others, eNom first accrued names its customers didn't pay for, and then, eventually began proactively investing. "There's nothing wrong with it or illegal about it," Kane said. The portfolio eNom built made the company attractive to Demand Media's founders. eNom's first duty will always be to its customers, so it would not try to compete with them, for instance, to acquire a name that was back-ordered through ClubDrop, its drop-catching service, Kane said. But if no customer was interested in a particular list of domains, he said, "I don't think there's any conflict of interest" in a registrar acquiring them.

Jonathon Nevett, vice president of policy for Network Solutions and chair of the registrars constituency for Icann, said it is not his company's "business model" to speculate on domains. However, he said, he saw nothing wrong with other registrars doing it, and said it was unlikely he'd ever pursue a ban on the practice through his role in Icann.

Several registrar executives emphasized that a number of domain investors, such as Frank Schilling, now own stakes in Icann-accredited registrars. Hence, they said, they're simply on the same footing as someone like Schilling. The point has some merit. However, many such investor-owned registrars don't offer registration services to the public. Schilling, for example, said his company, Name Administration, bought a minority interest in a registrar formed in 2004, Domain Name Sales, for the purpose of making certain that its portfolio was secure. That's because registrars have at times made errors or been deceived by so-called domain hijackers, resulting in domain owners' names being transferred to other parties.

Domain Name Sales doesn't register names for consumers, said Schilling. It does, however, have a few other clients besides Name Administration, he said.

Google, Amazon.com, and AOL, among others, have become Icann-accredited registrars for various reasons, but they don't use the registrars to sell names to the public. Google did it because it believed the information it would glean would help it improve the quality of its search results.[12]

Some investors like to own their own registrars so they can have direct connections to the registry to obtain expired domains, and so they only have to pay the wholesale price for names.

Schilling said he decided to take matters into his own hands in part because many retail registrars have become big investors. "It is beguiling that registrars who serve the public also invest in names for their own ends," said Schilling, who owned more than 350,000 names by 2007. "What is to stop retail registrars from making renewals on good domains prohibitively difficult or expensive in order to unseat their registrants and take over those names?" He added, "There is no defense like a good offense."

Some registrars agree that they would have a conflict of interest if they speculated on domains. Monte Cahn, CEO of Moniker.com, said Moniker isn't building its own portfolio for that reason. "We made a very important decision sometime ago," he said. "Do we want to compete with the customers we serve, or do we want to serve the customers with our services and make our money in a different way? . . . And I could look back and say, 'Well, maybe we should have been in the competing business, and competed with a Yun Ye and a Frank Schilling and a BuyDomains, and we would have been in a different [financial] position than we are today by owning a huge inventory and really monetizing the heck out of it.'

"But my partner [company president Eric Harrington] and I felt it was better and more ethical to serve our customers by providing the services to help them build up their portfolios and make them valuable, rather than doing it ourselves. And then there would never be a question of whose side am I on and where my interests really were." Cahn first got involved in the domain market in the mid-1990s by investing in about one thousand names, but that was before he became a broker and acquired a registrar.

Other types of companies that have traditionally served investors have moved into speculation, too. SnapNames, long focused on back-ordering names for clients, has begun building a portfolio through a unit called OregonNames.com. Ray King, co-founder and director of SnapNames, said owning a portfolio is a key part of diversification for the company in a rapidly changing business climate. "Most people in this space own domain names, and SnapNames' activity with OregonNames is no different," he said. "Having an inventory [of one's own domains] is generally a good thing."

Mason Cole, director of industry relations for SnapNames, refused to disclose how many names the company owned. "I can tell you for certain we own a tiny fraction of what someone like DirectNIC owns," he said. He also said the company "absolutely" did not compete with its customers on any name. "Any that we acquire will be well after anyone else seems interested in them and has a chance to acquire them," he added. "Or we acquire them through another channel."

"Crafty Businessmen"

SnapNames and other companies haven't escaped controversy in their speculative endeavors.

In April 2006, the European Union launched the much-anticipated .eu extension, a pan-European alternative to .com. It authorized a nonprofit organization, EURid, to administer the new domains. EURid invited companies throughout the world to apply to become accredited .eu registrars.

As registrars, they could snag names on behalf of customers during a so-called land rush, which took place over a few days. The idea was for each registrar to have an equal chance to grab a domain it wanted. The process was similar to the release of domains in the drop.

SnapNames and several other companies created a slew of registrars to increase their odds, even though only one company was really behind each of the new entities. SnapNames formed about thirty, listing either the company's corporate address or the home address of its chairman, Sudhir Bhagwan. The names of the registrars ranged from Bollywoodbabes.info to Bhagwan Enterprises to DomainRaker.net. It cost 10,000 Euro (about $12,000 at the time) for each registrar. For SnapNames, the expense came to more than $360,000. A review of a handful of the Web sites for the entities SnapNames created showed they all used the same template. Each entity said it "only handles volume domain registrations for a small number of clients."

Dotster, eNom, DirectNIC, and other companies also created many registrars for the land rush. When Bob Parsons, the flamboyant CEO of Go Daddy, found out what happened, he was livid. He'd noticed soon after the launch began that his company was unable to acquire many of the names its customers had requested. After investigating, Parsons went on his blog, BobParsons.com, and lambasted EURid. "What happens when you match an inept registry with crafty businessmen?" he asked. "A really large scam." He said that when he contacted EURid he was told everything about the numerous registrar accreditations was proper. "It was so obviously bogus," Parsons said later, "and I was the only guy in the world—the world!—who was saying anything."[13]

In a front-page article in The Wall Street Journal about the controversy, SnapNames' Mason Cole said his company acquired "several names for ourselves" in the .eu launch. He refused to elaborate.[14]

When asked for this book whether SnapNames obtained names for any customers during the land rush, and, if so, how many, Cole declined to comment. He also refused to share any specifics about how many names SnapNames obtained for itself. "I'm not going to be able to talk about EU," he said without explanation. (Snapnames in 2007 was acquired by Oversee. net, parent of domain-parking service DomainSponsor and a big domain-portfolio owner.)

It's unclear whether SnapNames breached any part of EURid's registrar agreement. The agreement said a registrar "may register domain names for its own use. However, it will refrain from 'warehousing practices,' that is, registering large numbers of domain names without being specifically instructed to do so by end users."

Patrik Linden, a EURid spokesman, said the agency didn't have a specific limit in mind. "Stating an exact number is not really possible," he said. For example, if a registrar had many trademarks it would be reasonable that it would need many names for itself, he said.

In any dispute, Linden said, it would be up to a court to decide whether warehousing had occurred. Several lawsuits were filed. In one high-profile case, EURid tried to block use of 74,000 domains won by three firms registered in Cyprus. However, a Belgian court ruled EURid's action was unlawful.[15]

Linden said he saw no other way the accreditation process could have been handled. "Not letting recently created companies become registrars would not have been fair, especially in the Internet business where development is quite rapid," he said.

More than a million domains were registered in the first few days of the .eu land rush, making it one of the biggest first-time offerings of a domain extension. As of March 2007, about eleven months after the land-rush period, about 2.6 million .eu addresses were registered. However, the value of such names is in doubt, according to several investors. Many Europeans are proud of their own country's suffix, and may not take to using .eu. The .eu suffix is also tightly regulated—for example, registrants are supposed to reside in the European Union. So far, it appears to be a highly speculative segment of the market. Brian Taff, vice president of corporate development at NameMedia, said at an industry conference that some buyers of .eu names had some major regrets about their purchases within only a few months. "There's a lot of friends of mine who speculated in .eu that are now trying to sell whole portfolios for less than the $14 per domain name that it cost them, so there's a risk," he said.

A few .eu names have sold for six figures, including hotels.eu and shopping.eu, which fetched $300,000 and $200,000, respectively, according to DNJournal.com.

Not surprisingly, some people who've registered .eu names are trying to capitalize on typographical errors in which Internet users leave out the *d* in ".edu" when looking for an educational Web site. During the .eu land rush, Bret Fausett, a lawyer who authors a blog about Icann, wrote that people had registered university names such as ucla.eu (University of California, Los Angeles), uark.eu (University of Arkansas), and vanderbilt.eu (Vanderbilt University). Fausett said it appeared that just about every .eu version of a major American university's name had been grabbed in the stampede.

Taste Tests

The domain market has never lacked for creative thinkers. It's filled with people eager to exploit every opportunity they can find to maximize their profit while minimizing their risk. Few techniques in that vein have been more controversial in recent years than "domain tasting."

To "taste" is to register a name for five days and evaluate how much traffic it gets and how much money it makes from ads. If the domain generates more revenue than the annual cost to register it, the investor generally keeps it. If not, the investor lets it go and receives a refund. Tasting exploits a rule that allows registrars to return to VeriSign within a five-day grace period any .com or .net name registered by mistake, and to recoup the $6 fee registrars must pay VeriSign, as well as the 20 cents they must pay Icann.

Icann, with input from VeriSign, implemented the rule in 2000 because some registrants made typographical errors when registering names. They would then ask the registrar to register the correctly spelled address and cancel their previous registration. In such cases, the registrar was saddled with the fee for the first name.

In the early 2000s—after the rule had been adopted but prior to the explosion of search advertising—a few investors, including Frank Schilling, persuaded a few registrars to allow them to sample names in blocks of ten thousand or twenty thousand. They typically chose to test names that had expired, but that they weren't certain would draw much type-in traffic. They evaluated the traffic and how often users clicked on text ads or affiliate links. Typically they kept a small portion of the names. The practice then was known as "batch testing" or "autodelete registrations." SnapNames reported colorfully on the phenomenon in its industry newsletter, State of the Domain, in the fall of 2001. It likened tasters to whales "filtering tons of plankton" and described the practice as "our industry's version of the binge and purge." According to Schilling, VeriSign cracked down on the practice because it viewed the large numbers of acquisitions and subsequent deletions as an abuse of the five-day grace period. The few registrars that had participated, which included Miami-based DotRegistrar (later acquired by Dotster), reluctantly stopped allowing tasting, Schilling said.

When pay-per-click advertising exploded in the mid-2000s, registrars and their clients revived tasting in a major way. And this time, VeriSign didn't clamp down. Jay Westerdal, who runs market-research firm Name Intelligence, said he coined the phrase "domain tasting" and registered domaintasting.com in July 2005, about a year after he first noticed the activity while monitoring statistics on registrations and deletions. "We thought it might be a fluke at the time," he said.

Only about 100,000 domains were tasted each day as of late 2004, Westerdal said. The figure surged over the next two years, reaching 4 million on some days. Some companies use sophisticated computer programs so they can rapidly register hundreds of thousands. Less than 1 percent of tasted domains are kept, Westerdal said.

Who tastes? Some registrars do it for their own portfolios, and some offer their customers an opportunity to do it—sometimes for a fee. Investors can't taste without a registrar's cooperation. And anyone wanting to test thousands of names needs an ample supply of cash. That's because VeriSign requires upfront payment of the $6 it receives for every name registered. Tasting 100,000 names, therefore, costs $600,000 upfront.

Critics contend tasting is a gross manipulation of the domain-name system driven by greed. They say the practice harms consumers and small businesses by reducing the number of addresses available for registration at any given point in time. Proponents, on the other hand, say tasting violates no Icann rules and merely reflects innovation in a competitive market. (At the time of this writing, some efforts involving Icann were under way to potentially put a stop to tasting.)

Go Daddy's Bob Parsons became one of the most vocal critics of the activity, which he called "kiting" rather than tasting. Parsons brought attention to the little-known practice in 2006 by discussing it at length on his blog. "Domain kiting is out of control and must be stopped," he wrote. "It benefits only those few organizations that are pillaging the domain name system. It takes millions of good names off the system, and makes them unavailable for the purposes for which those names were originally intended." Parsons said Go Daddy neither permitted tasting by its customers nor tasted itself.

Go Daddy even raised concerns about the activity when it filed documents with the Securities and Exchange Commission as part of a plan to go public in 2006 (a plan it later canceled). "If domain name tasting and monetizing or other market practices that could develop significantly diminish the number of available domain names that are perceived as valuable, it could have an adverse effect on our domain name registration revenue and our overall business," it warned.

Domain tasters evaluate names that have never been registered, as well as names that have just expired. To decide what to taste, many use computer programs to automatically generate huge lists of unclaimed names. Registrars that have participated in tasting include Belgiumdomains, Capitoldomains, and Domaindoorman (all part of the same Miami company); Dotster; Oversee.net's NameKing.com; and Intercosmos Media Group. Solares, the CEO of Intercosmos, said the company stopped offering tasting because "it caused too many headaches." Intercosmos had tasted for itself and offered the opportunity to clients. On at least one occasion in 2006, the company erred, and failed to return to VeriSign unwanted names within the five-day grace period. Some industry insiders said it was a major, costly blunder, but Solares brushed it off. "We did not get stuck with a bunch of bad domains," he said. "I am not sure how customers of ours have felt about the ones they got. However, they paid us for all they kept."

Close readings of VeriSign's monthly reports on domain activity reveal which registrars allow extensive tasting. A high ratio of deleted domains to retained domains indicates tasting. Following is a list of the registrars with the highest volume of tasted .com and .net domains from September 2006:

Registrar	Total names on Sept. 30	Names deleted in September
NameKing.com	1,619,672	6,554,531
Belgiumdomains	319,408	5,822,407
Domaindoorman	408,263	5,812,451
Capitoldomains	340,583	5,769,287
Name.net	218,036	2,014,880
ItsYourDomain.com	615,276	1,775,538
Spot Domain	342,110	1,774,635
Name.com	163,849	1,230,831

Interest in tasting has become so intense that speculators taste scores of names that have just been discarded by other tasters. Some names go "through six or seven companies before they're laid to rest," Westerdal said. "It's garbage tasting." Some companies taste a name, let it go, and then taste it again after it flows through other companies. John Berryhill, the domain-dispute lawyer, likens the tasters to dung beetles. "It's like an Eskimo fishing village with a whale," he added. "Every part gets used, there's this whole food chain, and there's nothing left."

Some tasters have gotten away with not paying for even the domains they liked by dropping them after five days and quickly re-registering them, with the cycle then repeating itself again five days later, according to Jonathon Nevett, the Network Solutions executive. Nevett said Network Solutions didn't allow its customers to taste domains. He said the company wasn't opposed to others allowing it; however, it was opposed to the version of tasting in which payment was continually avoided.

In its contract with Icann, VeriSign has a right to charge registrars a penalty for "disproportionate deletes" during the five-day grace period. Some critics have accused the company of supporting tasting because it makes money off the domains that are ultimately kept. VeriSign has said money has nothing to do with, and that it's following the rules approved by Icann. For its part, Icann said it's neutral on the activity, though it facilitated discussions on how to address the issue at several of its international meetings. Some critics claim Icann, like VeriSign, has little incentive to try to stymie the activity because it receives 20 cents for every name ultimately registered.

On his blog, Parsons called for an organized effort to persuade Icann and VeriSign to crack down on the activity. Borrowing an idea from Network Solutions, he said Icann could deter companies from tasting by making non-refundable the Icann fee. The cost would bring the "scheme to a screeching halt," he said.

Network Solutions' Nevett said VeriSign seemed uninterested in taking any action to deter tasting. "Having seen the language in [their] contract, knowing they have very strong language to take action if they wanted to and they've chosen not to, then I think they're at least copasetic with it," he said.

Moniker's Cahn said tasting is fine as long as companies actually pay for the names they keep after five days. He said he offers "VIP" customers the opportunity to taste through his registrar for a small service charge. "If there's an opportunity to help meet my customers' wishes and their need to increase the value of their portfolio, I will do it," he said. "There's now an established market for tasting, and I think that's a good thing, because it invites outside investment to our industry."

Although VeriSign took no action against tasting, registries for a few other domain extensions did. In August 2006, Nominet, the registry for domains ending in .co.uk (for the United Kingdom) restricted the number of names registrars could cancel to five per month or 5 percent of the total monthly registrations, whichever is smaller.[16] Public Interest Registry, a non-profit organization that runs .org, won approval from Icann in 2007 to impose a five-cent surcharge, per domain, for registrars deleting more than 90 percent of their registrations in a given month.

Tasting was just one of many unseemly practices that had been allowed to proliferate as a result of lenient regulation of the domain-name system. Another had been when domain speculators paid registrars to get preferential access to acquiring expired domains, to the detriment of average Internet users. Icann had been set up to reflect the interests of all Internet users, and to develop policies from the bottom up. While the intentions were noble, a bureaucracy emerged that was slow to respond to innovations that had potentially negative consequences for the broader Web community. Also, Icann couldn't make key policy changes unless its major constituents came forward with proposals. Some of the major constituents—notably registrars—were the entities that needed to be policed. Thus, there was less likelihood of action than if Icann had been an independent regulator. In some ways, the system wasn't all that different from the chaotic environment that characterized the early days of name registration under Network Solutions. And speaking of chaotic . . .

Chapter Eight

Shenanigans in Cyberspace

In May 2006, Neiman Marcus, a century-old, high-end retailer, filed a federal lawsuit accusing a company of massive cybersquatting. Usually, such cases don't generate many headlines, even in the technology press, because they're relatively common. But this case stood out because the defendant was atypical. It wasn't an obscure speculator. It was Dotster, one of the biggest domain-name registrars.

The case, which Dotster eventually settled, offered insight into the seedier side of the domain market, where companies eager to bolster profits cross legal and ethical lines. The case also underlined the difficulties the industry faces in trying to revamp its image. Domain investors hate the term "cybersquatters," and are correct to say that the term is often used unfairly to label all of them. But when the industry's seemingly reputable players collect scores of domains associated with well-known trademarks, as Dotster and others have done, it punctures the industry's credibility.

Dotster, based in Vancouver, Washington, began registering Web addresses for customers in January 2000, soon after Icann opened the registration business to competition. Its heritage was unusual. Columbia Analytical Services, an employee-owned operator of environmental-testing laboratories based in Kelso, Washington, created the registrar in an effort to diversify its revenue. The idea came from a twenty-two-year-old engineer, George DeCarlo, who was tapped as Dotster's general manager.

In December 2004, Baker Capital, a New York private-equity firm with more than $1 billion under management, bought Dotster from Columbia Analytical Services for an undisclosed price. Kevin Kilroy, a partner in Baker Capital and a former Hewlett-Packard executive, became Dotster's chairman. Flush with money from its new owner, Dotster began snapping up other registrars. It bought about ten in one year. But it also sought to increase its profits by building its own domain portfolio, just as other registrars were doing.

Some Dotster executives liked the idea of trying "tasting" as a way to identify valuable names to enhance the portfolio, according to people familiar with the company. In the second half of 2005, Dotster built an automated system to rapidly identify unregistered domains and test their ad-revenue potential, the company's CEO, Clint Page, said later in court filings. Dotster began tasting thousands of names. (For more on tasting and how it works, see Chapter Seven.) It picked names to test by looking at data showing which names Web users typed into their browsers to find relevant information. Such data can be gleaned from a number of sources, though it can raise privacy concerns. Google, for instance, says it doesn't study its users' type-in behavior because of privacy issues.

Dotster decided to engage in tasting "because companies have been devoting ever-greater percentages of their advertising and marketing budgets to online advertising," Page said in a court filing. Dotster's portfolio grew to several hundred thousand Web addresses.[1]

Dotster alerted its employees when it began tasting, Linette Ueltschi, then a Dotster customer-care specialist, said later in sworn statements in federal court. From at least the second half of 2005 until March 2006, the company didn't list any Whois information in its public Whois computer server for any of the names it registered through tasting, which is a violation of Icann rules, she said. Dotster instructed Ueltschi and other customer-care specialists to tell any third party that inquired about a name that it was registered to a "Dotster customer," she said in her court declaration, "even though both Dotster and I knew that the domain name was owned by Dotster." In late 2005 or early 2006, Dotster instructed customer-care specialists to start telling such third parties that the name was registered to a "Dotster affiliate," she said. Dotster also told employees to advise third parties that, thanks to a computer glitch, it couldn't provide Whois information. Ueltschi, who worked for Dotster for three years, was fired in March 2006, according to her statements.

Dotster fixed the Whois problem, by and large, by March 16, 2006, Page said in a court filing.

The company took precautions to avoid registering names corresponding to third-party trademarks or clear misspellings of such trademarks. Before it tasted a list of names, Dotster compared them to a "blacklist" of nearly 23,000 domains reflecting trademarks. "If a blacklist domain match was found," Page said in court documents, it "would be excluded from tasting." Dotster also assigned employees to review the list of names it had decided to keep after a tasting exercise, and discard any problematic addresses. However, "the process was not as effective as it should have been," due to "the volume of names and the time in which the employees had to complete their review," Page said.

In late 2005, David J. Steele, an intellectual-property lawyer in Newport Beach, California, was monitoring the registrations of domains associated with his clients, including Neiman Marcus. Steele, who was in his late thirties and worked for Christie, Parker & Hale, had a lot of experience in domain-name law. He also had computer skills that made it easier for him to track the activities of speculators than it was for other lawyers. Steele earned a bachelor's degree in electrical and computer engineering from California State Polytechnic University, and developed high-speed computer networks for about eight years before attending Loyola Law School in Los Angeles.

Steele noticed that neimanmarqus.com was registered on Nov. 11, 2005, but the Whois information didn't list the owner. Dotster was the registrar.

Steele sent Dotster an e-mail on Jan. 21, 2006, informing the company that at no time since neimanmarqus.com was registered had Whois data been listed for it. He asked the company to provide him with the Whois data and to tell him whether or not Dotster had a contract with a registrant for the name. And he said the registration of the name infringed the trademark rights of his client, Neiman Marcus. Dotster, coincidentally, also was the registrar Neiman Marcus used for its domains.

Ravi Puri, Dotster's legal counsel, said in a reply the next day that Dotster was the registrar—"not the registrant"—for the name. He said the company was disabling the site. He also said it would be happy to delete the name from its database or move it into an account for Neiman Marcus to manage.

Steele suspected Dotster was actually the owner. After his e-mail exchange with Puri, Steele found other domains that lacked Whois information and appeared to be registered by Dotster. Failing to list Whois information violated Dotster's registrar agreement with Icann. Steele also suspected Dotster tasted. In his office, he ran his own system of computers and custom software that allowed him to flag recent registrations of domains associated with his clients' trademarks and other companies' marks. It helped him build cases against Dotster and others.

In 2006, Steele noticed that many of the names that it appeared Dotster had registered pointed to sites filled with ads, as well a link that users could click to inquire about purchasing the name. When an investigator working for Steele's firm inquired about bergmangoodman.com, the investigator received a response by e-mail from Scott Fish, a Dotster employee. "This domain is available for $1,000 USD," Fish wrote. "It gets a good amount of traffic right now, and would be a great domain to brand."

"$1,000?" replied the potential buyer. "Really? Would you take $500 for it?"

The two sides settled on a final price of $800, and the name was transferred to the investigator. Payment was accepted at a Paypal account with the user name domains@revenuedirect.com. RevenueDirect is part of Dotster.

When he sold the name, Fish wasn't familiar with Bergdorf Goodman, which has a single luxury store in New York and a Web site, he said later in court documents. He didn't know the domain might infringe on a trademark; otherwise, he said, he wouldn't have offered it for sale.

Neiman Marcus and Bergdorf Goodman sued Dotster in federal court in Tacoma, Washington, on May 30, 2006, accusing it of violating the Anticybersquatting Consumer Protection Act, as well as trademark infringement, dilution, and unfair and deceptive trade practices. The companies sought an injunction to bar Dotster from continuing the activity, as well as statutory damages of $100,000 per domain and other financial damages.

In the suit, Neiman Marcus listed several dozen domains it alleged Dotster had acquired through tasting, and from which it was trying to earn ad revenue. The names included nelmanmarcus.com, neimanmarcuse.com, niumanmarcus.com, and borgdorfgoodman.com. No Whois information was listed for the domains. The complaint accused Dotster of trademark infringement because the sites displayed pay-per-click ads or pop-up ads for goods that competed with those sold by Neiman Marcus and Bergdorf Goodman.

Attached to the suit were exhibits listing roughly one thousand other Web addresses Dotster had registered that closely resembled the trademarks of other major corporations, including Walt Disney, Google, Yahoo, Verizon, and Wal-Mart. The names included disneychanne4l.com, google-eath.com, and walmartcds.com.

The case shed new light on the domain industry. "It's not just any cybersquatter, it's a registrar, which is a problem," said Ann Ford, an intellectual-property lawyer with DLA Piper in Washington, D.C.[2]

Shortly after receiving the suit, Dotster took down the sites and halted its domain-tasting program. It conducted a manual review of its portfolio and stopped displaying ads on sites that were likely to be confused with the trademarks of other companies. It also hired an outside company to evaluate its portfolio for possible trademark infringement. And it introduced new policies to filter names entering its portfolio.

Satisfied that it had the proper controls in place, Dotster resumed tasting in late July 2006, even as the lawsuit was pending.

In the ensuing months, Steele continued to find cases of Dotster registering names corresponding to trademarks of large companies. The addresses included unitediar.com, toyotasoutheast.com, playboymanshen.com, and ballyhealthspa.com. The defendants are "serial cybersquatters," Neiman Marcus said in a court filing. Dotster used its position of trust as a registrar "to conceal its unlawful activities," it said.

Dotster voluntarily stopped tasting in early November 2006, and has no plans to resume the activity, Page said in a court filing. The controls it had implemented weren't "satisfactory," he said.

The companies settled the lawsuit in March 2007. Dotster paid Neiman Marcus an undisclosed sum of money and agreed to a permanent injunction barring it from registering domains corresponding to Neiman Marcus and Bergdorf Goodman trademarks.

Several other federal lawsuits were filed against domain tasters in the wake of the Dotster suit. In August 2006, Wilmington Trust sued Chesterton Holdings, a California firm that had registered names associated with the financial-services company's trademarks. Wilmington Trust voluntarily dismissed the case after Chesterton Holdings transferred the names to the company. But even after the suit was withdrawn, Chesterton kept registering versions of its trademarks using automated tasting programs. The parties resolved those disputes out of court. "They have very sophisticated software, they just can't seem to program it correctly so it stops registering my client's domain names," said Camille Miller, an intellectual-property lawyer with the Philadelphia office of Cozen & Connor, which represents Wilmington Trust. "They must register five of ours a week. It is actually very annoying."

Chesterton Holdings tasted names through the registrar NameKing.com, owned by Oversee.net, one of the major companies in the industry and the parent of DomainSponsor. Josh Armstrong, general counsel for Oversee.net, confirmed in an interview that an employee of Oversee.net also was a manager at Chesterton Holdings. Oversee itself has a checkered legal past. It has been sued several times for trademark infringement by companies including Dell Computer and UnitedHealth Group; in those two cases, consent judgments were entered in favor of the plaintiffs.

In March 2007, Microsoft sued Maltuzi, a prolific domain taster based in Mountain View, California, for alleged cybersquatting. Maltuzi had registered more than 450 domains that were typographical variations of Microsoft products. Like Chesterton Holdings, the obscure Maltuzi had tasted with the consent of Oversee.net's NameKing.com. When asked if any employees of Oversee.net also worked for Maltuzi, Armstrong refused to comment. Microsoft and Maltuzi later reached an out-of-court settlement.

Dotster and the others are hardly alone in having registered many names corresponding to major corporate trademarks. Many domain investors own either misspellings of corporate trademarks, known as typosquatting, or correctly spelled variations of corporate names or brands.

Typosquatting is common because correctly spelled monikers are often already registered by corporations. Also, there are virtually an infinite number of typographical possibilities typosquatters can try to exploit. Typosquatting has been around for years. In 2000, Yahoo wrested 37 names from a typosquatting clan in an arbitration case. In 2004, a federal judge sentenced John Zuccarini, a notorious Florida typosquatter, to thirty months in prison on charges that he used misleading domains to deceive children into looking at pornography. Zuccarini earned as much as $1 million annually from his 8,000 addresses, which included bobthebiulder.com and dinseyland. com—misspellings of popular children's sites.[3]

At least a half-dozen Web sites offer a "typo tool" or "misspelling generator," enabling users to type in a correctly spelled term or Web address, such as "bankofamerica.com," and see a long list of typographical variations of the name. Some domain investors then try to acquire such names.

There are thousands of variations of some corporate names, and in many cases a large percentage is owned not by the trademark holder but by a typosquatter. For years, a number of big companies have tried to make "defensive registrations," snapping up hundreds of variations, including negative terms like DellComputersSuck.com. But the growing number of domain extensions—there are more than 240 worldwide—and the creativity of cybersquatters makes it tough to keep up, trademark holders say. "A corporation at this point is in a hopeless situation," said Sarah Deutsch, a lawyer with phone giant Verizon Communications. "The use of the hyphen, for example, introduces so many variations."

Typosquatting can be quite lucrative, according to domain speculators. Some names generate thousands of dollars a month in pay-per-click ad revenue. Why? Because some consumers make typographical errors when entering a corporate name into the address bar of their browser. In such cases, they will see a list of ads. If one of the advertisers listed is a company they're trying to reach, they'll often click on that ad to get to the advertiser's site.

Mixing It Up

Some of the biggest and most successful domain speculators have owned a mix of generic names and names that resemble the trademarks of corporations.

One is Anthony Peppler, the Indiana investor who grabbed many names in the expired-name market. "I walked on both sides," he told me.

Peppler has owned such names as datingtips.com and jobrecruiting.com. He also paid $15,000 for carryon.com, and said he is pumping money into its development as a child-safety portal. But Peppler has been embroiled in numerous legal battles and is emblematic of investors who have given the industry a negative reputation. In 2002, Syracuse University sued Peppler and his company, Realtime Internet, in federal court for registering syracuseuniversity.com. The site displayed a logo for the university with "TM" beside it, suggesting it was the university's trademark.[4] Peppler and his company agreed in a court-approved settlement to surrender the name to the university and to pay it $20,000 in attorneys' fees and statutory damages. He also settled a federal lawsuit with Remax, the real-estate company. Peppler has also lost a number of arbitration cases under Icann's dispute policy, requiring him to forfeit such names as linennthings.com, aolmediaplayer.com, mapquesst.com, and albertamotorassociation.com.

In 2007, Microsoft sued Peppler and companies he was affiliated with in an Indiana federal court, alleging cybersquatting and trademark infringement. The company said the defendants owned or once owned at least 95 domains that were variations of Microsoft trademarks, including microsoftoffice2000.com, outlookexpress.com, microsoftmoney.com, and hotmailpassport.com. The parties later reached a settlement that included a permanent injunction barring Peppler and the other defendants from registering or using any domains that are identical or confusingly similar to Microsoft's trademarks.

Peppler said that when companies contact him to tell him he has registered a name that infringes on their trademark, he usually simply transfers the name. Peppler said that what upsets him is that he has lost several arbitration cases over generic domains. "To me, this is railroading," he said. "It's unfair."

One of the most troubling cases, Peppler said, involved militarylife.com. Downey Communications, the publisher of a magazine called Military Lifestyles, filed a complaint under Icann's dispute-resolution policy against Modern Limited, a Peppler-run company, in April 2004. Peppler registered the address on May 30, 2002, according to a copy of the complaint. He displayed advertising links on the site for military products and services. Downey Communications said it began using the "Military Life" trademark on Oct. 9, 2002 on its Web site, MilitaryLifestyle.com—nearly six months after Peppler registered his address. Downey contended that militarylife.com was confusingly similar to its existing trademark for Military Lifestyle, as well as its pending "Military Life" mark. It also said Peppler's company had been the "subject of numerous Icann complaints" regarding "the questionable registration" of more than 2,200 domains that look similar to well-known trademarks and names.

Peppler's lawyer, Ari Goldberger, argued that Downey's action was "a case of blatant reverse domain name hijacking," according to the arbitration panel's ruling. Goldberger said Downey failed to mention that prior to filing its complaint, the U.S. Patent and Trademark Office had made a final decision to refuse to register "Military Life" as a trademark. "The PTO's refusal to register the mark flies smack in the face of complainant's allegation that the mark 'Military Life' is 'inherently distinctive' and 'entitled to the maximum level of protection afforded to any trademark,'" Goldberger wrote.

Two of the three panelists ruled in Downey's favor, awarding it the domain in June 2004. The dissenting panelist, Diane Cabell, a director of the Berkman Center for Internet & Society at Harvard Law School, wrote that Downey had failed to show that Peppler used the domain in bad faith because it hadn't used "Military Life" in commerce until after Peppler registered the name. "The fact that [Peppler's company] has, as part of its extensive domain registration enterprise, occasionally registered names that are similar to other marks, does not mean that all of the 2,200 registrations are acts of cybersquatting," Cabell wrote. "Each registration must be assessed on its own merits. Because almost every common word in the English language forms a part of some trademark registration, it is difficult not to use terms that appear in someone else's mark."

Some domain investors and legal experts say the UDRP process has been biased in favor of trademark holders ever since it began. More than 80 percent of cases are won by the challenger. Some experts say that's to be expected, because companies tend to file cases they're likely to win.

Shadowy Movements

Cases of alleged cybersquatting appear to be on the rise. The number of domain disputes filed with the World Intellectual Property Organization, which arbitrates more than half of the complaints handled under the Icann dispute policy worldwide, rose 25 percent to 1,823 in 2006 from a year earlier.[5] That marked the highest number of complaints since 2000. The National Arbitration Forum in Minneapolis, meanwhile, said its case load grew 21 percent in 2006 from a year earlier.

Trademark holders are concerned about domain tasting, among other recent developments, WIPO said. "While electronic commerce has flourished with the expansion of the Internet, recent developments in the domain name registration system have fostered practices which threaten the interests of trademark owners and cause consumer confusion," said Francis Gurry, WIPO's deputy director general, who oversees its dispute-resolution work."[6]

Cybersquatters use a number of techniques to avoid detection by trademark holders. One way is to provide phony information in Whois records. That's against Icann rules, but enforcement by registrars is lax, in part because it requires a lot of resources. Another way is to use a Whois privacy service. The services allow domain registrants, for a few dollars a year, to keep their personal information from being listed publicly in the Whois database. It's similar to paying to keep one's phone number out of the phonebook. Proponents of Whois privacy services say they help Web-site owners avoid spam and other unwanted communications, such as an unannounced visit at a home or business. In addition, some companies like to shield their domain registrations to keep competitors from learning of a planned business strategy. Some trademark holders have had to file lawsuits and obtain subpoenas in order to learn the identity of a domain owner.

Another common technique of cybersquatters is to incorporate in a foreign jurisdiction or to reside offshore. That can make it more difficult for trademark lawyers to locate a cybersquatter and win a lawsuit. For instance, if a company can't establish personal jurisdiction in the U.S. for a cybersquatter, it can't win financial damages in a suit under the federal anticybersquatting law, though it can win rights to the domains.

Faced with arbitration cases filed under the Icann procedure, some cybersquatters never respond, presumably because if they e-mailed a response it could make it easier for trademark holders to trace their whereabouts and ascertain their behaviors. Also, they'd have to pay a lawyer if they tried to fight each case.

No one really knows how much money major cybersquatters make, though industry insiders say there are cybersquatters making millions. "It must be a good business model, because so many people are doing it for a reason," said Camille Miller, the lawyer who represents Wilmington Trust.

Embarrassing Situations

When public companies and buyout firms began pouring investments into domains, they all sought to improve the image of the market. All said, for example, that they would take steps to make sure their portfolios contained no trademark-protected names. Many also tried to avoid owning adult-oriented names, believing it might appear unseemly.

The mere presence of the bluebloods improved the industry's image. However, some of the companies acquired domains related to trademarks, raising questions about their business ethics and making them vulnerable to high-profile lawsuits. The actions also tarnished the industry's reputation yet again.

One offender was iREIT. The Houston company rapidly acquired dozens of portfolios of smaller investors. When doing an acquisition, the company said its general practice—and the practice often used by its peers—was to eliminate from the deal any names that carried potential legal risks.

In a January 2007 e-mail interview, Bob Martin, then iREIT's CEO, said, "We take a very strict policy against holding . . . potentially legally sensitive assets in our portfolio. While we are not able to review all of the 400,000-plus domains that we have purchased, we use a combination of techniques to filter our portfolio."

A month later, however, I analyzed a list of addresses owned by iREIT, using a simple spreadsheet program, and found that thousands corresponded to trademarks of major corporations. I checked dozens of the sites to see whether they were active, and all displayed pay-per-click ads for products or services related to the names. More than thirty addresses were Google-related typos, such as googiearth.com and googlrmaps.com. iREIT also held several typos of Starbucks, such as starbuckds.com and starbuckscofee.com. Howard Schultz, the chairman of Starbucks, was the co-founder of Maveron LLC, one of iREIT's major investors. And Dan Levitan, also co-founder of Maveron, was on iREIT's board.

According to Whois records, iREIT had owned many of its trademark-related names for only a few weeks. However, it had owned some for months. For example, ebayinc.com, which mirrored the corporate name eBay Inc., had been in its portfolio for at least ten months. The site displayed ads related to auction sites, including eBay. iREIT deactivated the sites after I listed them on my blog. In a phone interview, Martin said the company was still refining its system of identifying "legally sensitive" domains and purging them. "We know that typos of domains that are potentially legally sensitive are not something that have lasting value," he said. Martin added, "This is definitely a challenge the industry faces in a major way." iREIT's president, Craig Snyder, who joined Martin in the interview, said the company planned to expand a relationship with a partner that had recently helped it eliminate a significant number of potentially problematic addresses. It also was developing internal screening tools.

"We are confident that in a short time, we'll have a good handle on these issues," Martin said. "I'll never say we're going to be 100 percent perfect."

I contacted several of iREIT's directors for comment. Steve Blasnik, the president of Perot Investments, the investment firm affiliated with former presidential candidate Ross Perot, politely declined, saying he typically doesn't do interviews. Maveron's Levitan didn't respond to inquiries by e-mail and phone.

In March 2007, just a few weeks after my blog entry exposed iREIT's practices, Verizon sued the company in federal court, accusing it of massive cybersquatting and trademark infringement. The suit, filed in iREIT's hometown of Houston, charged the company with operating more than ninety domains that were typographical variations of Verizon's trademarks, such as verizonwirelessgames.com, virizonpcs.com, and verizonwirelessreabates.com. Verizon said iREIT displayed pay-per-click ads on the sites for various products competing with Verizon's. The suit also claimed iREIT operated thousands of other domains corresponding to other companies' trademarks, including bankofanmerica.com, disnelyland.com, and ebayonlineauctions.com. The suit also claimed iREIT intentionally provided "material and misleading false contact information" when registering some of its names.

The case was a big embarrassment for iREIT. Martin soon left the company and was replaced as CEO by Snyder. "I think the board felt, and he probably felt, that it was better to have somebody else run the company long-term," Snyder told me months later. The trademark problem, as well as the company's ownership of adult-oriented domains, were key factors in Martin's departure, said Snyder. Owning such names "is incongruous" with the goal of the company and its major financial backers to one day cash in on their investment through an initial public stock offering, Snyder said, noting that Wall Street wouldn't look favorably on a portfolio with legal problems and sex-oriented names. iREIT also left the Internet Commerce Association, a group Martin had helped create. The Washington, D.C.-based group, founded in 2006, lobbied for the interests of domain investors in Washington and within Icann. Its code of conduct, adopted in 2007, requires members to "follow accepted trademark law and respect the brands and trademarks of others." Martin resigned as the group's president in 2007.

Snyder worked on cleaning up iREIT's portfolio, focusing on generic names. "It has come a long, long way in becoming the best portfolio it can be," he told me.

Verizon and iREIT settled the lawsuit in late 2007. iREIT paid Verizon an undisclosed fee and agreed to a permanent injunction barring iREIT from registering or using any domain that is identical or confusingly similar to Verizon's trademarks.

I also discovered that Marchex, the Seattle-based public company, owned and was displaying pay-per-click ads on some names related to trademarks, such as ibestbuy.com, chasemortgagega.com, and carnivalsinglescruises. com. The company had acquired the addresses when it purchased Yun Ye's portfolio in 2005. When I pointed out the names to Marchex in late 2006, it deactivated them. "Thanks for bringing these domains to our attention," Ethan Caldwell, general counsel, wrote in an e-mail. "Marchex continues to review and analyze domain names it purchased in bulk for the express purpose of identifying and subsequently eliminating any which do not fit into our long-term strategy. The domains you have identified do not fit into our core strategy of building sites from domains which are either commercially descriptive or have generic characteristics which enable Marchex to build highly relevant, useful, and compelling content."

Caldwell also said the addresses were part of a dispute with a "third party." He said he was unable to elaborate. But in a filing with the Securities and Exchange Commission, Marchex disclosed that it was in a dispute with Ye's Name Development "over potentially trademark-infringing domains." Pending the dispute, an escrow agent was "holding the balance" of the $25 million in cash that Marchex had placed into escrow in connection with its purchase of Ye's domains. Marchex said the money would remain in escrow until a determination was made as to whether Name Development had to pay anything to Marchex to indemnify it for legal liabilities. The $25 million represented about 15 percent of the total price of about $164 million paid for Ye's portfolio.

In 2007, Name Development and Marchex reached an accord. Name Development agreed to return to Marchex 250,000 shares of its Class B stock, worth about $5 million at the time of the 2005 sale, and Marchex released the rest of the balance in escrow.

When Marchex purchased Ye's list, it also acquired many pornographic names, such as adult-sex-fetishpics.com and adultxxxgalleries.com. It sold most of them within eighteen months because it didn't want to own such names, Caldwell said. Many were purchased by Grant Media LLC, a San Francisco-based adult company run by Gary Kremen, the former owner of sex.com. Caldwell declined to say how much money the sales generated.

Google and Yahoo: Co-conspirators?

Critics contend Google and Yahoo encourage cybersquatting, and benefit from it, because ads they sell appear on many Web addresses corresponding to trademarks. Google counters that it removes sites from its advertising network if the trademark holder contacts it. Yahoo says it proactively removes sites as soon as it learns about them, even if isn't contacted by the trademark holder.

Critics say the companies and their partners—such as domain-parking services—aren't doing enough to screen such sites, which proliferate on the Web. "It's hard to reconcile Google's support of this activity with their 'Do No Evil' motto," said Ben Edelman, an assistant professor at Harvard Business School who's done extensive research on cybersquatting.

In response, a Google spokesman said in an e-mail: "It's difficult to create an automated technology to determine what is and is not trademarked, so we rely on the trademark holder to let us know."

It's unknown how much of the pay-per-click ad revenue in the domain market comes from sites related to trademarks. For analysts, hazarding an estimate is filled with pitfalls. First, it's tough to measure which names clearly are trademark-protected. Second, domain holders and ad companies rarely share much information about the revenue of individual domains, which would be necessary to calculate an estimate.

Some marketers wary of the parked-domain channel say much of their concern stems from having their ads appear on typosquatters' sites. "Click fraud, typosquatters, domain kiting—those things add up," said Jon Lisbin of Point It, the Seattle search-marketing agency. "A percentage of the domain channel is people who are in it strictly to make a quick buck. They're not really into this to help searchers find information." He added, "I'm not saying I don't like domain parking, I just think it needs to be cleaned up and be more transparent."

Several top executives in the domain market have openly criticized the continued rampant speculation in trademark-protected terms, saying it casts a cloud over the market. "Perhaps the greatest disappointment of 2006 was that despite all the progress we've made and the success we've shared, the domaining community has yet to gain control of their seedy underbelly," Matt Bentley, chief strategy officer at Sedo, the name broker, wrote in a year-end review published on Sedo's Web site. "Despite increasing crackdowns, there are still a frighteningly large number of people choosing to chase the quick and dirty buck via typosquatting, cybersquatting, or click fraud, rather than building a legitimate domain portfolio."[7]

Several individual investors who focus on generic names said the cybersquatters undercut their profit-making opportunities. "If you consider the PPC [pay-per-click] market to be a pie, there's a certain amount of money in that pie, and I'm competing for that," Dan Cera, a successful domain investor in Vancouver, Canada, said during an appearance on *Domain Masters*, an online radio talk show hosted by Monte Cahn of Moniker.com, in September 2006. "Right now I'm competing with guys who are taking shortcuts, who are monetizing typos and monetizing trademarks. That's their business, it's just that I'm not sure that those are the cleanest, purest, nicest forms of traffic, and if I'm competing with those, they're really taking money out of my pocket. So my advice to people would be to have an ethical approach: spend your money on good names."

Cera said domain investors who hope to one day sell their portfolios should steadfastly avoid trademark-related addresses. "If my exit strategy is to sell, I can't really think of any sort of self-respecting organization that's going to want to buy into a pile of potential legal issues," he said. Trademark holders "are catching up with people. And I've been saying for a long time on [a domain forum] and elsewhere that somebody is going to be the Martha Stewart of this industry. And they're going to hang somebody out and make an example of them, and in a good sense I can understand why."

The domain market will always have a dark side. But more industry leaders like Cera and Bentley are speaking out about the problems with cybersquatting. If investors pay heed, the entire market will benefit. Advertisers will feel more comfortable buying ads, and Wall Street will be more eager to invest in domain companies. There likely will be more money to go around. It's something for newcomers to think about as they weigh their leap into the market.

Chapter Nine

The Future

Is it too late to invest in domain names?

Let me twist around that question for a moment. Is it too late to invest in real estate? Stocks?

You can probably guess my answer. No, it's not too late. Some people think it's too late because they think of domains as one-time buys—that if you failed to register a name when it was first available at a registrar's Web site, you missed out. But that's not the case. There's a growing secondary market for Web addresses, where investors buy, sell, and, in some cases, swap names. Some investors are buying domains and flipping them a few months later for a nice profit.

Wherever there's a marketplace, there are opportunities to exploit differences in opinions about the value of the assets for sale. Plus, the domain market is still in its infancy, just like the World Wide Web. Domains are expected to appreciate in value over time as more people use the Web and do business on it. The number of Internet users will grow to 1.8 billion worldwide in 2010, up from about 1.2 billion, or roughly a sixth of the world's population, in 2006, according to the Computer Industry Almanac. Every new business that wants to operate on the Internet must start with a domain.

It's important to point out some caveats. The domain market, though still immature, is much different than it was when Scott Day entered it. And it's different than when Frank Schilling jumped in. In short, acquiring high-caliber names costs a lot more money than it did five or ten years ago. Keep in mind, too, that investing in domains is generally riskier than investing in other financial markets, such as real estate, stocks, and bonds. Why? Simply put, investment returns are less certain. It's an emerging market, with a relatively short track record. When names have sold, prices have been all over the map. It also can take months or years to find buyers, whereas other markets are much more liquid. On the upside, investors can generate cash flow from their names while they own them, just like in real estate, without costly overhead. Such revenue, of course, can fluctuate with changes in the Internet economy.

In this chapter, I'll explore the fundamentals of today's market, risks that investors should be aware of, and potential strategies for success.

Not Your Older Brother's Domain Market

In little more than a decade of existence, the market has changed dramatically, evolving in tandem with the Internet itself. The market now includes many large, well-heeled players, and most good names are in somebody's hands, instead of sitting at a registrar, waiting to be snagged. But many news articles published during the Internet mania of the late 1990s declared that "all the good names are taken." And yet many investors who didn't own names until two or three years later have done remarkably well. That should give any newcomer reason for optimism.

Some fundamentals from other financial markets apply. One very basic point is that if you have the money, you can buy good properties, just like you can buy oceanfront real estate in California or Florida. Some investors won't sell their names under any circumstances, but many are willing to sell if you offer a fair price. And you don't necessarily have to pay cash. Some companies, such as Fort Lee, New Jersey-based Domain Capital, offer financing to domain buyers. Now, a key difference from years past is it may be more difficult to generate a high return on your investment. As the market matures, it's harder to find names priced at a significant discount to what buyers can earn off them. "More people understand the value so people won't let their names go so inexpensively," said California investor Howard Hoffman. "A couple of years ago I could buy domains from other people relatively inexpensively. It's very hard to do now."

Heightened media coverage has played a part in that. There are now even magazines devoted to the market, including Modern Domainer and Domainer's Magazine, along with at least a dozen blogs, such as Domain Name News, Domain Name Wire and the Daily Domainer.

Newcomers need not buy so-called premium domains. Plenty of names change hands for a few hundred or a few thousand dollars. Domain brokers estimate that the median sales price in the secondary market is about $1,000. Investors also can still find some decent never-before-registered names, and pay only the registration price of less than $10 a year. The barrier to entry in domain investing remains relatively low.

One example of success in small numbers: Andrew Allemann, who was involved in the formation of iREIT and runs Domain Name Wire, bought decay.com in May 2006 on the registrar Go Daddy's auction site for $2,000. About two months later, he sold it on Afternic.com, another domain marketplace, for $2,900, giving him a nifty profit. But the person who bought it from him did even better five months later, selling it for $12,000 through Moniker.com.

Allemann also sold blogs.info for $6,000 in 2006, double the price he paid for it a year earlier.

What Should You Buy?

Every kind of investment comes with some degree of risk. If you buy a blue-chip stock like IBM, you're taking a risk. IBM is a stable, highly successful company, but fierce competition or poor management could prompt its profit growth to slow, causing its shares to decline. On the other hand, buying IBM stock comes with much less risk than buying the stock of a company that trades over the counter (instead of on a major stock exchange) for a few pennies a share and has never turned a profit.

Such variations of risk exist in the domain market. Buying a name ending in .com is generally less risky than buying one ending in another extension, such as .net or .info. Many successful domain investors stick almost exclusively to .com addresses. The .com extension has easily been the most popular choice of domain owners and Web users since the explosion of the Web. It has become ingrained in the American culture, and in many other cultures as well. Dot-com addresses have long been advertised on billboards and on television. When guessing at a Web address, most users try the .com version first. Dot-com names also have the best track record of being resold and of generating revenue from ads and e-commerce sales.

If you're interested in investing in domains and want to mitigate your risk, choose names ending in .com. If you focus on other extensions, earning a return on your investment is less certain.

That point was made on a panel at the Traffic East domain-industry trade show in Florida in the fall of 2006. Panelists were asked to explain how they would invest $100,000 in the market. Most said they would focus on .com addresses. "Dot-com is really where it's at," said Brian Taff, vice president of corporate development at NameMedia. "And it's going to be where it's at. My recommendation is to buy a Picasso—a $100,000 .com—or buy one hundred [addresses for $1,000 each], but don't buy them in dot-whatever. Buy them in .com."

If you're willing to accept more risk, you should explore alternative extensions. Risk and reward go hand in hand. A successful investment in a name ending in an alternative extension might generate a greater return than an investment in a .com name, since the .com market is more mature and bargains are harder to come by. Risk tolerance in domains is similar to risk tolerance in stocks, according to Tim Schumacher, co-founder of Sedo, the domain broker. Some investors favor stocks in new, unproven industries because they see greater potential for growth, as opposed to buying stocks in stable, slow-growth industries.

Some domain investors, using that line of reasoning, are pouring money into alternative extensions. The names are also cheaper than .com names. Others believe buying a few names in the other extensions is a prudent way to diversify their holdings, knowing that other extensions could become major thoroughfares as the Web expands. Some favor .de, Germany's extension, because the country has a vibrant Web economy. The .de suffix has become the second-most popular in the world after .com. To register a .de name, you must have an address in Germany.

When Ron Jackson, the publisher of DNJournal.com, began investing in domains in the spring of 2002, he stayed away from .com addresses because they were more expensive than others and the competition was fierce. "I could sense there were people who knew the business much better than I did and were much better financed than I was," said Jackson, "so I felt like I would get killed if I went in and tried to go head to head with these people. I didn't feel like I had the resources or the knowledge and experience at that time. But I did see an opportunity in new extensions. So I started buying them up like crazy with virtually no competition."

He built a profitable portfolio composed primarily of domains ending in .us (for the United States) or .info. He routinely sells names for $2,000 to $4,000 that he acquired for less than $100. For instance, he sold lend.us in October 2006 for $7,000, after buying it for less than $50.

It's not clear that the .us and .info extensions will be popular with Web users over the long run. One downside is many of the people registering such names are domain speculators, rather than businesses building full-fledged sites, which is essential to the extensions becoming more prominent in the eyes of Internet users. But some observers believe having a very good generic name ending in a less-popular extension will be superior in the long run to owning a mediocre generic name ending in .com. You may be able to sell the domain to a business that would like to have an easy-to-remember address it could use to market itself.

Jackson, a former television sports reporter, based his domain strategy in part on his media experience. In his days in radio, he saw the FM band go from nowhere to being as popular as AM. Jackson, who lives in Tampa, Florida, has 7,000 domains. He makes what he calls healthy returns from his portfolio. After struggling his first five months as a speculator, he began to rack up sales, and his portfolio became profitable in the fall of 2004, about two and a half years after he started.

Domains ending in .com account for nearly half of all addresses registered worldwide. Here's how other extensions stacked up to .com as of September 2006:

Extension	Registrations
.com	57,288,638
.de (Germany)	10,116,244
.net	8,259,567
.co.uk (United Kingdom)	5,296,911
.org	5,110,297
.info	3,559,469
.eu (European Union)	2,152,500
.nl (Netherlands)	2,045,027
.biz	1,491,461
.it (Italy)	1,247,891

SOURCE: Zooknic.com

A number of names ending in .net, which has long played second fiddle to .com among generic top-level domains, have sold in the six figures. In 2006, sex.net fetched $454,500, mortgage.net $149,000, and creditcards. net $118,500.

Now, if you've read the previous eight chapters, it almost goes without saying that, no matter what extension you choose, a good rule of thumb is to focus on generic, commercially relevant words. Category names such as "shoes," "computers," and "cameras," are ideal, if you can get them.

Too many investors buy gaudy or cutesy names. Scarcely a month goes by without a press release from someone declaring that they're selling hundreds of names all containing a phrase along the lines of "buy4less" or "liveontheWeb." Rarely do such names attract buyers, and certainly not at desirable prices. There are an unknown, but presumably large, number of investors sitting on money-losing portfolios filled with such names. Not all virtual real estate is such good real estate. Just like in the physical world, there are plenty of vacant properties that lie dormant for years, unable to attract interest.

Besides names that are too clever for their own good, you also should generally avoid buying names with hyphens (most Web users don't think of typing a hyphen) or numbers. And don't register names associated with the trademarks of companies. If you do, you could face some very expensive legal bills. To ascertain whether a trademark is associated with a name you're considering, do a search on the Web site of the U.S. Patent & Trademark Office. That's not foolproof, however. Some businesses have been awarded trademark rights by a state. Others have gained common-law rights to a mark through long use of it in commerce. You should do extensive research to minimize your legal risks.

Where do new opportunities lie?

One area to consider is geographic-oriented names, such as houstonlawyers. com or chicagoplumbers.com. As discussed in Chapter Six, analysts expect that "local search" will be a key growth area within Web advertising in the next few years. More and more Web users are searching for local information online, rather than sifting through dense phonebooks. And that's prompting more small businesses to buy Web ads. Companies like Marchex, which is focused on the local search market, have been sweeping up such names. But many can still be purchased, and they're generally less expensive than other generic terms.

Geosign, a domain-investment business in Canada, paid only $12,000 for both newyorkrestaurants.com and nyrestaurants.com in 2006. Ryan May, a Geosign employee, looked up the Whois record for one of the names, found out it was owned by a man named Michael Allen in New York, and e-mailed him to find out if it was for sale. Allen said he'd received several unsolicited offers over the years, but none approached what Geosign paid. Tim Nye, Geosign's CEO, felt he got a steal. Allen said some of his friends and his associates valued the names at more than $20,000, but "the true measure" was "what Tim was willing to spend." The case shows how it can be difficult for sellers to find buyers, and how there are still good deals to be had for enterprising investors.

Exploiting New Terms and Technologies

A tactic that has long been part of domain investing is keeping an eye on emerging trends and technologies, and acquiring a relevant domain before someone else does. It's perhaps even more important now, because so many names in the English language already have been acquired. Spotting emerging trends and technologies means paying close attention to current events, reading industry trade journals, and not being afraid to spend time talking to just about anyone you meet at a cocktail party.

"There are opportunities that open up every single day of the week," said veteran investor Rick Schwartz.

Andrew Allemann of Domain Name Wire is a big believer in the strategy. For example, he's invested in about one hundred domains related to pre-fabricated housing, or homes that are manufactured off-site. He believes pre-fabricated homes are moving "up market," poised to attract buyers from higher-income brackets in the coming years. He got the idea from reading Dwell magazine, which covers modern residential architecture and design and has showcased prefab houses priced at $500,000 and up.

Allemann, who is in his early thirties, looked at a list of the one hundred largest U.S. cities, attached the word "prefab" to the end of each city's name, and did a search to see which ones were available for the registration price. "Right now, I don't get traffic . . . even one hit a day" on those names," he said. "But I could see a time when that changes."

Allemann, who earns more than $100,000 in profits a year from his one thousand domains, including sales and pay-per-click ad revenue, also bought prefab.us for $800 in 2006. The seller? Ron Jackson of DNJournal.com.

Besides regularly reading Dwell magazine, Allemann subscribes to Wired, the cutting-edge technology magazine. In Wired, he regularly learns about emerging technologies, and registers a few names related to them. He also reads financial publications like the now-defunct Business 2.0, where he learned about bamboo shirts potentially replacing cotton, prompting him to register bambooshorts.com and bambooboxers.com.

"I still think there's a lot of room for people to succeed [as domain investors] at the micro-level," said Allemann. "People who think it's get-rich-quick, that's not going to happen anymore. It's being smart about what you're doing."

Another creative thinker is Jeff Burkey of Rochester, New York. A stockbroker with the online brokerage Scottrade, Burkey specializes in buying and selling domains that might be attractive to hedge funds—loosely regulated investment pools. Hundreds of new hedge funds are created every year, and many want to have a presence online. Burkey, also in his early thirties, buys previously unregistered domains, so his costs are low. His goal is to sell enough names to be able to start his own hedge fund. On his site, HedgeFundDomain. net, he lists more than a dozen addresses for sale, including Aviator Capital and Python Capital, each for $10,000. His first sale, for about $1,000, was optimuscapital.com, acquired by a money-management firm affiliated with a Japanese bank. It wasn't a huge amount of money, but it more than paid for all his domain registrations, the Web-hosting fees for his site, and other expenses. "I know a lot of the names I'm registering will be worthless, but I hope some will go big," he said. "I only need a few to hit [to have good investment returns]. If I sell one for $10,000 or $50,000, that pays for a lot of $10 registrations."

Keep in mind that new words are introduced to languages every day. Those are opportunities for domain investors. For instance, one of the big trends online today is the use of "wikis" to share information. A wiki is a Web site that lets multiple users add and remove content simultaneously. Thus, it's ideal for team projects in the corporate world, academia, and elsewhere. Just a few years ago, only a few people used the term. In late 2006, an entrepreneur reportedly agreed to pay nearly $3 million for wiki.com.

Still a Wild, Wild West

If you're interested in taking a buy-and-sell approach to domain investing, you must be prepared to deal with the market's liquidity problem. Whereas one can easily find buyers for stocks traded on a major exchange, it can be very hard to find buyers for domains. Speculators account for a large chunk of the buyers and sellers. Domain brokers and others are trying to persuade more small businesses and corporations to explore acquiring names in the secondary market. If they succeed, the market will expand and investors will have an easier time peddling their names.

The domain market is often likened to the real-estate market, "but it is a long, long way from real estate because the liquidity is not there," said Ron Jackson of DNJournal.com. Dan Warner, chief strategy officer at Dark Blue Sea, has estimated that only 1 percent to 2 percent of domains change hands each year.

Warner made a key point in an industry whitepaper when he said that a challenge for domain sellers is that many businesses would rather register a new name at Go Daddy for $8.95 than pay $1,000 for one in the aftermarket. Even if the never-before-registered name is less desirable, they figure, they can build a brand with it. "Most consumers do not understand the difference in value between domains until they have a need to improve their brand through a better domain," Warner wrote. So "until they have already established an interest in buying a domain, it is difficult to generate an aftermarket domain sale."

Warner is among those leading a movement to aggregate listings of domains for sale in a central place where buyers could view them all, like the Multiple Listing Service used in American real estate. Otherwise, buyers must look on many different sites that offer domain marketplaces. The system Warner is working on could also lead to much greater data on domain sales, which would make it easier for buyers and sellers to assign a value to a name.

What's the Right Price?

Figuring out what a domain is worth is difficult. Even veteran investors tell me they often go on a hunch when they decide to buy a name, rather than conducting a careful financial analysis. "Gut instinct!" is how Florida investor Sahar Sarid said he typically places a value on a name.

Determining values is challenging for a number of reasons. One is that no two domains are exactly alike, so comparing the price of one sale to another isn't apples to apples. Also, because most domain sales happen in private, there's limited pricing data available to buyers and sellers. Other markets, including real estate and stocks, have much greater transparency and more participants, so the market tends to be efficient in pricing the values of the assets.

How might you try to estimate a fair price for a domain? You could have the name appraised by an independent service. Appraisal services use a variety of factors. For example, Zetetic, an appraiser in Davis, California, measures twenty-eight variables, including whether the name ends in .com or another extension, how many letters the name has, and how many daily unique visitors go to the site. Zetetic also takes into account recent sales activity of other domains. It punches all the numbers into its formula, and spits out an estimate.

The way companies like iREIT, Marchex, and NameMedia price the portfolios and single names they buy from domain owners varies, but some rules of thumb have emerged that you could use as a starting point. In general, names are being purchased for five to twelve times annual revenue. Typically the revenue source is pay-per-click advertising. So, if you own a name that generates $1,000 in annual pay-per-click revenue, you might expect to sell it for $5,000 to $12,000.

Such valuation methods are in flux. As with any market, investors need to do extensive research to keep up with pricing trends. As the market expands, there will be greater transparency about sales, and the market will become more efficient in pricing domains.

Generating Cash Flow

Your chance of success in domain investing depends a lot on what you do with the names you buy. You could just sit on your names and hope a seller comes along. But that's not an ideal strategy. You want to start generating cash flow. Cash flow is how much money you take in, minus your expenses. As the investors described in this book have demonstrated, generating cash flow, rather than simply trying to resell names, is important to building a profitable portfolio. Some investors don't even worry about reselling domains. They buy names based on an estimate of how much they can earn from the names from ads, lead generation, leasing, or other revenue streams.

If you have a smart business idea or excel at generating content that interests other Web users, you might turn an otherwise lackluster domain into a large revenue producer. That's the beauty of Web addresses. They're malleable. You can change them from month to month, or even minute to minute. Unlike investors in physical real estate, you don't need to fret about zoning laws and making pleas to community officials to have your plans approved. You also don't need to worry about leaky water faucets or broken light fixtures. When Demand Media's Richard Rosenblatt had dinner with Frank Schilling in 2005 to discuss the industry, he told him the thing he loves about the domain business is that if you fail at one plan for a name, you can start over. "We get a redo!" he said with glee, Schilling recalled.

A key way to produce cash flow has been pay-per-click ads. But will that continue?

One of the biggest risk factors in the domain market is that Google, Yahoo, and other advertising networks might stop syndicating pay-per-click ads on so-called parked domains because of concerns over click fraud, typosquatting, and questions about the quality of the traffic. But a complete halt to such ads is unlikely, in part because a number of static, ad-laden pages, such as CNET's kids.com, generate good returns for marketers.

As long as marketers pay by the click for online ads, there will be cases of abuse, low-quality traffic, and angry marketers. That goes for all Web sites that derive revenue from pay-per-click ads, not just bare-bones sites. The question is whether this negative side to pay-per-click advertising will become so strong as to overtake the positive aspects. Google, which draws more money from pay-per-click ads than any other company, is well aware of the downsides to the model and has for several years been diversifying its revenue streams. It has explored cost-per-action advertising, for instance, and has also begun selling ads in other media, such as television and radio.

Major changes in Internet advertising driven by Google, Yahoo, Microsoft, and their rivals will have a profound influence on domain owners. Any investor wanting to generate cash flow from ads will need to anticipate and adapt to changes by the big ad brokers. One way to get prepared right now is to think about having more than just ads on your sites. Think of creating content that adds value for Web users.

Investors who pay close attention to the evolution of Internet advertising will be rewarded. Spending on Web ads in the U.S. jumped to a record $21 billion in 2007, according to the Interactive Advertising Bureau. "Offline advertising will all be online sometime in the next ten years," says Microsoft CEO Steve Ballmer. "That means there's going to be huge growth in online advertising."[1]

You should be mindful of new opportunities, such as a start-up that sells ads in a new way. It's not out of the realm of possibility that another Google will form in the next few years, profoundly altering the state of online advertising.

Also, pay close attention to how large brand advertisers change their approach to marketing. Many, including giants Kraft Foods and Pepsi, have been shifting more of their annual advertising spending to the Web from traditional media. Investors who own generic names relevant to a particular industry might be able to strike agreements with brand advertisers to run their ads on the domains, or redirect traffic to the marketers' sites. They also may be able to sell such a name to the advertiser if they can clearly articulate the benefits to ownership. Some domain investors have been frustrated by what they perceive to be ignorance about the importance of Web addresses on Madison Avenue and in corporate America in general. It's true that big corporations have embraced domains at a slow pace. However, the pace now appears to be increasing. Television, radio, and print ads, for instance, often mention a domain associated with the ad campaign. Burger King registered HaveItYourWay.com to promote its motto for selling hamburgers. Campbell Soup registered MySoup.com to offer sweepstakes and online games. American Express registered StopPong.com as part of its sponsorship of tennis star Andy Roddick and the U.S. Open; on the site, users could play a version of the old Atari game Pong.

Domain investors also should consider other ways to produce cash flow besides advertising and redirects. One area to consider is e-commerce, a fast-growing sector. Forrester Research estimates that U.S. online retail sales will rise by more than 50% to $268 billion in 2010 from $175 billion in 2007. Sales rose 21% in 2007 from a year earlier. Some veteran domain investors expect many of today's ad-choked pages to transform over time into e-commerce sites. NetShops, a successful Omaha-based e-commerce company that runs sites such as Hammocks.com, Cribs.com, and GrandfatherClocks.com, demonstrates how commercially relevant, generic domains can be used to sell products.

One of the beauties of e-commerce is that a perfect domain isn't mandatory for success. As a domain name, eBay.com wasn't an instant winner. But as a well-executed business concept, it was.

Creating e-commerce sites clearly requires more time and costs than pointing domains to pay-per-click ads. You're becoming a developer, not merely an investor. The level of risk, therefore, is much greater. However, if the plan is solid and properly executed, it may generate far greater returns over the long term. Marc Ostrofsky invested in Blinds.com, run by a Houston man, Jay Steinfeld, and helped turn it into a thriving seller of window blinds with annual sales of more than $45 million.

Navigation Changes

One risk factor in domain investing is that the way users navigate the Web could change in such a way that domain names diminish in importance. Makers of Internet browsers like Microsoft, for example, could alter browsers to make the address bar less prominent, while emphasizing a search engine or other tool. This could discourage users from typing in a domain to find relevant information, and thereby reduce traffic to sites dependent on type-in traffic. There's also the potential for Microsoft and other computer companies to make even more dramatic changes to computer and Web technology that could curtail type-in traffic. However, most experts don't expect any major changes to Web browsers or computer operating systems in the coming years that would profoundly affect the market. A key reason is that the system has long offered an effective way for users to find new sources of information, and for new businesses to get noticed. Computer companies recognize that. One also must keep in mind that domains have been integral to the successful operation of the Internet for more than twenty years now. There could be certain changes, however, resulting from concerns about Internet security, as a rising tide of cyber-criminals use domains to pull off their scams.

Perhaps a greater risk for investors is that Web users, acting independently, will shun the address bar in favor of search engines. There aren't good data on the percentage of Web users who search for information through the address bar. It's estimated to represent roughly 10 to 15 percent of all search activity. In a 2006 survey by Forrester Research, 38 percent of consumers said typing an address into the computer was one of the ways they'd found Web sites they'd visited in the past month. Vint Cerf, one of the pioneers of the Internet, has said a smaller percentage of people may search by typing in domains as search engines improve.[2] Still, he said, the volume of type-in searches may grow as the number of Web users increases.[3]

Some investors fear the proliferation of ad-loaded pages, which depend on type-in traffic, will prompt Web users to avoid guessing at domains over time. If they can't find what they're looking for on such pages, why go back? This is one reason many in the industry are calling for domain owners to publish not just ads on their sites but also relevant editorial content.

Publishing quality content also will mean that domain owners will be less dependent on type-in traffic in the first place. If you build a content-rich site, you can show up in the organic search listings of Google and other major search engines. That's a terrific way to draw traffic.

What It Will Take

If you decide to invest in domains, don't expect overnight success. Many of the investors described in this book worked tirelessly for years—often working seven days a week—to become successful.

"You have to have drive," said veteran Toronto investor Adam Dicker. "That's what separates individuals in this industry. And you have to be willing to commit quite a bit of time." If you want to make a lot of money in domains, "it's not going to be an eight-hour-a-day job."

Being clever helps, too.

Consider Michael Bahlitzanakis, the New York investor. In 2004, he noticed that prices.com was registered to a big cleaning company in Montreal called Montcalm, which wasn't using it. He cold-called the company and got a senior executive on the line. "I see you're not using this name, and I'd love to buy it," he told her. The executive asked him how much he'd like to pay. He said very calmly, "I think I can muster up $3,800 and wire it you." There was a pause. "You're telling me you are willing to pay $3,800 for it?" the executive said, apparently surprised at what she believed to be a substantial offer. Bahltizanakis kept his cool. The executive had no idea that he was low-balling her—big-time. Her company agreed to the deal, and he wired the money. Prices.com earns several thousand dollars a month in pay-per-click ad revenue, Bahlitzanakis said.

Until more people learn about the domain market and it matures, there will be many more stories like that one.

Where Are They Now?

What does the future hold for Scott Day, Garry Chernoff, Frank Schilling and other big domain investors highlighted in this book?

Many are moving into developing their sites, seeking to make them more valuable to Web users, and more profitable for themselves.

In late 2006, I visited Scott Day and his parents in Terral, Oklahoma. Scott and his father, Frank, showed me the watermelon shed where Scott first registered domains sitting at a dusty desk, using a dial-up Internet connection and an old Macintosh computer. Then Scott drove me out to his parents' house in his pickup truck. Frank followed in his pickup. Upon arrival, I hopped out of Scott's truck and looked back to see where Frank was. He pulled up right behind us. When he stepped out, he had a shotgun in his hands. He immediately lifted it up onto his shoulder and aimed it straight up into a tree. He fired, and a brown squirrel plopped to the ground. Frank grabbed it by the tail and chucked it somewhere.

"Why'd you kill that squirrel?" I asked.

He said, "The dang things have been getting on my roof."

Scott laughed and shook his head. "That's dad," he said.

A little while later, Frank pointed out where some wild hogs had been rooting in his yard, tearing up the soil and causing him fits. Then I got a sense for how this rural-dwelling family has been reshaped by the Internet. Inside the house, his wife, Jeannie, was sewing on a machine adjacent to her laptop computer. She said she used the laptop to shop online, and was planning a Web site to sell her handiwork. The site is aptly named SewDay.com. Out in the living room, Frank had a laptop handy on a coffee table.

Scott's parents are immensely proud of him. Scott, who is in his mid-thirties and lives in nearby Waurika, sits on the local school board, teaches Sunday school at his Baptist church, and is known by just about everybody in town. His house is easily the biggest in Waurika, but most residents have no clue what he does for a living, he said. When they ask, he keeps it simple: "I work on the Internet." Stacy Day drives a Volvo with Oklahoma plates that say, "DOT COM."

Near the end of my trip, I visited the office of DigiMedia, where Day is president. The office occupies the eighth floor of one of a few tall office towers in Wichita Falls, Texas, about a forty-minute drive from Day's house.

Day is building a small media business on top of his portfolio. He's hired more than a half-dozen Web-site developers to add content to many of his sites. On MovieReviews.com, for example, users can review any movie, and others can rank the quality of their submissions. I interviewed Day in his large office surrounded by glass walls and big windows. If he looked out to his left, he could see most of Wichita Falls, a town of about 100,000. To his right, he could see through to the reception desk, occupied by his sister-in-law. Though times are changing, Day's company remains a family business.

Still, the office is a far cry from the old watermelon shed. I asked Day if he missed being on the farm with his father. He nodded. "Maybe I get to go back and work alongside him," he said. "He's taught me everything that I know that I am."

I asked him what his goals were for DigiMedia. He did not talk about going public one day and trying to shake up the online media business. His response was typically humble and brief. "We want to see if building a media company goes forward," he said. "We want to build on our foundation." When I pressed him to say what his favorite domain is, he said he couldn't answer that. "It changes from time to time," he said.

A little while later, Day drove me to the Wichita Falls airport, so I could catch a flight home. We got to talking about how his life had changed with his success in the domain market. "I don't set goals anymore," he said. Then he looked me square in the eye and said, "I don't think God could bless me anymore than he has."

Garry Chernoff, the Canadian who battled Day in the expired-domain market in the late 1990s, is relishing life. He said he now makes more than $1 million a year from his portfolio of about 3,200 names. A few years ago, he bought an 8,500-square-foot house on ten acres overlooking Okanagan Lake in Penticton. He spends much of his time lifting weights, woodworking, and riding his dirt bikes in the hills around town, just as he did as a kid.

"I thank my lucky stars to have such a life now," he said. "It's so much fun, and it's so easy. There's very little upkeep. I'm making money right now while I'm talking to you, but I don't have to physically do anything."

But Chernoff, who's in his mid-forties, said he planned to start developing his sites, after being inspired by the Traffic West show in Las Vegas in the spring of 2007, where many investors talked about the importance of adding content and enhancing the experience of Web users.

Chernoff said he'd sell his portfolio if the price was right. Some major companies in the industry have looked at both his list of names and the numbers of unique visitors they attract, he said. But no one has offered what he believes to be a fair price. "The industry is still so young," he said. "I can make a lot more money selling a name one at a time to an end user. These guys all want traffic stats. For 95 percent of the names I've sold, the buyers didn't ask for traffic stats."

Frank Schilling no longer works twenty hours a day. Having built his domain empire on Grand Cayman Island, he's been able to slow down and spend more time with his wife and children. His company, Name Administration, owns more than 350,000 sites. Revenue tops $20 million annually, with 90 percent falling to the bottom line.

Schilling continues to build the business. He's adding content to thousands of his sites. PersonalLoans.com, for example, explains the differences between secured and unsecured loans, and helps users understand credit scores and debt consolidation.

In 2007, Schilling started a blog (frankschilling.typepad.com), where he shares some of his secrets to success and reports on news in the industry. The blog is part of his way of sharing knowledge with other investors. He, too, benefited from mentors when he began, and wants to give something back. Investors have flocked to the blog to read his observations and ask questions. Schilling also helped launch the Internet Commerce Association, a trade group for domain investors.

Schilling remains bullish on domains. He believes there will be investors in the future who will surpass his accomplishments by spotting new opportunities and exploiting them. "The one constant since the dawn of the commercial Internet is type-in traffic," he said. That makes him most bullish on .com addresses, but he encourages investors to explore buying names in extensions for countries whose Web economies have strong growth prospects, such as .de for Germany or .cn for China.

Schilling continues to compete in expired-name auctions, and said he finds bargains all the time. In 2007, he grabbed homeforeclosures.com for $90,000. He said he expects the name to earn back that money from ads in three years. He said other recent scores include rumcakes.com ($4,100) and joystick.com ($65,250).

Anybody can access lists of soon-to-expire domains and compete in auctions, taking advantage of deals that arise. Put in the research and time, and you, too, could build a profitable domain portfolio.

"The opportunities are here and now," says Schilling. "In the future, having a great domain will be a hugely valuable thing. It will be an asset you pass on to your heirs."

Appendix I

Big Deals

The Twenty-Five Largest Reported Sales of Domain Names*

Rank	Domain Name	Price	Year
1.	porn.com	$9,500,000	2007
2. (tie)	business.com	$7,500,000	1999
	diamond.com	$7,500,000	2006
4. (tie)	asseenontv.com	$5,000,000	2000
	korea.com	$5,000,000	2000
6.	altavista.com	$3,350,000	1998
7. (tie)	loans.com	$3,000,000	2000
	vodka.com	$3,000,000	2006
	wine.com	$3,000,000	1999
10.	creditcards.com	$2,750,000	2004
11.	autos.com	$2,200,000	1999
12.	computer.com	$2,100,000	2007
13.	express.com	$2,000,000	1999
14. (tie)	mortgage.com**	$1,800,000	2000
	seniors.com	$1,800,000	2007
16. (tie)	cameras.com	$1,500,000	2006
	tandberg.com	$1,500,000	2007
18.	men.com	$1,300,000	2003
19.	vista.com	$1,250,000	2007
20.	scores.com	$1,180,000	2007
21.	chinese.com	$1,120,008	2007
22.	bingo.com	$1,100,000	1999
23.	wallstreet.com	$1,030,000	1999
24.	fish.com	$1,020,000	2005
25. (tie)	beauty.cc	$1,000,000	2000
	guy.com	$1,000,000	2007
	if.com	$1,000,000	2000
	linux.com	$1,000,000	1999
	rock.com	$1,000,000	1998
	topix.com	$1,000,000	2007

*   This information, current as of the end of 2007, is based on published news reports, as well as data collected starting in 2004 by DNJournal.com, the industry's main trade publication. It should be emphasized that this list only contains sales that have been publicly reported, and where the specific sales price, rather than a range, has been confirmed. Most domain sales occur privately, and often the parties are prohibited from disclosing the details. It should also be noted that in some transactions, the buyer acquires not just a domain, but also other assets. This list is focused on sales of domains only.

** included the sale of hipoteca.com, Spanish for "mortgage"

Appendix II

Resources for Investors

If you want to invest in domain names, you'll need to do your homework. There's a lot to learn. To help you get started, here's a sampling of Web sites that offer services and information.

Registrars
These sites let you register domains.
Dotster: www.dotster.com
Go Daddy: www.godaddy.com
Moniker: www.moniker.com
MyDomain: www.mydomain.com
Network Solutions: www.networksolutions.com
Register.com: www.register.com

Aftermarket Sites
These sites list domains for sale.
Afternic: www.afternic.com
BuyDomains: www.buydomains.com
Domain Name Aftermarket: www.tdnam.com
Fabulous Domains: www.fabulousdomains.com
GreatDomains: www.greatdomains.com
Sedo: www.sedo.com

Drop-Catching Services
These sites let you bid for names whose owners have let them expire.
NameJet: www.namejet.com
SnapNames: www.snapnames.com
Pool: www.pool.com

Parking Services

These sites offer "domain parking," enabling you to list advertisements on your domains.

DomainSponsor: www.domainsponsor.com
Dotzup: www.dotzup.com
NameDrive: www.namedrive.com
Parked: www.parked.com
Skenzo: www.skenzo.com
TrafficZ: www.trafficz.com

News Sites and Blogs

These sites provide news and information about the domain market.

Domain Name Journal: www.dnjournal.com
DomainNameNews: www.domainnamenews.com
Domain Name Wire: www.domainnamewire.com
Domainer's Magazine: www.domainersmagazine.com
DomainNews.com: www.domainnews.com
DomainTools Blog: blog.domaintools.com
Modern Domainer: www.moderndomainer.com
Seven Mile (The official Frank Schilling blog): www.sevenmile.com

Forums

These sites let domain owners discuss, buy and sell names.

DNForum.com: www.dnforum.com
DomainState: www.domainstate.com
NamePros: www.namepros.com

Research Sites

These sites allow domain owners to research such information as who has registered a domain, sales prices, and whether a name has been trademarked.

Better Whois: www.betterwhois.com
DomainTools: www.domaintools.com
DNSalePrice.com: www.dnsaleprice.com
U.S. Patent and Trademark Office: www.uspto.gov

Dispute Resolution

These sites provide information and services related to domain-name disputes.
Icann Domain Dispute Resolution Policies: www.icann.org/udrp/
National Arbitration Forum: http://domains.adrforum.com/
World Intellectual Property Organization: www.wipo.int/amc/en/
domains

Acknowledgments

Writing a book is a lonely, agonizing and yet incredibly rewarding process. One of the things that made this book rewarding was getting to know the many interesting people in the domain market and hearing their stories. This book would not have been possible without the willingness of several major domain investors to open up their lives to me. I will be eternally grateful for that.

I'd also like to thank some fine fellow journalists who reviewed drafts of this book and offered ideas to enrich it: Carl Bialik, David Goldenberg and Michael Myser. Each helped me refine paragraphs and section titles, and answer questions I'd failed to tackle. I'd also like to thank Peter DeMarco, a fellow newspaper reporter, who tracked down federal-court documents that helped strengthen the book. Thanks also to Bill Grueskin, Jason Anders and Marcelo Prince, who hired me to write feature articles for The Wall Street Journal Online, where I stumbled onto the domain market and came up with the idea for this book. I'm also grateful for the support and encouragement of my agent, Jack Scovil.

Finally, I'd like to thank my family for supporting me on this journey. My parents inspired me to chase my dream of being a writer from the early days of high school. They cheered my efforts, often in comforting phone calls, while I worked hastily to get this book finished. Lastly, I want to thank my wife, Tanya, and my daughter, Greta, for their many sacrifices. Tanya cooked meal after meal and did the dishes, too, even though the latter is my duty. And she fell asleep in front of the television alone too many nights while I worked in the adjacent room. She also stayed up until 2 a.m. the night of my deadline, helping me tweak entire chapters. Greta, who was only seven months old when I began the project, sat in my lap while I did interviews and played in my office by herself on late afternoons and Fridays when it was my duty to watch her and she should have been getting much more of my attention. Thanks to both of you for brightening my life immeasurably everyday.

A Note on Sources

This book is based largely on interviews with more than a hundred people intimately familiar with the domain market. They include investors, Internet advertising executives, intellectual-property lawyers, Wall Street analysts, and current and former employees of Internet registrars and registries. Interviews were conducted by telephone, e-mail, instant messaging, and in person.

Many interview subjects spoke candidly on the record about the marketplace and its history. But because of the secrecy of the industry and the sensitivity surrounding certain subjects, some sources spoke only on condition of anonymity. When I chose to use information from such sources, I contacted other sources for corroboration. Passages in the book rarely rely on a single unidentified source, and when they do, the source was a person with firsthand knowledge of the event or information described.

I want to thank each person who spoke with me. Many took hours out of their busy schedules to help me understand complex topics.

Given the faulty memories of human beings, whenever possible, I checked publicly available documents to verify information. I consulted Whois data, court records, domain-dispute rulings by arbitrators, real-estate records, Securities and Exchange Commission filings, and business incorporation records. Of particular help was the Internet Archive, which offers a free online tool allowing researchers to see how Web sites looked at various points in time. Some sites block the Internet Archive from taking "snapshots" of their pages, but nonetheless the archive provides a vast wealth of information. Also of immense help was DomainTools.com, a research site run by Jay Westerdal and his company, Name Intelligence. It lets researchers view historical Whois data and download—with some limitations—lists of domains belonging to single entities.

I also consulted more than a dozen books on the Internet economy, as well as hundreds of articles in newspapers, magazines, and on the Web. Many articles and books are cited in the text and are listed in the following endnotes.

Endnotes

Chapter One

1. Katie Hafner, "A Net Builder Who Loved Invention, Not Profit," *The New York Times*, October 22, 1998; *PR Newswire*, "Dot.com Celebrates its 21ˢᵗ Birthday," June 21, 2004.
2. *Los Angeles Times*, "He Created the Net—Really," March 1, 2001; Rex Bowman, "Boucher Trounces Opponent in 9ᵗʰ," *Richmond Times-Dispatch*, November 8, 2000.
3. Robert H. Zakon, Hobbes' Internet Timeline, at: http://www.zakon.org/robert/internet/timeline/.
4. Ibid.
5. Ibid.
6. Milton L. Mueller, *Ruling the Root* (Cambridge, Mass.: MIT Press, 2002), 110.
7. Joanne Cleaver, "Trademarks Do Not Guarantee Internet Domain," *Crain's Chicago Business*, October 9, 1995.
8. Mueller, *Ruling the Root*, 112.
9. Ibid, 112-113.
10. Joshua Quittner, "Billions Registered," *Wired*, October 1994.
11. M.A. Stapleton, "Careful What Names You Invoke on the World Wide Web," *Chicago Daily Law Bulletin*, December 26, 1996.
12. *PR Newswire*, "The Princeton Review Relinquishes Controversial Internet Name," October 5, 1994.
13. Quittner, "Billions Registered."
14. Mueller, *Ruling the Root*, 121.
15. Tim Blangger, "In the Spirit of Gumby, Boy Keeps Web Name," *The Morning Call*, April 22, 1998.
16. David M. Kelly and Elizabeth L. Mitchell, "Dot.com: A New Property Right?", *Intellectual Property Today*, November 1996.
17. *Intermatic Inc. v. Toeppen*, a federal lawsuit (N.D. Ill. 1996), http://www2.bc.edu/~herbeck/cyberlaw.intermatic.html.

18. Ellen Rony and Peter Rony, *The Domain Name Handbook: High Stakes and Strategies in Cyberspace* (Lawrence, Kan.: R&D Books, 1998), 507.

19. Mueller, *Ruling the Root*, 113.

20. Mike Allen, "Seeing Ad Dollars, C-Net Multiplies Web Sites," *The New York Times*, September 16, 1996.

21. James Romenesko, "Auction of Internet Name Could Make St. Paul Man Richest Kid on Cyberblock," *Saint Paul Pioneer Press*, May 2, 1996.

22. Available online through Archive.org: http://web.archive.org/web/19980115045724/watermelons.com/packer.html.

23. Mike Mills, "Internet Domains That Haven't Paid Registration Fees May Find Their Sites Deleted by Herndon Gatekeeper," *The Washington Post*, June 22, 1996.

24. David S. Hilzenrath, "Internet 'Enhancement' Fund Remains Untouched," *The Washington Post*, January 11, 1997.

25. Jim Puzzanghera, "Online Race for Political Domains," *San Jose Mercury News*, June 7, 1999; Alan Elsner, "Bush-basher sites put out of sight," *Reuters*, June 15, 1999.

Chapter Two

1. Garry Chernoff, *50 Idiot-Proof Ways to Make Money on the Net* (Self-published: 1997).

2. David Adlerstein, "The King of Domains," *South Florida Business Journal*, September 22, 2000.

3. Jeff Houck, "Want Web Address? Talk to the Landlord," *Palm Beach Post*, August 16, 1999.

4. GreatDomains.com, Steve Newman, and Susan Wels, *Domain Names for Dummies* (New York: Hungry Minds, 2001), 31.

5. Laurie J. Flynn, "Prototype Internet Name is Sold for $100,000-plus," *The New York Times*, May 12, 1997.

6. *Business Wire*, "Internet Name Sold for $150,000," June 4, 1997.

7. James Romenesko, "Masters of Their Domain," *Saint Paul Pioneer Press*, May 27, 1996.

8. Elizabeth Keest Sedrel, "Wall Street Traded for Easy Street," *Albuquerque Journal*, April 30, 1999.

9. Ibid.

10. GreatDomains.com, Newman, and Wels, *Domain Names for Dummies*, 34.

11. Enrique Rivero, "So What's in a Name? Lots for Web Site Owner," *The Daily News* of Los Angeles, August 3, 1999.

12. Chris Gaither, "A Prescription for Riches?", *Wired News*, July 21, 1999.

13. Ibid.

14. Chris Gaither, "Tadpoles Hopping onto Drugs.com," *Wired News*, Aug. 13, 1999.

15. Houck, "Want Web Address? Talk to the Landlord."

16. Andrew Pollack, "What's in a Cybername? $7.5 Million for the Right Address," *The New York Times*, December 1, 1999.

17. Mueller, *Ruling the Root*, 144.

18. Julia Angwin, "Do Cyberspace Court Panels Favor Trademark Holders?", *The Wall Street Journal*, August 20, 2001.

19. Jeri Clausing, "In New Forum for Domain Name Disputes, Trademark Holders Dominate," *The New York Times*, Cyber Law Journal online edition, May 19, 2000.

20. The arbitration ruling is available online at: http://www.wipo.int/amc/en/domains/decisions/html/2000/d2000-0054.html.

21. Angwin, "Do Cyberspace Court Panels Favor Trademark Holders?"

22. Aaron Baca, "City Man's Domain-Name Auction a Bust," *Albuquerque Journal*, December 24, 1999.

23. Judith Schoolman, "Names to Net Millions," *New York Daily News*, December 21, 1999.

24. Baca, "City Man's Domain-Name Auction a Bust"; Schoolman, "Names to Net Millions."

25. Ibid.

26. Hobbes' Internet Timeline, by Robert H. Zakon, at: http://www.zakon.org/robert/internet/timeline/.

27. Declan McCullagh, "Domain Name List is Dwindling," *Wired News*, April 14, 1999.

28. Jennifer 8. Lee, "At Least Some Domain Names Draw Money at Net Auctions," *The New York Times*, July 15, 1999.

29. Wendy Tanaka, "Deep Cuts at 2 Area Internet Companies," *Philadelphia Inquirer*, January 3, 2001.

Chapter Three

1. Kate Fitzgerald, "Demand for Domain Names Falls Without Brand Support," *Advertising Age*, November 27, 2000.

2. Alex Pham, "Domains Don't Net as Many Buyers," *Los Angeles Times*, December 29, 2000.

3. Ibid.

4. P.J. Huffstutter and Karen Kaplan, "Virtual Real Estate Is a Buyer's Market," *Los Angeles Times*, July 29, 2002.

5. Karen Kaplan, "GreatDomains.com Bought by VeriSign," *Los Angeles Times*, October 26, 2000.

6. Lee Hodgson, "Domain Name Goldrush Part 1—The Rules of Play," *Sitepoint*, February 19, 2001 (Online only: http://www.sitepoint.com/article/name-goldrush-1-rules-play).

7. Susan Stellin, "Rivals Say VeriSign Still Has Advantage," *The New York Times*, April 9, 2001.

8. Ibid.

9. Ibid.

10. Ibid.

11. Ibid.

12. Ibid.

13. Lyn Berry, "Playing the Domain Game," *Denver Business Journal*, May 18, 2001.

14. Ibid.

Chapter Four

1. John Battelle, *The Search* (New York: Portfolio, 2005), 100.

2. Saul Hansell, "Clicks for Sale," *The New York Times*, June 4, 2001.

3. Battelle, *The Search*, 111-112.

4. Ibid, 104-105.

5. Chris Gaither, "Search Engines are Powering Ad Revenue," *Los Angeles Times*, May 24, 2004.

6. Andrew Goodman, *Winning Results with Google AdWords* (Emeryville, Calif.: McGraw Hill/Osborne, 2005), 36.

7. Lane Anderson, "Traffic Patterns—Enterprising Scam Artists Exploit the Typo for Profit," *Ziff Davis Smart Business for the New Economy*, December 1, 2000.

8. *Business Wire*, "Google Acquires Applied Semantics," April 23, 2003.

9. Lee Hodgson, "Domain Name Goldrush Part 3—Wild Wild West," *Sitepoint*, June 22, 2001 (Online only: http://www.sitepoint.com/article/goldrush-3-wild-wild-west).

10. The email is available online at: http://www.icann.org/announcements/icann-pr10aug01.htm

11. Aliza Earnshaw, "SnapNames Inks VeriSign Deal With Major Potential," *The Business Journal of Portland*, January 11, 2002.

12. Ibid.

13. VeriSign's justification for the system is described online at: http://www.icann.org/bucharest/vgrs-wls-justification-28jan02.pdf.
14. Icann's discussion paper addressing the issue is available online at: http://www.icann.org/registrars/redemption-proposal-14feb02.htm.
15. Ibid.
16. Congressional testimony by Paul Stahura, July 31, 2003, archived by Federal Document Clearing House, Inc.

Chapter Five

1. David Heath and Sharon Pian Chan, "Dot-con Job—Part 2: Cashing Out" *The Seattle Times*, March 7, 2005.
2. Mark Memmott, "Cheney Error Sends Net Users off Track," *USA Today*, October 7, 2004.
3. Ibid.
4. Ibid.
5. *Business Wire*, "Marchex Announces Asset Acquisition," November 23, 2004.

Chapter Six

1. John Cook, "Marchex Solidifies its Web Presence," *Seattle Post-Intelligencer*, November 24, 2004.
2. Ibid.
3. Ibid.
4. Ron Jackson, "The Marchex Story," *DNJournal.com*, September 2006.
5. Robert Weisman, "Internet Stealth Company Steps Out," *The Boston Globe*, June 12, 2006.
6. Ibid.
7. Paul Sloan, "The Man Who Owns the Internet," *Business 2.0*, June 2007.
8. Eric Engleman, "Stashing Names Might Yield Big Revenue," *Puget Sound Business Journal*, May 19, 2006.
9. E-mails between Blake Bookstaff and William Marquez, cited in *Bookstaff v. Marquez*, a federal lawsuit, 3:06-cv-00085, U.S. District Court for the Eastern District of Tennessee.
10. Chris Sewell, "Spelling Trouble," *Telephony*, October 14, 2002.
11. David Hayes, "Lawsuit Accuses Sprint of Fraud," *Kansas City Star*, April 11, 2002.
12. Paul Sloan, "Masters of their Domains," *Business 2.0*, December 2005.
13. Julia Angwin, "For These Sites, Their Best Asset is a Good Name," *The Wall Street Journal*, May 1, 2006.

Chapter Seven

1. Ron Jackson, "Behind the Scenes in the $3 Million Sale of Vodka.com," *DNJournal.com*, December 2006.
2. Ibid.
3. Paul Sloan, "Staking a Claim on Domains Beyond Dot-Com," Business 2.0, August 2006.
4. Lee Gomes, "All the Good Ones Have Been Taken—In Domain Names, Too," *The Wall Street Journal*, July 19, 2006.
5. Kieren McCarthy, *Sex.com* (London: Quercus, 2007), 40-43.
6. Chris O'Brien, "Internet Maverick," *San Jose Mercury News*, September 17, 2006.
7. Rachel Konrad, "Sex.com Hijacker Pleads Poverty After Fleeing to Mexico," *Associated Press*, February 27, 2007.
8. Ron Jackson, "Rick Schwartz: Domain King or Royal Pain?", *DNJournal.com*, March 3, 2004.
9. Sara Kehaulani Goo, "Click Fraud Threatens Foundation of Web Ads," *The Washington Post*, October 22, 2006.
10. As a member of the media, I didn't pay the admission fee.
11. Kevin J. Delaney, "Web Domain for Sale in Really Hot Locale: Hell.com Takes Bids," *The Wall Street Journal*, October 27, 2006.
12. Bob Tedeschi, "Now that Google Can Sell Domain Names, Will it Expand its Business Beyond Search Services?", *The New York Times*, February 7, 2005.
13. Paul Sloan, "Who's Your Go Daddy?", *Business 2.0*, December 2006.
14. William M. Bulkeley, "In Europe's Auction of New Web Names, Strife and Confusion," *The Wall Street Journal*, August 30, 2006.
15. Thomas Crampton, "What's in 74,000 Names? Big Money," *The International Herald Tribune*, October 6, 2006.
16. Emma Barraclough, "Leaving a Bad Taste," *Managing Intellectual Property*, October 1, 2006.

Chapter Eight

1. Corilyn Shropshire, "Web is No Bottomless Pit for Dot.com Name Seekers," *Pittsburgh Post-Gazette*, August 16, 2006.
2. Declan McCullagh, "Dotster Named in Massive Cybersquatting Suit," *News.com*, June 5, 2006.
3. *Playboy*, "Lolipp.com," September 1, 2004.
4. John O'Brien, "Syracuse University Sues Web Company Over Site," *The Post-Standard*, April 7, 2002.

5. *Associated Press*, "Cybersquatting Complaints Rise 25 Percent, U.N. Says," March 12, 2007.
6. World Intellectual Property Organization, "Cybersquatting Remains on the Rise With Further Risk to Trademarks from New Registration Practices," March 12, 2007.
7. Bentley's year-end review is available online at: http://www.sedo.com/links/showhtml.php3?Id=1373

Chapter Nine

1. "Ballmer Makes Big Bet to Get to 'Next Level,'" Robert Guth, *The Wall Street Journal*, February 4, 2008.
2. "Domain Roundtable," Ron Jackson, *DNJournal.com*, April 27, 2006.
3. Ibid.

Printed in the United States
117835LV00003B/316-324/P

9 781436 332279